DON'T DRINK
THE WATER

D0895869

DISCARDED

185 main st.
Yuma Az 85364

RICHARD JENSEN

Yuma County Library District
350 3rd Avenue
Yuma, AZ 85364
928-782-1871
www.yumalibrary.org

Published by
Tempo Distributors
12190 East Arabian Park Drive
Scottsdale, Arizona 85259

Copyright © by Richard Jensen, 2000
All rights reserved

ISBN 1-55056-777-2

First printing, 2000

Printed and bound in Canada by
Friesens Corporation
Altona, Manitoba,
R0G 0B0

The front cover photo is shown by permission from
Marianne Caroselli of Fair Oaks, Texas, the creator of this
beautiful life sized sculpture entitled "Puppy Love."

MAR 0 3 2005

Dedicated to the memory of my parents and all of Standard's early pioneers who set the path and prepared the way for my generation.

PREFACE

Having been born during the only depression of this century and having survived the fears and intimidation's of a global conflict, I have been emboldened to chronicle the places and times of my youth. This writing adventure which is focussed on my journey through childhood was undertaken despite the fact that my own personal involvement in the era under review was minuscule and of absolutely no importance. Notwithstanding this inconsequential and undistinguished lifestyle, growing up at a time when horses were still regarded as a vital source of energy offered a special education and a unique challenge. Moreover, the pioneer schools that dotted the prairies offered an odyssey of events that are unparalleled in today's world but are still well worth remembering. While it is true that my own country school experience was short- lived, and provided only a minor part of my upbringing, its parochial nature characterized the entire interval of my youth. Also, being among the last to partake of these pleasures, I feel a particular need to relate some observations that emanated from this period of transition that impacted all small towns and cloistered communities.

From a national perspective, one could argue that the somewhat insular venues for the episodes of my early life were trivial and devoid of any meaningful contribution. While that may appear to be the case, in reality my community and others like it, were the veins and arteries that gave our land its initial prosperity. Indeed, it was these small rural centers, largely populated by first generation immigrants, that fostered the spirit and character of our modern society. More importantly, the standards set by these early settlers as evoked today, remains the taproot for Canada's morality and conscience. It is my sincere hope that my narrative has not diminished nor tarnished this understated truth.

My early life was filled with a spectrum of events that fueled my dreams and fantasies for the future. The seldom predictable outcome of these happenings provided much of the adventure that accompanied these nearly forgotten incidents. Although there are sure to be differences, I would be surprised if many of my contemporaries have not suffered many of the same trials, savored similar triumphs and endured many of the feelings and emotions which I have endeavored to describe in the text. Perhaps this review will gladden a few hearts with rekindled memories.

At the very outset, it was my purpose to inform my children of their roots and to familiarize them with the shape and genesis of their being. In writing this largely historic account, I soon discovered that it was a lot of fun to relive the road just past and muse over so many of its heady and memorable events. It is hoped that my children and perhaps a few others will find some enjoyment in it as well.

I am indebted to a number of my classmates who helped sequence the blur of so many school teachers. Also my sister, Irene, assisted in fleshing out and restoring my memory relative to a few of the more weighty affairs which while distanced by time, played a roll in my formative years. Finally, without continuous encouragement from my wife, Irene, I may not have finished the project. Moreover, her talent and perseverance were put to the test as she deciphered, and typed the entire manuscript from innumerable pages of my hand written scribble. Her preliminary edit was equally important in getting the story into its final form and to the printers.

DON'T DRINK THE WATER

THE EARLY YEARS

The ballast in one of the overhead florescent tubes was sizzling and there was a faint flicker in the bluish white light that illuminated the room. The surroundings were particularly Spartan with but three padded chrome chairs randomly scattered on the expansive tile floor. The peeling plaster and exposed water pipes in the far corner gave the windowless office an extraordinarily bleak appearance. There were no pictures, and except for the Canadian Coat of Arms and a bank calendar, the walls were absolutely blank. The date on the calendar, a full month behind, showed June, 1953, suggesting that the room was seldom used.

It was in fact July 4, 1953 and I was in Edmonton cooling my heels in a government office building. Actually, I was on the fourth floor of an old Jasper Avenue furniture store in which a few federal agencies maintained an Alberta presence.

Grade Twelve Departmental Examinations had been completed during the week just past. Results would not be available until early August but as far as I was concerned, there could be no turning back. School was out and for the moment at least, any thoughts of additional school house learning were out of the question. Mr. Bragg, my high school teacher, had given me a ride to Edmonton the day before. Although the trip was long and we had shared an automobile for over six hours, education had not been a part of our adult conversation. Now at last, in Alberta's capital, I was on my own and had finally broken with the school cycle. With luck, I would complete the break and earn my independence as I

1

embarked on a career as a weather observer with the Department of Transport.

In point of fact, application for employment had been made with the D.O.T. in May, well in advance of my final high school exams. The appropriate government forms had been picked up during an earlier but brief visit to the Calgary Quonset hut, air terminal and weather office. Mr. McQuarrie, the senior Calgary meteorologist, had been especially helpful, showing me the entire weather station and explaining the work of a weather observer. He provided details on the thermometers, barometers, balloons and other more interesting paraphernalia that generated the data needed to draft up the weather maps. Satellite surveillance was yet to be developed and these large charts, prepared daily, showed the location of the weather systems throughout Canada and most of the United States. Using these as a guide, it was simply a matter of predicting the direction of the weather fronts - presto, a weather forecast.

The visit had been most intriguing and had convinced me to apply for employment with the Department of Transport. What could be more simple than watching the clouds and a few thermometers?

In response to my application, preliminary affirmation had been received from the Alberta Director early in June. This communication also invited me to Edmonton for a final adjudication as soon as grade twelve exams had been completed. Initially, it had been assumed that this meeting was simply a formality to determine if I had the usual number of arms and legs. Now sitting and waiting on one of the government issue chrome framed arm chairs and waiting for the final judgment, I was not so sure.

Earlier in the morning I had been of good cheer, and filled with joyous expectations for the future. Arriving in good time for my appointment, I was immediately ushered into a very crowded boardroom. The large table, surrounded by government issue imitation leather padded chairs, totally filled the available space. This made movement around the set up a bit awkward and since I was invited to sit at the far end, away from the entry, a modicum of gymnastics were required to gain my position.

With typical government inefficiency, I soon found myself trapped by what seemed to be a whole herd of rather corpulent gentlemen. None had suit coats, but each to a man wore a vest which in some cases left generous sections of dress shirt exposed between the poorly fitting vest and trouser top. Also with their arrival, the room took on the mixed smells of government issue lead pencils and stale cigarette smoke. It would seem that my interview was to be conducted by a panel of nine senior examiners. While it should have been obvious that I was blessed with the usual number of arms and legs, it was now clear that there was a more sinister reason for the meeting. Apparently this overkill, and role of the nine, was to ensure that the ranks of government would not be infiltrated and contaminated by some unworthy interloper. It no longer seemed to be a simple formality.

The meeting, or more properly "the interrogation," lasted well over an hour. As you might expect, there were a multitude of questions, which for the most part, were easily answered. Most of the panel members were pleasant and made no obvious attempt to intimidate me. Their queries were of a general nature regarding my interest in sports, favorite subjects, recently read books, etc. Unfortunately the preemployment application form asked if the prospective employee had command of any language other than English. While this question was clearly intended to determine a competence in French, I had in the blank space provided, penned in the word "Danish." Wow! Was that ever a mistake.

To my horror and surprise, one of the panel members was of Danish extraction. As best remembered, his name was

Olsen and seemed to be more Danish than King Christian himself. This was emphasized as he proudly advised that his Danish talents had been put to good use during recent negotiations with Denmark. Apparently he had been loaned to the United States government when that country made arrangements for their Thule, Greenland airbase and weather office.

Wouldn't you know it, here I was trying to look good and had taken the liberty of exaggerating my language competence by claiming that I could speak a second language. When Mr. Olsen started to ask questions in Danish I was dead. While I had some notion of what he was saying, I hardly dared to risk a reply with my limited Danish vocabulary. Although he and everyone else soon determine that my second language was for all practical purposes a fraud, he continued with his diatribe and increasingly sarcastic questions. It soon became obvious that he was showing off to his colleagues who could not understand any part of the exchange. My muted replies, usually a mixture of shabby English and Danish, seemed to fuel his eagerness to shame me further. His tenacious badgering made it clear to the entire forum that I had made an improper claim by overstating my skills on the preemployment application. Mr. Olsen was enjoying himself but I was made to look like an absolute fool. In my cramped space at the end of the table, there was little to do but squirm and endure the humiliation for having made this over zealous language assertion.

When, after what seemed an eternity, and the inquisition was finally over, I was directed into an adjacent room. Here in the quiet but otherwise drab surroundings there was time to be alone with my thoughts. Having just undergone such a grueling examination, I was emotionally drained and felt the need for a little time to reflect on the events just past.

It was certainly no exaggeration to say that this, my first ever important job interview had been a catastrophic disaster. Sitting pensively while waiting for the final verdict, I could do little else but reflect on my foolish error. I promised myself that never again would I overstate my competence in a second language. Also there was time to consider the future, which at the moment was filled with uncertainty. Whatever the outcome of the days examination, it was certain that the life ahead would be very different from the past.

First of all, I was leaving the comforts of home and the security of loving parents. Also, as I was now destined to become a city dweller, a wholesale change in my lifestyle was a certainty. An urban life would require the development and honing of a totally different set of attitudes and defenses. Farm life and country living would give way to the clamorous rigors of traffic, busy sidewalks, strict schedules and new relationships. Most disturbing, my childhood and the early years of my youth would soon be little more than a happy memory.

Up to now everything had been a delightful and generally happy experience. To be sure, there had been brief moments of discomfort and disorder, but these were few and far between and were not a fair measure of the years past. These unhappy incidents and mishaps were more than offset by a whole host of joyous occasions and memorable times which in better circumstances could easily bring on a smile and leave a strong feeling of well being.

****

As shown on my application for employment and for the record, I was born in Calgary, Alberta, Canada, right in the middle of the Great Depression. It was raining like a jungle monsoon when Mother was admitted to the Calgary General Hospital. Simultaneously, the Barnum and Bailey

Circus was in town and as far as is known, this was their last ever appearance in Western Canada. While this fact is totally irrelevant, there were times when Mother wondered if the hospital had inadvertently gotten me mixed up with a circus monkey.

My birth on June 4, 1934, was somewhat overshadowed and badly preempted by the Dionne quintuplets, all of whom had come into the world a week earlier. Although things went rather well, my triumphant arrival received absolutely no publicity. The quintuplets were most certainly to blame for that omission, since the newspapers were filled with the more exciting story of Cecile, Yvonne, Marie, Emily, and Annette.

Dr. Richardson, a seventh son of a seventh son, and the family physician, must have done a good job since I arrived right on time and weighed in at 9 pounds, 2 ounces. I have since been advised that this hefty package made me the biggest baby in the hospital - literally. It is now lost forever, but for years I had in my possession, Dr. Richardson's "Paid in Full" receipt for medical services rendered "$25.00."

I of course don't remember my birth, but do have some early recollections of Dad planting trees around our old farmstead and weatherworn house. Actually this happened at two very distinct and separate times. Not surprisingly, there is no claim to knowledge of the first planting, which took place during the spring of 1934, the year of my birth. It would be nice to think of it as a commemorative event, but it is more likely that the need for a shelter-belt was the true motivation. I have long since reluctantly accepted the fact that this first effort to create some shade on the otherwise desolate Canadian prairie was not of my doing and therefore, I now and forever, renounce all credit for this legacy of arboreal life.

This is not so for the followup beautification project. The second shade fest came about three years later and there is little doubt that it is this momentous event which still comes to mind. Moreover, by this time I was a full participant and old enough to get in Dad's way. It is certain that my presence was an irritating nuisance as he carefully paced off each spot for the placement of a willow or poplar twig. All of the saplings that were planted had been gleaned from Alfred Petersen's wonderful grove of trees, just one half mile to the south and any misalignment as they grow today can easily be credited to my interference.

****

The memories that I carry of my childhood, or more accurately the recall of my youth, may be subject to some question. I do nonetheless, have a very clear sense of many events which occurred in my fledgling years. Most of these are not recollections of earth shattering adventures or traumatic episodes, they are simply a collage of many occasions and things, which although somewhat fuzzy, are still suspended in my mind.

Along with Dad's trees, I harbor very strong impressions of a dog by the name of Ringee. As recalled, the dog in question was a large black and white collie that believed his mission in life was to keep me awake by barking most of the night. Whether it was the dog barking or me crying, it soon became clear that one of us would have to go. Although the law was substantially on my side, it is probable that Mother and Dad had at least some debate on the matter.

In the end, and after weighing all the factors, my parents decided that a good night's sleep was worth more than the protective watchfulness offered by Ringee. After all, and perhaps more importantly, they had just paid Dr. Richardson $25.00 to bring me into this world. Besides, Ringee had discovered that chickens made good sport and his palate was rapidly developing a strong addiction for fat hens. Notwithstanding the farm fowl, it would be nice to think that

Mother and Dad would have made the right decision in keeping me rather than the dog. We will never know for sure.

Apparently Ringee's demise caused my sister, Irene, to inquire of his whereabouts. At this, Dad was obliged to advise that Ringee had experienced a fatal accident when he inadvertently ran into the head of a ball peen hammer. This explanation satisfied both Irene and the few nervous but still surviving chickens.

With growing up comes a lot of learning. At some point, there was the need to learn the nuances of drinking from a glass, eating with a fork and spoon, and perhaps later, developing the skill required to tie ones own shoe laces. These essential talents come in the first few years and are all a piece of cake compared to the business of potty training.

I don't recall just when potty training started, but I will never forget when it ended. I was probably two and a half to three years old. Mother had dressed me in my favorite, and probably only pair of overalls. They were blue with red bias tape trim and had two fairly large buttons on the front bib suspender attachment. No doubt there were side vents with the same type of buttons. Memory is a bit fuzzy but I seem to recall that there was also a front bib pocket, just like Dad's; you know, the pocket where he kept his roll-your-own tobacco and paper, and as you might expect, a fair bit of wheat chaff mixed with a bunch of mostly burnt match sticks.

It was probably right after breakfast when this sordid but important learning experience took place. I was walking from the kitchen to the living room and remember thinking what a bother it would be to go to the outdoor privy or upstairs to the potty. Boy, was that ever a mistake! The sensation was certainly unpleasant and the results exceeded my wildest expectations. Thunder and lightning could not have been worse, and I instantly knew that there was big time trouble ahead. Also I was smart enough to know that Mother would not approve, and with the sudden change in the weather, or more appropriately, the local climate, it was impossible to escape. Besides, my speed had been reduced to absolute zero. High gear was completely out of the question and even a slow walk would have betrayed my guilt.

Filling one's pants is probably one of nature's cruelest accidents, but when you are approaching three years of age, mothers show little sympathy. Sure enough, Mother soon had me by my ear and although there was good reason to believe that more was coming, it was certain that the rest of the punishment would have to wait, at least until the area reserved for the next phase was cleared up.

After all of the preliminaries, which for reasons of a painful memory will not be disclosed, I was sent to bed until my only pair of overalls could be laundered. It seemed that it would take forever for those pants to dry.

****

It is difficult to remember each and every event that occurred during these early growing up years. On the other hand, it is hard not to recall some of the really important moments when major learning took place. In some of these learning situations, best results often required the help of a firm but fair hand strategically applied by Mother or Dad to a point of my learning.

There were of course many learning experiences and in fairness to my own innate ability, only a few needed a physical application. Although a spanking was not a part of it, by far the most memorable lesson came with the building of the chicken house.

While the time is relatively unimportant, my sister and I agree that Dad built the chicken house in the summer or fall of 1937. By that time I was a few months past my third birthday and can easily recall that Gotfried Beck, one of Dad's school friends from the old country, was there to help.

9

He is easily remembered since he had a very deep voice and while shingling the roof, claimed to eat the nails that he held in his mouth. I didn't really believe him but the claim had some credibility since the nails continued to disappear.

Construction of this magnificent addition to the farmstead is worthy of mention for several reasons. First and most obvious, it is probable that the chickens were happy to vacate the old barn and obtain their own more comfortable accommodations. Moreover, can you imagine the joyous feelings of the cow, Bessy, and horse team, Nancy and Beauty, when they were able to evict all of those noisy co-tenants with whom they had been obliged to share their quarters. Also, it had to be a treat for them not to have a chicken in the manger, laying eggs right on top of their lunch.

For me, the chicken house was important for a very different reason and although I suffered quite a few nasty moments, there is good and continuing reason to be particularly grateful for it's construction.

To place the building on a sound footing, a concrete foundation was built. As a first step in constructing this foundation, Dad and Gotfried hauled a few loads of sand and gravel from a municipal sand pit that was located about three miles south of the farm. This task was accomplished with the help of Nancy and Beauty, who made several trips with the old lumber wagon. It wasn't long before a neat pile of sand appeared right near the sight of the chicken house. Wow! What a temptation for a three year old to play and run through this delightfully soft pile of beach aggregate.

Now Dad didn't mind a bit of messing in the sand pile just as long as it wasn't spread all over the yard. In short, I was allowed to play in it but it was clearly understood that it would more or less stay in a conventional heap and thus remain usable for construction of the chicken house foundation.

You have no idea how much I enjoyed this new recreational area. With hardly any effort, it was possible to make roads, dig a hole, engineer a tunnel, or even shape a mountain or hill. The bad part was the location. The sand pile was of course near the site of the proposed hen house, and that was a long, long way from our living quarters and my normal area of activity. Would it ever be great to have this keen stuff close by and maybe even in some shade. If it was in shade, it would be much better than the loose dirt on the hot, south side of the house where I often played. Besides, it would be much cleaner.

Now it just so happened that I had a little red wheelbarrow capable of holding ten to fifteen pounds of sand. Put another way, my wheelbarrow would probably hold one big shovelful if Dad was wielding the shovel. Sure enough, the Devil made me do it. I loaded up my wheelbarrow and took off for the house for what was going to be the best play area in all of Christendom. Unfortunately, the house was a very long way off and with a heavy load of sand, a guy gets mighty tired. About half way, I decided that building a new play pen was much too difficult, so the load was lightened by dumping the sand - all fifteen pounds. It may not have been much, but there it sat, a neat little pile right in the middle of the yard.

It wasn't long before Dad noticed this small but anomalous spot on the square. He wasn't really upset, but invited me to explain my intentions for this major expenditure of effort. Knowing that the rules had been violated by scattering sand away from the pile, and fearing the worst, I denied any involvement. Dad of course knew the truth, but pretended to accept my denial. It was clear however that my story was a fabrication and I was totally miserable. Telling a lie is no fun and I began to suffer terribly. Dad was aware of this and hoping for a clean breast of things, made yet another inquiry. Once again innocence was claimed, asserting that I had absolutely nothing to do with the sudden appearance of this new bump in the yard. This made matters even worse. While my denials continued for some time, Dad was cleverly using this small and relatively unimportant episode to teach me a much needed lesson. Finally, after hours of extreme discomfort filled with guilt and shame, I finally admitted responsibility. This confession or embellished admission of guilt went along the lines that I had forgotten, but now suddenly remembered something about the load of sand mysteriously appearing in my wheelbarrow. Now, with great and sudden revelation, it came to me that I had indeed dumped it on the way to the house. Dad knew how much I had suffered and accepted this rather confused confession. I was much relieved and will never forget the cleansing and lifting of guilt that came over me when finally the truth had been told. While Dad may have added a few words of admonishment regarding the value and merits of honesty and truthfulness, they were unnecessary since the guilt and suffering told me all that I ever needed to know. To this day, the episode of the chicken house is one of the most important learning experiences of my life.

It has been said that everything one needs to know can be learned in kindergarten. Well, I never went to kindergarten, but have always maintained that the chicken house served as a splendid substitute. It is certain that kindergarten could not have taught a more meaningful lesson than that conveyed to me back in the summer of 1937.

****

Apart from the agony of the sand, I got into very little trouble during my early years. I was however, not always very clever and did cause Mother and Dad a few anxious moments with my stupidity.

For example, one evening I was playing with a box of brass harness rivets. These metal fasteners, used to repair the leather traces on Nancy and Beauty's harness, were about the size of a 22 caliber bullet. They were shiny, bright and smooth, and were also about the size of my nostrils. That fact should be irrelevant but since they fit so well, that is exactly where I put them, not one but two, one in each nostril. Very soon they were beyond my reach and the more I tried to dig them out, the worse things became. I of course knew of my predicament but said nothing to anyone. Fortunately, Mother and Dad noticed that my breathing was rather unusual and realized that something was seriously amiss. They soon found the problem, but as their efforts to remove the rivets were also futile, we all piled into the old Chev for a visit to Dr. Fletcher's Drug Store in Standard.

Although it was late in the evening, Dr. Fletcher was most obliging, leaving the comfort of his home, for the back of the drug store where he maintained an examination room equipped with a few surgical instruments. With the help of his fancy tongs, the rivets were soon removed.

It is probable that the whole experience was somewhat painful but while this has long since passed from memory, I still savor the taste of the vanilla ice cream that followed.

Once again, timing is at question, but it is certain that the hen house was finished and most likely there were a few scraps of lumber left over. In any event it was later in 1937, during a rainy period when Dad built a playhouse for we kids. We had no idea that it was under construction and it is probable that it was meant to be that way, since it was fabricated right in the middle of the garage, away from our prying eyes.

Neither Irene nor I realized that such an important project was underway. We even failed to notice that the car had been left out in the rain for several days. Wow, were we ever surprised when the weather cleared up and Dad pulled this fine playhouse out of the garage, leaving it no more than twenty yards from the front door of the house.

The playhouse was approximately four by seven feet in size. It was some four feet high at the eaves, increasing to about five and one half feet at the very peak of the roof. It also featured a pretend chimney right on top. The windows on each side were of real glass and the door at the front was about forty inches high. These dimensions may seem a bit cramped, but you can be sure that the size was just right for two small children, not yet old enough to attend school.

During the winter, when it was too cold to enjoy as a plaything, Mother and Dad used it for meat storage. This worked extremely well as even a short lived chinook would not thaw the stored meat. This usually included an entire pig, butchered sometime during late fall or early winter.

Speaking of that, the business of butchering was always a gruesome and messy process. First of all there was the cruelty of death for the pig. Fortunately, living on a farm had to some extent exposed and hardened me to the finality of life. Once the animal was killed, the butchering operation included scalding the carcass so that the pigs bristles could be scraped off. When that job was finished, the hanging porker had a human color and texture, offering a macabre scene that always reminded me of a very dead, but naked person.

I was always glad when Dad lowered the dead hulk and carved it into hams, roasts, and bacon. They made good eating and were well worth the frightful spectacle of the hanging pig.

For several years, the playhouse saw a lot of use and took on a home-like atmosphere when Uncle Fred, Mother's brother-in-law, gave us a child- sized table and chair set for Christmas. Later, this was further improved when Dad made a small cupboard for Irene's tea set and various miniature pots and pans. On that occasion, Dad built me a birdhouse.

For many years, this small sanctuary was fastened to the pole that eventually held our radio aerial. I always hoped that a robin would nest there, but all that it ever housed were some very lucky English sparrows.

*************.

One of the most notable memories of my early years was the visit of Grandmother Jensen from North Dakota. I will never forget the excitement that preceded her arrival. More importantly, her visit, or at least the period of her stay, was for me a great renaissance. At the very least, I learned that the world in which we lived was much larger than our somewhat parochial community. After all, North Dakota was far away in the United States, a totally different country.

Grandmother Jensen, known as Anna Margarette Sorensen before she married Rasmus Jensen in 1892, was scheduled to arrive in Standard just before the Christmas of 1937. I was three and one half years old and had outlived the embarrassment of potty training and the misery of being careless with rivets and sand. To be honest, by this time I assumed that my worldly life had been exposed to most of the really vital human experiences. More to the point, after three and one half years, what else could possibly be new and important for my further development?

By this time, I had figured out that the big and previously frightening scissor shapes in the snow that always flanked and followed Dad as he did the winter evening chores were in fact moving leg shadows cast by the kerosene lantern which he was obliged to carry.

Also, I had learned that warm was usually good and that hot could at times be bad. No doubt this revelation emerged one day when Mother was dressing me near and in the warmth of the coal heater that stood in the parlor. I always enjoyed getting dressed in winter and in order to help

Mother reach all of the buttons, I was privileged to stand on a dining room chair, you know, one with a big black square of soft leather on the seat. This was all very nice except for the big chrome ring that stuck out and encircled the lid of the heater. In this elevated position my bare bottom was at exactly the right height to make contact with this part of the heater's ornamentation. Although frequently used by a youngster as a point of learning, a bare touche is not a good part of the anatomy to be employed in the study of thermodynamics and the physical principles of heat transfer.

Perhaps the most important discovery for actual self preservation came in the summer just past when I had made the very astute observation that rain would bring on salamanders. Irene and I called them lizards, and we were sure they came out of the sky with the rain and lightning. Sure enough, after every thunder shower, salamanders would appear in or near the standing pools of water by the old cave root cellar. The root cellar, almost in disuse, was located past the barn, back in the most distant corner of the yard and well beyond Dad's newly painted chicken house. Mother was afraid of them, so we kids were fairly certain that these three to four inch slithering, slimy looking monsters were life threatening.

Happily, the old root cellar was well beyond our normal range of planetary research and discovery. Not so however for the dugout cellar which was right smack dab under our house. Here Dad stored several tons of coal to fuel our stove and the parlor heater to which I carelessly turned my back. Anyway, can you imagine our concern when Irene and I spotted one of these dinosaur remnants in a dark coal filled corner right under the floor on which we walked and played. You can be sure from that moment on, we were extra careful to check under our beds each night before we went to sleep. Clearly this diligence and care paid off since no salamander ever came up from the cellar to get us.

16

But back to Grandmother's arrival; she was due to arrive after dark one cold winter night. Her coming would be a first visit with Dad since 1918 and a first ever with Mother. You should have seen them if you think I was excited.

Mother, Dad, Irene and I all put on our warmest coats and boots before getting into Dad's 1930 Chev, whereupon we headed south to Gleichen and the main line of the C.P.R. No doubt about it, our train station in Standard was important, but the really big one, and for all I knew, the biggest in the world was in Gleichen. Being only sixteen miles south of the farm it was, that day at least, the most important one since Grandmother was soon due to arrive.

We got to Gleichen early, so Irene and I passed the time by sliding back and forth on the big wooden benches that were located in the warmth of the station waiting room. It was fun, and made easy by our heavy woolen coats which were really slick on the varnished and contoured surfaces of these huge pew like seats.

Finally, after what seemed to be a terribly long wait, the big clock on the wall showed some movement and the station agent announced that the train was approaching. Dad took me by the hand and led me outside to the station platform. It is certain that Mother had an equally good grip on my sister's hand as we all moved out into the frosty winter air. Apart from the shock of the cold, I was not at all ready for the events that followed and the shattering experience of meeting my first train. First of all, the brightest light that you could ever imagine was rapidly approaching, This was really scary as it grew nearer and nearer. It seemed as though it was going to lead the rushing and oncoming train right over the platform on which we were standing. Fortunately, at the very last minute, this painfully bright light slipped by only to be replaced by an incredibly noisy roar, whosh, clank, and burst of wind. With all of this we were totally enveloped by a swirl of blinding, hissing steam. Wow! What a commotion. For a moment I had been certain that the train would knock us over and sweep our entire family into its big steel wheels. Even with Dad holding my hand, I was terribly frightened, and had no doubt that we had all just survived a near death experience.

Finally, the big locomotive and its tender rumbled its way past the shaking wooden deck on which we were standing, and which I now reasoned to be much too narrow for use by any sane person. If in fact it was the intention of the Canadian Pacific Railway to settle and bring civilization to the West, they certainly had a strange way of going about it. Who would wish further exposure to such a trauma?

As the big train finally came to a stop, and the white steam rolled out and cleared from under the platform's overhanging roof, one could see that a small stool had been strategically placed right in front of the door leading out from a passenger car. Apparently this was intended to make it easier for Grandmother and the other passengers to disembark.

The first guy to get out of the train was all duded up in a dark blue coat and a matching hat trimmed with a considerable amount of gold braid. He appeared to be important but when he turned to face us, I could hardly believe my eyes. I don't actually remember Grandmother getting off the train but I will never forget my first encounter with a black man. I had never before seen an African American. Up to that point, my visual experience had been essentially limited to the pale faced citizens of Standard who were mostly of Danish origin. At the very worst, the toeheaded men of our town may just have emerged from the coal mine north of town, and if so, they probably needed a bath or at least a good face washing. I knew that coal could make you dirty and can recall thinking that this man's appearance had something to do with the big black locomotive which used coal and had, just moments before, nearly killed us.

Grandmother's visit started with Irene and me getting a bunch of new toys. Memory is a bit fuzzy, and in all probability, these gifts were withheld until Christmas, which came a week or so later. In any event, the most memorable gift that I received from Grandmother was a wooden train set. This toy train didn't need and didn't have tracks. It did however, include tenders, coaches, and two locomotives, one of which looked like the original Tom Thumb. Unlike the one in Gleichen, my miniature trains were not at all threatening.

The various parts of my toy trains had been carefully crafted and assembled by Uncle Chris, Dad's second eldest brother. Uncle Chris was a master carpenter and a truly remarkable person who could do almost anything.

At this point, it is perhaps worth mentioning that Chris emigrated to the United States in 1911 when he was seventeen years old. Apparently he started his career in Detroit as a machinist but soon gravitated to his love of carpentry and woodwork. To start this new venture, Chris left Detroit and relocated to Kenmare, North Dakota, a small town just a few miles south of the Canadian / U.S.A. border.

Chris was apparently quite successful since he was able to help Grandmother and three younger brothers move to the United States later in 1915. By then, Chris had rented a house for himself and all of the new Jensen immigrants arriving from Denmark. These included my widowed Grandmother, Carl, age eighteen, Dad, age sixteen, and Alfred, the youngest who was then fourteen, having been born in 1901, just two years before Grandfather Rasmus passed away in Horning, Denmark.

John, the eldest Jensen, had followed Chris to America and was twenty two years old when his mother and brothers joined them. By that time, he was in college, well on his way to becoming a Lutheran pastor. John pursued a theological career after being strongly influenced by Jens Dixen, the founder of Brorson High school in Kenmare. Apparently this was a fine Christian School, designed to assist and educate new Danish immigrants. Dad briefly attended the school and no doubt it proved to be helpful since it provided him with a formal exposure to the English language.

Moving to the United States was a natural outcome for Uncles John and Chris. Both were American citizens since they had been born in Toledo, Ohio in 1893 and 1895 respectively. This curious happenstance came about when Grandfather Rasmus Jensen immigrated to America in 1880.

As the son of a farm worker and a stone cutter by trade, Grandfather was aware of his limitations in the heavily regimented society of Denmark. In contrast, America promised limitless potential to everyone regardless of their socioeconomic background. For those willing to work, social differences mattered little and this was most certainly of great appeal for many early immigrants.

Following his lead, Grandmother Anna Margaretta Sorenson, Grandfather's fiancee, came to the United States two years later and the two were wed in Toledo on June 2, 1892.

I have no knowledge of the struggles which this young couple endured but do know that they walked right into a brief but severely depressed economic period. Workers outnumbered jobs and there is little doubt that their new life together was most difficult. In the end, they decided to abandoned their plans and dreams for a life in America. It was with great disappointment that they returned to Denmark with their young family in the spring of 1896. By this time Grandmother, always quick and eager to learn, was reasonably fluent in English.

Although the foregoing chronicle was unknown to me in 1937 and may seem out of sync with my story, it had considerable relevance when Grandmother came to visit.

Before continuing however, it is equally vital to know about my mother's parents, Lars and Anna Rasmussen or as I knew them, Bedstefar and Bedstemor, (the Danish equivalent of Grandfather and Grandmother). They, along with their entire family of six children, Rasmus, Anna, Christian, Edward, Ingaborg, and Olga emigrated to America from Falster, one of Denmark's several islands. While they all touched the shores of the United States in 1909, en route, Rasmus and Ingeborg contracted a fatal respiratory illness. Both children died in the immigration facilities on Ellis Island, New York.

With what must have been very heavy hearts and much despair and uncertainty, Bedstefar and Bedstemor moved to Askov, Minnesota, where they settled on a small farm. After loosing two children, it is impossible to imagine the courage and resolve required by these new arrivals as they stuck with their North American plans. Frankly, I don't think that Bedstemor ever fully recovered from the loss. Perhaps their pain was eased a bit when Mother was born in 1910 and was given the names of her deceased brother and sister, Ingeborg Rasmine.

It was not long after Mother's birth when Bedstefar came to the realization that the rocky soil of northern Minnesota would not support a growing family. Once again, Bedstefar and Bedstemor packed up their children and belongings, this time heading north to Canada and Standard, Alberta, a relatively new community that was seeking settlers.

Without question, the move to Standard in 1914 was made easier by the fact that most of the settlers in the area were of Danish extraction and that this was the language of local commerce. Here at last, the Rasmussens could prosper and raise their family which had now expanded to include two additional daughters, Karen and Agnes.

Dad emigrated to Canada from the United States in 1917. Both he and his brother Carl arrived in Standard with little money but great expectations for the future. They had in fact taken advantage of a "land seekers fare" (one cent per mile) promoted by the railroad which was endeavoring to settle the virgin land of Western Canada.

Dad pursued a farming career, working for several farmers in the area before striking out on his own. He commenced this new endeavor on a half section of land, five and one half miles south of Standard.

Although the farm was eventually acquired outright, during the first several years, Dad rented the land from the Canadian Pacific Railway (C.P.R.). A look at history reveals that in 1885 the C.P.R. tied Canada together by building a national coast to coast railway. This no small feat was outrageously expensive when compared to the paltry economic rewards of the time. To assist with the financing and in consideration for the courage and vision exhibited by the founders and investors, twenty five million acres of land bordering the right of way were granted to the C.P.R. In an effort to provide economic viability for the railway, these lands were subdivided into farm parcels which were then sold or rented to the early pioneers taking up residence in Western Canada. To assist, and to accelerate settlement, the C.P.R. often built a few buildings and other needed amenities on some of the farmsteads. This usually included a house, a barn, a well and some fences.

Although Dad's farmstead was not prebuilt by the C.P.R., it did include these essential items. It had in fact been previously occupied by earlier pioneers, Mr. and Mrs. Willard McDowell, who had dug a well and built a house, barn and outhouse. When Dad took over, these few buildings were far from new, and all were badly weathered. By today's standards, the house was barely habitable, and had never seen a drop of paint on its cedar clad exterior. Strangely enough, the barn may have been painted at one time but had been allowed to deteriorate to a rusty brown color. Its largely earthen floor was worn to uneven levels, showing years of use by both cattle and horses.

The boards that made up the outdoor privy, also unpainted, had shrunk leaving nearly inch wide cracks through which one could peer while enjoying the comfort and ambiance of its interior. This was great in the summer, but these voids also gave entry to drifting snow in winter. Sitting on the bench and finding the required toilet tissue, a snow covered Eaton's catalogue, was never high on my list of favorite things to do.

As for the well, this one hundred and sixty foot, steel cased shaft could produce an enormous amount of water if required. In the very early days, its stream was always rust filled but with increased usage, this cleared up to become a pristinely clear and chilled water source. Its less favorable attributes were only of interest to those not immune to its medicinally cleansing action.

About the time that Dad went farming on his own, he met and became interested in Mother. They were wed on December 21, 1931. Since there was no money for a honeymoon, they immediately moved to Dad's farm which was only three miles south of Bedstefar's farmstead. It was also here that I grew up. In this handy dandy cloistered environment, it is not surprising that my early years were in constant contact with Mother's family and the Danish language.

In those early days, Danish was much more common on the streets of Standard than was English. Indeed, I believe that I was baptized in the Danish language, and in fact Nazareth Danish Lutheran Church continued to have some Danish services until I was twelve years of age.

Although he eventually spoke and understood a fair amount of English, Bedstefar retained Danish as his language of choice until his death in 1955. In deference to Bedstemor, he always spoke in that tongue if she was nearby. To the best of my knowledge, she never became even slightly comfortable with English, and indeed I don't recall that she ever seriously tried to speak the language. Almost every word that she spoke to me was in her native tongue. In truth, Bedstemor was never totally happy in America and to illustrate this fact, she wrote several very melancholy poems in the Danish language. These sad ballads told of her love for Denmark and the family that she left behind. The following is a translation of one such poem.

A   Song

I traveled over salty waters
With my friend so dear,
To far and foreign countries
Only the memory I bring with me.
But the memory has power
And I never shall forget
Even if I never hereafter
See my homeland again.
And when in loneliness I dwell
My thoughts go to my home,
And from my breast a sigh escapes
It's for the home I hold so dear.
I think of Father and of Mother
Who still are living there
And of my sisters and my brother
Whom I sincerely hold so dear.
I remember the happy times
The days of tender youth,
I spent with my girlfriends
Before I traveled here.
I think of the bliss and happiness
With you to be reunited.
If only God would decide
To make my prayer come true.

In light of the foregoing, it should not be surprising to know that my entire but limited vocabulary was Danish when Grandmother Jensen arrived in 1937. Undoubtedly she was surprised and perhaps a bit disappointed to find that her Canadian grandchildren were illiterate numskulls, and as Danish as King Knute, (whoever that might be).

I do not specifically recall the transition, but her arrival brought the English language into our home and into my life for the first time. No doubt she realized that the Danish language would not cut it in the real world and as a consequence, Irene and I fell into a heavy duty English immersion course.

When Grandmother returned to North Dakota, we all continued to speak English, the language of the land. Actually, Mother and Dad were more comfortable with the official language so the change over was easy for them. Sadly, my Danish vocabulary is now akin to that of a somewhat retarded three year old. It doesn't make it on the streets of Copenhagen, Arhus, or for that matter, a job interview in Edmonton.

Grandmother was an incredibly resourceful woman. She had to be since she was a very young woman when Rasmus, her husband, died. For the many years after being widowed, she made her living and that of her children with her craft skills. Sewing was her strong suit. If it was to be made of cloth, Grandmother could make it. If a needle and thread were required, she knew how to use them. Years later, and the last time I saw Grandmother in her small but tidy room in a senior citizen's home in Minneapolis, she still had her treadle sewing machine. What's more, she could still use it.

During her visit to Canada in 1937, she seemed always to have a needle and thread in her hand. It is certain that anything that needed mending got mended. If it didn't need fixing, she would stitch on some embroidery work.

After a few months, and for sure by the time she returned to her home in the USA, every pot, vase, ashtray, armchair, ornament, lamp or whatever was standing on or covered with a doily. Moreover, all of the pillows and pillowcases were decorated with carefully stitched embroidery. Perhaps more importantly, all of my sister's dolls and stuffed toys had been outfitted with a wardrobe of fine clothing. After all, it is not proper to have naked dolls laying around.

With all that skill and interest in sewing and crafts, I have never understood why Grandmother dressed as she did. She looked to be as old as God. Then, and in all succeeding years, she always wore a long black dress with almost no frills. There was never any obvious makeup and her graying hair was made up into a large bun at the back of her head. This looked fine but I once saw her with her hair combed out straight. Wow! Was it ever long. "Rapunsel! Rapunsel! Let down your hair." This fairytale character had nothing on Grandmother.

Apart from her talent as a seamstress, Grandmother Jensen was very comfortable in the kitchen and prepared the first frekadella that I ever tasted. For sure, this is the best way to prepare ground meat. No doubt, someday an enterprising Dane with talent in front of a stove, will simulate McDonald's with a national frekadella franchise operation. I can see it now - Frekadella - Billions Sold.

Grandmother's visit to our house came to an end sometime in late winter or early spring. We all missed her very much. It was the first time in my life that I experienced the empty feeling that always comes when someone loved and important goes away.

****

The snow melt came on so suddenly that the small creek just north of our house filled to overflowing. While the water ran high for only a few days, it was long enough to flood over the road and wash out the small culvert that was designed to carry the water under the slightly elevated muddy trail. Actually, this became an annual event and it was quite exciting to wake up and see a virtual river where the night before the valley had been dry or snow covered. It was in fact a very small, mostly dry, tributary of the Crowfoot Creek. For a few days each spring this hardly noticed water course could become a mighty river.

With the culvert gone, there was no way for us to leave our farm. The road south was always too muddy, and the washout prevented any movement north toward Standard. Although the spring floods offered only a brief period of isolation, it did feel strange and prison-like to know that we could not leave the farm.

After a few years filled with spring time intervals of almost certain isolation, Dad would anticipate the thaw and leave the 1930 Chev north of the creek, well above the high water mark. When the main flood subsided, usually within a few days, we could cross the washout on planks to our car and the world beyond. Walking on the bouncy narrow planks was a bit scary while water was still rushing through the canyon-like chasm below. Notwithstanding the narrowness of this escape route, it surely beat the idea of being locked in.

Not surprisingly, the continuing onslaught of the depression had left many farmers with their municipal taxes dangerously in arrears. For better or for worse, there was as a consequence many locals who would gladly undertake various types of road repair to work off the burden of a municipal obligation. In short, there was very little money for the payment of taxes but for an indebted land owner there was a keen willingness to work. With this incentive it didn't take long before the municipal district sent an eager farmer to repair the washout. In the spring of 1938, this was accomplished with a team of horses and a dirt scraper.

Over the years the almost annual repair filled the washout with soil from Alfred Petersen's pasture. To this day, the scars of these annual operations are still visible on the otherwise undefiled prairie.

****

Each year, after the warm breezes of spring had milked the white out of the hills north of town and the angry runoff had made it's way through the Crowfoot Creek to the Bow River, Dad would begin his work in the field..

In 1938, farming was not easy and that meant working with the old John Deere Model D tractor. Now this was a machine with a personality all of its own. Apparently Dad had some understanding of this often balky apparatus since he was the only person who could steer it. The tractor had only two cylinders and it went "Putt - Putt - Putt," as it wobbled and clanked along at about two miles per hour. The big drive wheels had steel lugs that dug little holes in the ground. The front wheels had rims of steel that belted the entire radius in such a way that it could grip the surface and be navigated through soft or hard soil.

As I remember, the fuel was a mixture of distillate, gasoline and water. To stop preignition, the water was mixed with the combustible fuels and it required many gallons to fill the radiator and water jacket which doubled as a supply tank for the water injection. Although the paint was badly faded, there was still a faint glimmer of green and the yellow "John Deere" logo was still more or less visible.

To start the infernal thing, Dad would prime each cylinder with gasoline. He would then spin the large fly wheel until the magneto could produce enough spark to ignite at least one cylinder. As both cylinders started, the smoke and fire would blast out of the front side of the machine through a curved but horizontal exhaust port. Even though I was very small, I could easily reach up and position my hand in front of the warm discharge, which with each blast, was strong enough to knock a mitten flying. That was lots of fun and on a cold, still day, this horizontal exhaust manifold could jettison perfect smoke rings with every blast of a piston. If Dad was working with the tractor in the quiet of the yard, these smoke rings could travel an enormous distance as they expanded and skimmed above the ground.

Dad almost always stood up when he was working with the tractor. Since the tractor employed a hand clutch and had a very poor response on the steering wheel, it was seldom that he used the steel seat fitted behind the wheel, and above the small well worn plank floor. I think it was for this reason that Mother sensed something was very wrong when Dad came home from the field that spring day in 1938. It may have been the first and last time the seat was ever used.

It was well before lunch, a most unlikely time for him to come home. The exact details are rather sketchy but I do recall that he was incredibly sick. Mother helped him into the house, and with the pain that had overtaken him, it was a wonder that he had been able to drive home with the tractor. My memory of the immediate events that followed are a bit fuzzy, but Mother's obvious concern and Dad's equally obvious agony made Irene and me realize that something was terribly wrong.

Once inside, Dad laid down on a bed in the hope that the pain would subside. It didn't, and it soon became apparent that serious help was needed. There was of course, no telephone system linking us to possible aid. On reflection, and to this day, I don't know why Mother didn't get into the old Chev and go for help. After several hours of waiting and watching Dad's deteriorating condition, Mother sent Irene and me to Alfred Petersen's farm for assistance.

Their house was slightly less than one half mile from ours, and was hidden in a beautiful grove of poplars. Irene and I had never before ventured that far from our house but we knew it was an emergency, so off we went in an almost panic atmosphere. While we had, with Mother and Dad's help, discovered a patch of crocuses just a few days earlier, on this urgent occasion, there was no stopping to look at them or the ubiquitous buffalo beans that grew along the roadway. I was still a few days short of being four years old but knew instinctively that this was a serious journey. After all, I had never before seen Dad sick, and felt certain that Mother would not have sent us away unless things were really bad.

We ran into Alfred Petersen's yard and up to their front porch. Except for the screen, their front door was open and we could look right through the kitchen into the parlor. We could even hear the living room clock ticking. For a seemingly very long time, we stood outside and shouted into what turned out to be an empty house. In spite of our strongest wishes and very loud voices, no one responded to our pleading. I still recall the urgency of our call and how terribly empty the house seemed to be.

Finally, Irene persuaded me that we should abandon Alfred and Edna's house and go another third of a mile south to the Ray Green farm. This farm was hidden by a slight rise in the road but we both knew it was there. Going further south was a major move for me since that would put us at odds with Mother's specific instructions. In any event, we had only gone a few hundred yards and were just about to loose sight of our farmstead when we saw a car turn into our yard at home. What a relief for both of us. We knew this would allow Mother to summon help, and we quickly turned back toward home.

The events that immediately followed are lost from memory, but it turns out that it was Mons Hansen who happened by. Mons, one of Dad's good friends, quickly arranged for Dr. Fletcher to come out and examine him.

Unfortunately, Dr. Fletcher could do very little but diagnose the problem as acute appendicitis.

It was nearly dark when Jim Smith, a Standard grain buyer and John Deere agent finally took Dad to Calgary in his nearly new car. The make and model of Mr. Smith's car is unknown but somehow he managed to fold the front passenger seat over in such away that Dad could stretch out on something akin to a hospital gurney. Blankets and pillows made up the bed with head to the rear and feet to the front. Dr. Fletcher joined with Mr. Smith and off they went to the Holy Cross Hospital in Calgary.

En route, the pain that Dad was experiencing suddenly vanished. Had it not been for Dr. Fletcher's urging, it is highly probable that he would have persuaded Jim Smith to return home. It is fortuitous that Dr. Fletcher's advise prevailed since the unattended ruptured appendix would have caused deadly peritonitis.

Naturally, it was all very confusing at the time but I have since learned that in those days a ruptured appendix most often resulted in death. Antibiotics were still to be discovered and early treatment was the only way to restore health. Dr. Richardson, the same doctor who brought me into the world, was the attending physician and surgeon. Apparently, the required appendectomy took place right after Dad was admitted to the hospital.

The following day Bedstefar drove Mother, Irene and me to Calgary for a visit with Dad. We were most anxious to see him and getting there seemed to take forever. Indeed, the trip was rather slow since the highway was unpaved and Bedstefar's old Graham Page was not particularly speedy.

Our first visit with Dad was quite a disappointment since he was still recovering from the anesthetic. Actually, Irene and I visited more with Dad's roommate than we did with him. Mr. Ashton, who shared the room at the Holy

Cross, seemed very talkative. We wished that Dad could be just as well and cheerful.

It's hard to remember how often we were able to go to Calgary but it was heartening to note that with each visit, Dad was somewhat improved. Unfortunately, Mr Ashton was getting progressively worse. Despite his rapidly deteriorating health, he would always share candy, apples and oranges with Irene and me. We enjoyed each visit with him and were sorry when he was no longer with Dad. We didn't know it then, but learned much later that he had died even before Dad was released from the hospital.

In the absence of antibiotics, Dad was required to stay in the hospital for seventeen days. During this time, we saw a lot of Dr. Richardson who was almost always present. He was genuinely pleased and proud of Dad's recovery. He of course knew how serious his patient's condition had been and how fortunate it was that he had survived.

In due course, Dad returned home still much too weak to take care of the spring seeding and other essential chores. These elements of farm life were handled by Mike, our hired man. Mike was in fact, one of Bedstefar's helpers whom we were able to borrow from time to time throughout most of that summer. While Dad was in the hospital, he did all of the required field work and kept up with the livestock as well. Mike was truly a likable man and a tremendous help during the days of Dad's convalescence.

We almost lost Dad in the spring of 1938 and I have often wondered how our lives would have been affected if Dr. Fletcher had not convinced Jim Smith and Dad that a trip to the hospital was required even though the pain had subsided. Indeed, would the good doctor have gone with Dad to the hospital had he not been a close friend and teammate during the early days when they played soccer together? Also, was it Divine intervention that caused Mons Hansen to turn into our yard at that moment in time? I am especially thankful

32

that the old John Deere was able to bring Dad home from the field that spring day. Finally, we were all grateful for the medical skills of Dr. Richardson.

****

As you might expect, there are many early vignettes that come to mind, but very few, like Dad's appendicitis attack, were frightening and unhappy. Having been born into a family with loving and caring parents made those early years a time to be treasured. Also, growing up on a farm was an additional bonus since there was always a new calf or a litter of baby pigs to take on as new pets. In the spring, the baby chicks were fun to hold and pet but one did need to be careful as their toilet manners were deplorable.

Raising chickens was never a high priority but having fresh eggs and an occasional Sunday lunch drumstick made the endeavor worthwhile. Apart from the several hundred baby chicks that were brought from a Calgary hatchery and that matured in the artificial warmth of a coal fired heater, there were always a few barnyard hens that found a place to lay and hatch eggs on their own. These new arrivals were a pleasant surprise and grew up in an entirely different, but more natural way. Typically, they would suddenly make an appearance as five to ten fluff balls, bumbling around the feet of their incredibly protective mother.

While mother hen made every effort to keep her brood together, scratching and clucking through a weed patch was almost certain to result in the temporary loss of at least one baby chick. Sympathy notwithstanding, returning one of these plaintive and incessantly peeping vagrants was fraught with risk. Good intentions were always misunderstood and getting to close to the distraught mother hen was sure to be rewarded by a handful of painful pecks and scratches.

I was always amazed with the survival of these essentially vagabond, homegrown chicks. In time they feathered out, became leggy chickens and eventually blended into the adult flock. This growth was possible despite the many hazards of the barnyard which included minor elements such as a water filled hoof print or a peck from a jealous rooster. Even the resident mouser shaved the chicks odds of reaching maturity.

Speaking of cats, the discovery of a new litter of kittens was always a big kick. This was especially rewarding since it usually required some major exploring by Irene and me. For some reason unknown to us, the mother cat always chose the most difficult of places to give birth to her kittens. Marco Polo's travels could not have been more exciting than was our search for them. It often involved the entire farmstead. After their discovery, they frequently disappeared only to reappear a few weeks later in an entirely new location, but now with eyes wide open, playfully tumbling over and around each other.

****

Undoubtedly, one of my most vivid and happy childhood memories is evoked when I reflect on our church and our family's involvement within it's doors. Nazareth Danish Lutheran Church was and is the only fully organized church in Standard. The first pioneers had barely unloaded their wagons when the church was founded. It was, and remains today, a cornerstone for virtually the entire community. Its ongoing success is characterized by a willingness to accept change, even though at times this proved to be painful. This was especially so for the early membership and founders of the church who over the years were obliged to accept a transition from their more comfortable native tongue to English.

In the very beginning its ministry was directed exclusively to the Danish community. At or about the time of my birth, Reverend Beck, the then leader of the flock, was obliged to inject an occasional bit of English into his services. Later, with the arrival of Pastor H. Christensen (about 1938), English began to assert itself. By the time he accepted another call, and was replaced by Reverend Jorgensen in 1944, every other Sunday service was conducted in English. In 1954, the name of the church was changed from Nazareth Danish Lutheran Church to Nazareth Lutheran Church of Standard.

Throughout this period, our family was continuously involved, enjoying many close friendships with other persons sharing the faith. I will always cherish these relationships and will forever be grateful to Mother and Dad who ensured that Irene and I attended church, Sunday school and confirmation classes. To this day, I am certain that this is the most meaningful and important legacy of my youth.

Putting spiritual values aside, the social and fellowship elements provided by our church were for the most part quite remarkable. While this was personified in many ways such as potluck dinners, pie socials etc., nothing could match the incredible Sunday, after church dinner parties that were truly a marvel of culinary excellence and social outreach. These gastronomical delights followed a pattern that hardly varied from year to year or from family to family.

Starting with the church service, it was easy to spot a family that had on that particular day, scheduled a dinner party. With apparent approval of the minister and contrary to the admonitions of the third commandment, it was guaranteed that the lady hosting the party would be home preparing the food, and would be absent from the morning service. It was equally predictable that her husband would be there, proving that all was well to his congregational guests who were also certain to attend.

Mother and Dad's food fests were typical of the many parties that followed a Sunday service. Invitations would embrace an entire family, young and old. The formal meal, served in the dining room could accommodate about ten guests. Irene and I along with any other children in attendance would be obliged to eat in the kitchen. There, the conversation was usually much less mature and rarely as interesting. As a bonus however, manners were not as rigorously adhered to and second helpings were less of an embarrassment and easier to obtain.

The meal, carefully prepared, always featured delicious salads and multiple vegetable dishes, all of which were generously served. Pork or beef was the usual entree but on at least three occasions wild game birds were provided as a special treat. Desserts were invariably outstanding and were punctuated with copious amounts of coffee.

Cleaning up usually involved all of the women, who immediately following the meal, invaded the kitchen and the dish pan with tremendous resolve. While this was underway, the men made for the soft furniture of the living room, settling in for a lot of conversation and a relaxing smoke. The ladies had hardly completed their chores when afternoon coffee and goodies would suddenly appear. Here again the sandwiches, cakes and cookies were plentiful and delicious.

There were of course many Sundays when we neither hosted a party nor were we invited to one. These blanks in the rotation were not uncommon and were effectively used to recharge ones batteries and allow Mother and Dad to review their calendar for forthcoming events. On reflection, there were probably a few unlucky church members who were seldom included and were not among those on an almost perpetual invitation list. Happily, these were few in number. Our family was not among such a minority and it's hard to think of a church family that has not been in our home or we in theirs. The food was always great but the fellowship was even better. With all of this who wouldn't develop a strong sense of belonging?

****

I didn't mind that Danish was so pervasive in our community but there were times when I wished it would go away. This was especially so during those early years when every summer, usually on a miserably hot day, we went to "Folkfest." This midsummer Danish ritual was always hosted by the nearby congregation of Dalum. Denmark could not have been more Danish than was this small enclave of blonde immigrants from Jutland and Sjaeland. The pastor, Reverand Rasmussen, a tall striking figure of a man who always wore black and a praestekrade (fluted collar), was the author and captain of this pasture carnival.

I was never quite sure what "Folkfest" was about except that it was staged in a deep alderbrush filled coulee, immediately behind Reverand Rasmussen's country home. It was hot, dusty, lousy with flies and mosquitos and there was no place to sit. If that wasn't bad enough, the entire program was in Danish with the likelihood that anyone speaking a word of English would be hung, drawn, and quartered. It was an incredible bore. To this day, I will never understand why my folks, or anyone for that matter, would attend this astonishing festivity. I was much too young to protest or opt out but going to "Folkfest" ranked with a trip to the dentist.

****

While there was the hardship of the "Great Depression," a worry for Mother and Dad, I was largely sheltered from these concerns and certainly did not miss any meals. After all, we grew most of our own food including an occasional pig, some chickens and of course many eggs.

When the old cow gave birth to a new calf there was also fresh milk, cream, and butter on the table. We could and did, on a few occasions, grind our own flour. A trip to the Gleichen flour mill could even yield a blended cereal not unlike "Sonny Boy Cereal," a well known Alberta breakfast food that featured several grain types including some very tasty flax seeds. It was not bad if you didn't mind mush for breakfast.

Mother was a natural gardener and spent many summer hours tending and weeding her garden. For sure, some of her happiest moments were spent looking for the first signs of growth each spring. She preferred flowers but this did not detract from the attention she gave to the almost vital business of growing vegetables. These frequently grew next to a row of flowers - petunias, African daisies and marigolds.

Speaking of flowers, Mother seemed intent on growing hollyhocks. As a child, I was never sure whether a hollyhock was a tree or a flower. It was in my view, a total mistake of nature. They grew to a height of about ten feet with a particularly unpleasant sticky trunk. It is probable that an axe was required to clean up each fall after the frost. The flowers were not bad but seemed always to be the first frozen and were as a result, very ugly through most of the autumn. In their defense however, they were tall like trees and in combination with a few equally tall sunflowers may have created something of a shelter belt.

Dad handled most of the heavy work and was as a consequence a major contributor to the success of the vegetable garden. With this joint effort, our diet always included an abundance of home grown produce. There were potatoes, carrots, peas, beans and all manner of equally important garden items. While these were all excellent, the tomatoes were by far the most notable and memorable. They were truly the best you could ever imagine. Although somewhat short-lived, for a few years we also had a strawberry patch that was the envy of the entire community.

Now it happens that in addition to all of these good things, there was rhubarb - lots of rhubarb. This is a plant of some notoriety and it is little wonder and very fitting that the dictionary includes in its definition, a quarrel or squabble. It is possible that rhubarb in small amounts is not bad. Unfortunately, that is not how we got it. In my memory, it came frequently as jam, frequently in pies, frequently in sauce and frequently in almost everything. Apparently it is a select source of vitamin A. That being true, I should have a lifetime supply of this important growth vitamin somewhere in my system. Were it not for a partial genetic inheritance of Bedstefar's diminutive five foot one inch stature, my enormous rhubarb ingestion would probably have seen me grow to a height of seven feet.

We had at least six large plants on the farm. One was considered sweet (none were sweet) and at least one was tart. Three of these overused plants grew right alongside the cow and horse pasture, and even with continued use, grew to enormous proportions.

Now when the grass within the pasture was chewed short it didn't take the animals long to figure out that there were still a few good morsels outside the fence. Even though there were four strands of barb wire, Dad never raised an animal that wasn't smart enough to reach out a foot or so to collect the many tender shoots of grass that were outside the fence boundaries, well beyond the range of trampling hooves.

The Jensen rhubarb plants were well within easy reach of the cows and horses and they chewed the grass right up to and around the stalks of these infernal plants. Clearly however, their taste was most discerning, since they left intact every green leaf on the rhubarb, just the way God had grown it. Could it be that cows and horses are smarter than humans?

As a side issue, it is a fact that rhubarb makes a dandy pot cleaner. After cooking this Asian herbaceous import in an aluminum sauce pan, you can almost use the pan's bottom for a mirror. Rhubarb sauce can slick up a pot better than Ajax and you don't even need elbow grease. It can be assumed that this well known garden item pays the same dividend to one's stomach. The defense rests.

****

But lets go back to the spring and summer of 1938; Dad's convalescence and recovery was going along very well so Mother and Dad decided a little vacation might be in order. We were not needed at home since Mike was available to feed the cows and chickens and do the required field work. Nancy and Beauty were in the pasture and only needed water every few days. That is to say, their water trough, a gas drum cut in half, contained a supply that could last for several days. This homemade water source was used in the pasture for many years but was finally replaced by a small earthen dam that held rain and snow runoff. The resulting pond also served as a skating rink in early winter.

Who knows where the money came from but off we went to Sylvan Lake, just west of Red Deer. It was my very first vacation and since Mother and Dad had missed out on a honeymoon, it was certainly their first holiday trip of consequence.

We stayed in a very small red roofed cabin in Sylvan Lake town which was right near the beach. The cottage had a single room with two beds, a small table and chair set, and a cook stove that used wood for fuel. I remember bringing in the fire wood from the kindling pile out behind the cottage.

Sylvan Lake has a delightful sandy beach and in those days, not a lot of folks to enjoy it. Unfortunately, the water was another story. It was plagued with weeds and myriads of hair snakes. Being about a foot long, and approximately the thickness of a hair from a horse's mane, these curious wonders of nature virtually dominated the water. They were in constant motion and as we waded into the lake we could feel these funny things touching and bumping into our legs. As far as we knew, they were totally harmless, but made the whole idea of swimming a bit unpleasant. Dad was able to swim and Mother could float but Irene and I didn't get our faces wet as we didn't much care for the incredible number of black hair snakes.

It was a great trip and was early enough in the year for a few ripened saskatoon berries. They were right along the roadside and Mother was able to pick some during a brief rain shower. She stayed in the dry comfort of the car as she reached out through an open window to the fruit laden branches. Using Dad's hat as a container, it wasn't long before she collected enough berries for our supper dessert.

It was a very restful few days which undoubtedly did a great deal for the restoration of Dad's health.

Now it turns out that Mother had started to loose her hair some four years earlier at the time of my birth. Everyone in the family knew about it but the Sylvan Lake trip was my first real awareness of just how serious the problem had become. After each trip to the beach and the lake, Mother would return to our one room cabin and comb her hair. This would literally produce handfuls of loose hair and generate bald spots all over her head. I honestly believe she could have removed all of her hair if she had continued combing. From that time on, she almost always had at least one bald spot somewhere on her scalp. Because she was distressed and embarrassed by this hair loss, it became a continuing and major trauma for her. In the many years that followed, Mother made countless trips to various doctors in the hope that some cure could be found. She tried lotions, herbs, salves and diets but nothing seemed to work. We all felt very sorry for her, since in her youth, she had been blessed with beautiful heavy auburn hair. I suffered with her and felt somewhat responsible, since the problem seemed to start with my arrival.

In total, we spent about three days at Sylvan Lake. We then motored east to the town of Stettler where Dad had a school friend from Denmark. There may have been some prior arrangements for this visit but I really think it was a spontaneous decision that triggered this extension to our vacation. In reality, the trip to Stettler added very few miles to the overall distance of our travels. It did however offer an alternate way home and provided an opportunity for everyone to see a little more of Alberta.

Traveling in the old 1930 Chevrolet was an experience that was both good and bad. It was a two door car so Mother and Dad could place Irene and me in the back seat, knowing that we could not fall out. The roads were not paved, and there was a considerable amount of dust that sifted into the car as we bumped and rocked along. Road dust had long since soiled the plush seats and despite a good deal of care and cleaning, they always had a dusty smell. They were certainly no fun to lie down on. This may be the reason that Irene and I rarely sat down during our travels. In any event, we both enjoyed a car ride and almost always stood up, holding on to the backs of the two front seats. They were both designed to individually fold forward when someone was entering the back seat of the car. In a frontal accident, this configuration would have allowed the seats to flip forward, throwing the driver and front seat passenger right through the windshield. We were of course, unaware of this design flaw and thankfully, no such accident occurred. Also, in those days, seat belts were for airplanes only. No one thought that such a safety device was required for an automobile.

The gap between the two front seats was about five inches wide. For Irene and me this opening, right in the middle, provided a prime standing location. Not only was it more comfortable, it also positioned the lucky occupant right between Mother and Dad and provided an outstanding view through the front windshield. Now who could blame us for wanting that? Clearly however, we could not both enjoy this location of choice and there was often a struggle or should I say, disagreement between Irene and me for this desirable territory. We were not necessarily rough but when the Chevrolet was traded off for a new car in 1947, the tops of the front seats were in absolute shambles. Over the years, our small hands had totally destroyed the plush coverings.

We arrived in Stettler during the afternoon and after a brief search and a few inquiries, Dad located the home of Andy Andersen, his old school friend from Denmark. The initial greetings were extremely cordial and somehow we were persuaded to stay for several days. I didn't much care for this since we all slept in their living room, and that put me on the floor. Also, Irene and I were expected to play with the Andersen kids, Jimmy and Nellie. They were about our ages but their tire swing in the back yard was almost always occupied by one of them while Irene and I supplied most of the push-power. In truth, it was much more enjoyable to visit the shop where Mr. Andersen worked. He was a mechanic, charged with the responsibility of maintaining the equipment in a flour mill.

Dad enjoyed the visit with his "Old Country" friend but to the best of my knowledge, the renewed relationship led to little more than the annual exchange of Christmas cards.

****

After returning home, Dad's strength continued to improve. With this, Mike's job at our farm played out during the late summer. We didn't see him again until autumn when Bedstefar's big threshing machine helped with the harvest.

Harvest, the successful culmination of hard work and a considerable amount of worry, was truly an exciting time. This drama of the stubble fields began with Bedstefar's big wood sided threshing machine coming down the road toward our farm. This was followed by several wagons, each pulled by a team of horses. What a sight! What a parade! The whole crew numbered about eight men, most of whom were driving a team of horses.

Uncle Chris always operated the tractor while Bedstefar drove his antique truck. The model of this ancient International Harvester vehicle is unknown but judging by its appearance, it must have arrived with the Mayflower. It certainly was old and may well have been used in the move to Canada from Minnesota in 1914.

The engine was constantly laboring and even when its wooden box was empty it sounded like it was about ready to expire. In truth, the most lively parts of the entire rig were its front fenders which shook with every beat of its coughing engine. It most assuredly was not built for speed and it looked the part. Streamlining was not a consideration in its design as both the cab and engine housing were about as square as a shoe box. The tires, fixed on wooden spoked wheels, appeared to be of solid rubber and the side windows and windshield were fixed in an absolutely vertical position. Compared with Elmer Wirt's new Fargo truck and Standard Transport rig, Bedstefar's relic should have been in a museum.

As bad as it sounds, it was part of the threshing outfit and it was always an incredible thrill whenever Bedstefar invited me to join him in the cab. Once inside, the grinding sounds intermingled with the uncertain gasping of the engine was even more ominous. Sitting on the well worn interior seat, it was possible to see the moving earth through the cracks in the floor boards. I surely wished that Bedstefar would get a new truck.

Anyway, when the parade of harvest equipment turned into our yard it was really something and it made me feel extremely important. Imagine all this stuff and people coming to our house. The threshing machine, all folded up for moving, was being pulled by Bedstefar's McCormick Deering tractor. Both Dad's John Deere and Bedstefar's four cylinder puffer were equipped with a pulley wheel that was necessary to drive the threshing machine, but for some reason, Dad's unit was never used. It maybe that the old John Deere didn't have adequate muscle to power this cumbersome but marvelous piece of harvest equipment.

The threshing machine was made of wood and steel. The wooden parts were a faded red while all of the metal, including the folded down straw blower, was of galvanized steel. So that it could be moved from place to place, it was mounted on four medium sized spoked wheels of steel. When it was in operation, Bedstefar's tractor stood about twenty yards away pulling an equally long belt that extended to the machine, and right in line with the bundle rack. This was folded out so that bundles of grain could be simultaneously tossed into the apparatus from either side. On one side, the horses bringing in the bundles were required to stand right next to the power belt, which was zipping by at a great speed. They were not always keen to do this, and at times, the wagon driver entering the machine on that side would experience some difficulty in getting his team to behave.

The machine itself, reminded me of a huge dragon since there were large jaw-like knives that reached out and chewed the bundles into digestible pieces as they were conveyed toward the mysterious inner workings. It looked very dangerous and there was always a concern that someone would fall into the bundle carrier. The noise was enough to scare me, and that combined with the shaking and banging, kept me from getting too close. Besides, it was unpleasantly dusty since every crack in the wooden sides produced little puffs of chaff and dust that filled the surrounding air.

The inside of the machine was a mystery but somehow the grain and straw were separated. The grain was elevated into a little box that was affixed to the end of a pipe about fifteen feet off the ground. Whenever the box was full of grain, it would dump into another spout that drained into the storage bin. Meanwhile, the straw would blast out of a big galvanized tube like a cannon shot. This resulted in a huge stack of straw that Dad could use to bed the livestock throughout the winter. When the snow came, Irene and I used it as a soft hill on which to slide down with our sled or toboggan.

Early in his farming endeavor, Dad did not have a proper granary to house the crop. Basically, it was dumped right on the ground, but was confined by a bin made of pig wire, tar paper and straw. The straw was carefully placed along the inside of the wire grid, which in turn, supported the tar paper. With all of this careful engineering, the bin was strong enough to hold the grain. When the harvest was completed, Dad would cover it with straw, thus protecting the grain from rain and snow. With its vertical sides, such a bin took on the appearance of a huge straw hat.

Clearly, I was much too young and small to be of any help during these early harvests. Once in a while however, Mother would let me stay out in the field after she had served afternoon coffee to the crew. This was really great and of course I promised not to stick my fingers into the whirling belts and shakers. If being around the machine became tiresome, I could sit in Bedstefar's truck or go with Dad and his hayrack into the field for a load of bundles. His wagon was different from all the others since it had two large beams that protruded out behind. Pretending that they were horses I could sit on one of them and ride for hours. If Irene happened to be there, we could each have a pole to sit on. Unlike the back seat of the car, there was lots of room for both of us.

Since much of the work at harvest was done by horses, it was not possible to work into the late hours of each day. After all, the horses were in need of a drink and rest just as much as were the men who drove them. At about five o'clock, Uncle Chris would shut down the tractor and loosen all of the belts on the machine. This was the signal for everyone to quit for the day. The quiet that ensued was almost deafening. For the first time since lunch, one could hear the crickets and grasshoppers. Off in the distance, the quiet jingle of loosened harness could be heard as the horses headed home through the afternoon's autumn dust and haze. They were looking for some oats, a good drink of water, and some rest.

We didn't have a pump engine at that time so it took a lot of work on the old pump handle to get enough water for the horses and men. It seemed that some of the men could drink almost as much as the horses. Also in preparation for supper, all of the workers washed up at an outdoor basin set up for that purpose. The routine never seemed to vary as each soiled harvester would fold under his shirt collar before vigorously scrubbing his face with both hands. This was always accompanied by a lot of snorting and blowing which appeared to be an essential part of the hygienic process. I was impressed and for several years tried to emulate these bubbling sound effects. In due course I learned that the nose noises had no cleansing influence but they did prevent one from drowning.

The water from our well was always cold and I was convinced that it offered the best drink in the world. Years later, after leaving home for long intervals, I discovered other attributes much less inviting. While it was still cold and could still quench a thirst, it also provided the benefits of a good dose of salts. Today, my advise would be "Don't Drink The Water."

My most cherished memory of those early year harvests was Mother's cooking. To keep everyone happy and working, she prepared meals just like the ones we had for Sunday company. They were so tasty that Irene and I could easily have wondered if the minister was coming. While the horses were munching on oats and hay, all of the crew members were seated in our living room at a big table especially set up for the occasion. More importantly, there was often one empty seat at the table and at those times, I was thrilled to sit and eat with the men. As you might expect, much of the table conversation was about a possible war in Europe.

Typically, Mother would serve a chicken lunch with all of the trimmings. For supper, we would feast on roast beef or pork, mashed potatoes and gravy along with a variety of garden fresh vegetables. This would be followed by lots of coffee and a choice of at least two types of pie, one of which was probably rhubarb. I would of course choose either apple or lemon if one of these favorites was on the menu.

Memory is less than perfect, but it is likely that most of Dad's 1938 crop was harvested with a threshing machine. It is possible however, that a small portion of the grain fields saw action from Bedstefar's new Holt combine. This was truly a magnificent machine. It could cut the grain and thresh out the kernels all at the same time. The operating crew was much reduced but it did require two able bodied men to make sure everything was running properly. One man had to ride the combine in order to look after its engine, the cutting bar, and of course the business of spanking the grain away from the straw. His partner had to drive the tractor which pulled this huge hunk of galvanized metal around the field. It may have been a major improvement over the threshing machine, but it was certainly much less fun. As a child, I much preferred the excitement of horses, wagons and lots of men. To make it worse, Mother didn't have to cook those wonderful meals for such a small crew.

****

After harvest, we were almost always fitted with a few new items of clothing for winter. Being a bit smaller than Irene, I was in line to inherit a few articles of clothing that no longer fit her. In most cases this turned out well and I didn't mind if the hand-me-downs were without specific gender. Overshoes, scarves and even a hooded snowsuit was quite acceptable. Sadly, the legacy of Grandmother's visit of the year just past, had given Irene's woolen mittens a distinctively feminine appearance. As I recall, they all had little animals or flowers carefully embroidered on their cuffs. They were warm but I always felt that the fluffy kittens showing on the back of my wrists were unnecessary and at times, in the presence of other boys, downright awkward.

Happily, everything was not second hand and while there may have been other new unused apparel, I will never forget the usual two sets of underwear. What a treat they were. This was the real McCoy - genuine fleecy long johns with a fashionable trap door at the back. They were so warm and comfortable and equally important, they were brand spanking new!

As usual, all of our new duds came from either the Simpson's or Eaton's Winnipeg distribution centers. These large retail companies never failed to send one of their mail order catalogues each fall. It was always a big day when one arrived and before the more serious business of ordering winter clothes could begin, Irene and I would hurry a look at the toy pages. What a marvelous selection there was. At least six pages were devoted to dolls, teddy bears, building blocks, toy guns, trucks, cars, tractors, and games. These pages were meant to dream over.

****

There probably was never a time when I wasn't interested in guns and hunting. It was late in 1938, when after his convalescence, Dad bought a 22 rifle, a real honest - to - goodness firearm. While I enjoyed my toy pop guns and pistols, I always knew that they weren't real and much preferred to ogle the new Browning pump that was safely positioned on a nail over the stairwell in the old two story house. It was beyond my reach and a chair would not sit on the stairs. Maybe if the legs were shortened on one side? Anyway, to make matters worse, and as an added aggravation, I wasn't even allowed to touch the gun when Dad took it down to oil and clean it, or to shoot at an occasional marauding coyote.

It sure did feel good to know that we had a gun in the house. I knew what a firearm could do, since someone in past years had used our house for target practice. There were three neat bullet holes in one of the closet doors. These gun shot markings had apparently arrived before Dad moved in and before he and Mother were married.

At or about the same time that Dad bought his rifle there was more and more talk about war. Everyone was murmuring about that ugly guy, Hitler, who now occupied Austria and had taken over the Sedeten frontier. Naturally, I wasn't fully aware of every German move but even a four year old has ears and an ability to become frightened. With this growing fear of war, I was mighty glad that we had the comfort of a gun for protection. There was every reason to believe that Dad could shoot Hitler or his sidekick Mussolini should they ever risk a visit to our farm. To this day, it is certain that Mother and Dad never realized how reassuring it was for me to know that there was a rifle hanging over the stairs. When the war finally broke out almost a year later, its importance was further noted when Dad was obliged to register the rifle with the RCMP in Strathmore. (To avoid the risk of political tyranny within Canada, these firearm registrations were carefully destroyed in 1945, after the war.)

I had become aware of war and its horrors long before I should have. Although fighting had not yet started in Europe, I had obtained some sense of people killing people while leafing through Bedstefar's "Book of Knowledge." This massive encyclopedia was filled with interesting pictures and it was always fun to thumb through several volumes and glean some ideas and stimulate some thought from the many varied illustrations. Reading was a skill yet to be acquired but this did not detract from the entertainment value of these weighty books. Also, a visit to Bedstefar's and Bedstemor's house could at times be quite boring. After Grandmother's visit, when English became the language of choice, we kids were seldom included in the Danish conversations. Besides, no one was terribly interested in the learned opinions of a four year old even though I thought they were pretty good. A look through one of the books with pictures made a better pastime and was usually more entertaining.

Now it is certain that a young child who has grown up in a sheltered environment is unlikely to know very much of man's inhumanity to man. Oh sure, there were moments of anger and small fights with Irene. There may even have been an occasional flair of temper with Mother or Dad, but these rare moments were not to be compared with the killing and the brutal activity of a war.

I will never forget the first picture that I ever saw of men in mortal combat. It was in the "Book of Knowledge" which showed a painting of some medieval battle. The scene depicted a clash between two armies fighting at very close quarters. The men armed with swords and knives were

51

cutting off limbs, heads and other body parts. The picture showed men standing in the gore of battle with dead soldiers lying all about. Some of the dead and dying were without limbs and were often positioned under equally mutilated bodies. Those that were not dead were in the act of dying or were in the process of killing someone. It was a terrible picture and I was more that a little upset with this disturbing discovery.

Taking the open book to Uncle Chris, I clearly remember him studying the scene for a moment after which he reluctantly advised that the picture illustrated a war in progress. So now, I understood what everyone was talking about or at least I thought I did. Working from this premise it was clear that such a battle would be the end of me, Mother, Dad, Irene, and all of my uncles, aunts, cousins, Grandmother Jensen, Bedstefar and Bedstemor. It was not a pleasant thought, leaving me with some doubts about the effectiveness of Dad's protective rifle. I was scared.

Adding to my fears, Mother and Dad had acquired a radio a few months earlier. In many ways it was a terrific device since it could mysteriously bring music right into our home. It could also bring news of the European conflict.

The radio, quite a large piece of furniture, stood in the living room. Mother and Dad had bought it from Stan Wanvig, a mechanic who ran Reliable Motors in Standard. The radio was new and included as a bonus gift, salt and pepper shakers each shaped like the RCA Victor dog. For years these salt and pepper shakers stood on one of Grandmother's doilies on top of the radio.

To make the radio work, a long wire aerial that was hooked to the back, extended outside through a storm window's air hole. The inside of the radio had electrical workings including vacuum tubes, B batteries, and A batteries. When the radio was turned on, the tubes glowed like the wick of a candle that had just been blown out. The batteries occasionally ceased to work and required replacement or recharging at Stan's garage in Standard. Because the batteries were short lived, playing the radio was more or less restricted but included the Sunday sermons of Premier Aberhardt, and Saturday's Hockey Night in Canada with the Toronto Maple Leafs and Foster Hewett. Week days always featured a few soap operas like Oxydol's Ma Perkins, and more importantly, the CBC news.

The CBC news came on at noon at least six days a week. While this broadcast was in progress, Dad insisted on total quiet so that not a word would be missed. This was all well and good, except in the close quarters of our home, I also heard every word of these frightening and nasty reports. Hitler and Mussolini were virtually in our living room every day. Invariably, each broadcast included a brief but poignant announcement from the BBC direct from London, England. These bulletins, usually a flood of war rumors, were even more ominous and foreboding.

With all of these appalling and alarming messages on the airwaves, it should come as no surprise that nearly everyone was talking about a possible war in Europe. These conversations made it easy to conjure up the image of men fighting men as depicted in Bedstefar's "Book of Knowledge."

If memory serves, war gossip was growing in intensity for at least a year before Hitler made a move on Poland in September, 1939. This period more or less coincided with Dad's convalescence and recovery from appendicitis. The combination of these two events represents an inordinately large portion of my early years and provides some of my most vivid childhood memories. Clearly however, my life was not dominated by war talk and there were many other events and circumstances which were of significance and which evoke many happy thoughts. I look back on these with great pleasure.

****

Christmas, my favorite holiday, came and went and was as usual, filled with great joy and celebration. As was our custom, all of the local members of Mother's family celebrated Christmas Eve at Bedstefar and Bedstemor's house. This meant that we, the Holms, along with uncles Chris and Edward were always there. On rare occasions, if the weather was suitable, the Andersens and the Molgards, living in Calgary at the time, would travel to Standard. When that happened, all of the Rasmussen cousins were together at once; did we kids ever have a blast.

Bedstemor was a fine cook and the celebration always started with a spectacular meal. Turkey was the main entree but Danish tradition was always satisfied with the addition of a roasted goose. The meal was served in the huge dining room and if there was space, we kids were allowed to sit with the grownups. I don't ever remember when we didn't all eat too much.

After the meal, it was the practice to sing a number of Christmas carols. Initially, these were mostly sung in English but gradually a few Danish ones were included. This was especially so if uncles Martin and Fred were present. In those days, before Dad permanently lost his singing voice during a severe winter cold, that trio could virtually rattle the windows with their boisterous singing of songs from the old country.

In due course, Bedstefar would light the candles on the Christmas tree. This was done very carefully so that the tree and the many paper decorations would not catch fire. The decorations included a few silver streamers but were for the most part, paper garlands and glass figures. Also, there were a fair number of Danish flags hanging from the tree. These included at least one very long string to which was attached a whole series of little red and white Danish flags. With all of this Scandinavian memorabilia, we had every reason to assume that Jesus was Danish and that Bethlehem was a suburb in the hills outside of Copenhagen.

The celebration continued with all of the cousins holding hands and moving around the tree in one big continuous circle. More carols were sung, but by this time they were mostly Danish. If Aunt Olga was there, she would play the piano, otherwise Mother would do the honors. "Glagelig Jule" was the most popular choice but Bedstefar would almost always find a way to deviate from the Christmas theme for at least one of his favorites, "Hils Mein Far og Mor." This was a very sad song about a sailor far from home. The story tells of a swallow that falls onto the deck of a ship far at sea. The lonesome sailor implores the little bird to fly back home to Denmark where it is to greet the seaman's mother and father.

Tears always came easily for Bedstemor and this song always touched her. No one ever made a comment as she slipped away for a little cry. We all knew how much she missed her family back in her homeland.

I was always glad to see the candles on the tree burn down so that we could stop dancing around the tree and get on with the really important business of opening our presents. There was a terrific assemblage of gifts since every family provided at least one parcel for each of the little ones. Typically, we small tykes would each receive a gift from the Holm's, the Molgard's, the Andersen's, uncles Chris and Edward, Bedstefar and Bedstemor, and of course, our own parents. These gifts could be almost anything from a Japanese toy with sharp edges to a set of dishes. At that time Japan was not known for it's craftsmanship and a toy of their making could, with luck, last until New Year's Eve. I was once given a toy alligator that sparked a flint when it was pushed along the floor. The flint was depleted long before the Christmas Eve celebration was over, and of course, I made a valiant attempt to repair the problem. After taking it apart to replace the flint, the cheap metal tabs that held it together, fatigued and broke off - end of toy. I also recall Cousin Lars getting a toy tea set. He opened it upside down and every cup and saucer smashed on the floor. In the end this mattered little since Lars was not terribly interested in pretend tea parties.

The gift I best remember from this particular Christmas was a pop gun received from Mother and Dad. It resembled Dad's new rifle and made a very satisfactory "Bang" when fired. In miniature, it resembled the real thing and if necessary it may have been able to scare Hitler. With this new equipment, it wasn't many days after Christmas that I went hunting.

****

It was late in the afternoon on a clear cold day when I ventured out into the wilds of our farm yard. Fresh snow covered everything and it was tough going. I did however manage to get past the spot, where in summer, Mother had her vegetable garden. This was well beyond the place where Dad parked most of the farm implements. Everything was frozen solid but there was hope that I would be able to spot a rabbit or maybe even a coyote. Any one of these dangerous beasts that occasionally appeared near the farmstead would provide a splendid target for my new gun. Unfortunately, there was no game in sight so it occurred to me that trapping one of these wary animals could be a reasonable substitute for this particular excursion.

Dad was trapping the occasional weasel and even better, I knew where the trap was set. So that there would be something to report when I returned to the warmth of the house, I bravely ventured forth to check on the set to see if there was something in his trap. No doubt about it, Dad knew how to catch weasels. Though somewhat unorthodox, he would place a chicken head in a soup can. This, positioned horizontally in the snow with a trap at the open end got marvelous results. This scrumptious bait was sure to lead the unfortunate weasel right over the open trap.

Upon reaching the set, I apparently didn't believe my eyes, even though it was obvious that the trap was clamped open and there was no evidence of a weasel. To be absolutely sure however, it seemed appropriate to place my mittened hand into the trap. Snap! Now I was caught. Not only did it hurt but I was sure that I would die. After all, it was well known that any animal caught in Dad's traps was soon dead.

Well, if this was the end, I certainly wasn't going to go quietly. I started to howl as loud as possible. Happily, Irene heard the commotion and came over to investigate. She provided little immediate comfort, since she also thought I was a goner. Despite this poor prognosis, she quickly ran to the house to report on my predicament. In the end, it didn't take Dad long to come to my rescue. He quickly opened the trap and set my hand free. The woolen mitten, probably knit by Grandmother, had permanently imprinted yarn marks into my tiny cold fingers.

The incident was never forgotten but after a good supper and the assurance that I would not die from the trap, I felt much better.

****

It may have been the somewhat drafty house or it may have been something going around, but whatever it was, Mother had an almost continuous bout of tonsillitis during the winter. Irene and I were not sick nor were we troubled by inflamed tonsils, but getting rid of them was popular and seemed the right thing to do. We all went to the hospital together and once again saw Dr. Richardson.

Irene and I tried to be very brave and promised the good doctor that we would be on our best behavior. When making this promise, we had reason to believe that Mother would be with us throughout the ordeal. Unfortunately, she was assigned to an entirely different ward. We were not expecting this and feeling utterly abandoned, were more than a little troubled. Dad stayed with us for a while, but when he left our best intentions quickly turned into a big bust. While waiting in our room for the surgery, we screamed and hollered so much that a frustrated nurse finally gave us each a spanking. Later Dad claimed that our crying could be heard several floors down and as far away as the front entrance to the Holy Cross Hospital.

Irene and I stayed in the hospital for one night. At this point, after our tonsillectomy, our throats were too sore to holler so we were quiet for a change. Dad came early the next morning to rescue us from our loneliness. Were we ever glad to see him and our very own clothes which he carried with him. Even at this early age, we didn't much care for the hospital gowns that opened at the back. After visiting Mother, who was obliged to stay in the hospital for a few extra days, we went to the Empress Hotel where we were treated to a dish of ice cream and my first ever taste of tomato juice. It hurt to drink and swallow but the taste of this new discovery was terrific.

Now the entire event may easily have been forgotten except that Irene and I each got a new toy. I received an orange teddy bear and Irene was given a new doll. The teddy bear still lives, and to this day it can still utter a not so fierce growl when tipped over.

****

With the arrival of spring, it was time to cut the arms and legs off the long johns that had kept me warm throughout the cold days of winter. I always liked spring since it brought on so many new things. Apart from the new leaves and the return of a few migratory birds, there were some equally important but perhaps less noticeable changes. The ruts that had been frozen into the road and our driveway since that last chinook in February were finally smoothed out. A lost toy that had been buried in the snow since November would reappear. The often frosty storm windows that had become stained to an unpleasant opaqueness could finally be removed and stored until fall, when once again they would be welcomed as a protection against the invading cold of winter. Not only could we get more fresh air, we could once again see through the windows with only a modicum of interference. Finally, and perhaps more importantly, I could stop wearing that miserable, heavy woolen coat that was so stiff and uncomfortable.

****

My first brush with real unpleasantness occurred late in the spring of 1939. Bruce Larsen, a two year old neighbor boy, was killed in a farm accident. Bruce's parents, Margaret and Harold, lived just one and one half mile south of our farm and were among Mother and Dad's best friends. We saw a lot of them and since Bruce was only a few years younger than me, I played and scrapped over toys with him on many occasions. Despite some difficulty with our communications, I saw him frequently and considered him to be a good romper room playmate. We usually had a good and boisterous time together. I have no doubt that our friendship would have continued and perhaps flourished into adult life, had he lived.

We were all terribly shocked by this tragic death and for many days there was real gloom and sadness in our home.

****

Up until at least my fifth birthday, Dad was my only barber. When a haircut was required, I was obliged to sit nearly naked under a towel which was wrapped tightly around my neck. Also to attain some height, I would find myself perched on a pot or tub which had in turn been placed on top of a kitchen chair. Can you imagine what such a throne would do to a tender bottom? For a brief period "Made in Canada" was embossed right on my butt.

This precarious setup was usually positioned right in the middle of the kitchen floor so that the falling hair could easily be swept onto a dustpan. Dad used a pair of hand clippers that pulled out as much hair as they cut. Adding to my agony, he also used what must have been a very dull pair of scissors. They pulled and pinched each time a lock was clipped. In summer, the entire sordid event usually took place outside where the hair could fall among the weeds.

Now it turns out that Frank Kroon, the local barber, had his shop in the same building as the Standard Pool Hall. To enter his business establishment, it was necessary to first go through Magnus's emporium of snooker, pool and bowling. Magnus also had a confectionery setup, which at a later date, proved to be the source for the coldest and tastiest Pepsi Colas in Alberta. They were served from a freezer of cold water that must have been maintained at a temperature approaching that of ice.

But back to Frank's barber shop which was, for all practical purposes, a part of the pool hall. This created a real problem for me since for all of my tender years, Mother had been telling me that a pool hall was a nasty place. For sure and certain entering such a place was at the very least, a venial sin. I knew that Mother was probably right so it was with considerable uneasiness that I first visited Frank's barbershop. Dad was of course with me but it still seemed wrong. As we approached, I tried not to notice the back of the building which housed many of the Devil's playthings - pool tables, bowling allies, and the like.

The barbershop itself was a model of efficiency. The centerpiece was clearly the barber chair. Compared to the wooden chairs at home, this one was huge and it featured all sorts of doodads. It could pump up to nearly any height, it could swivel, it could fold back. For total comfort, the arms, the seat, and the back were padded with leather. It even had a special pillow - like device that came up when the chair was folded back. On reflection, this appendage looked somewhat like the whiplash protector on a car, but that little rear view obstruction had yet to be invented.

The room had a long cupboard which more or less filled one side. The top of this cupboard featured an array of clear bottles, each containing fluid of a different color. The wall above the cupboard was mirrored which made the room appear to be twice as large as it really was. It also had the illusional effect of doubling the number of bottles on the shelf. Wooden benches were pushed back against at least two of the remaining walls and there was a small radio in one corner. Hanging from the chair and the cupboard were two leather straps that Frank seemed to snap every once in a while. I later learned that these were used to sharpen the many straight razors that were carefully folded and placed next to the numerous combs and scissors laying on the cupboard top. Leaning against the one remaining wall, next to a big brass bowl with a flared top, was a rather large cutting board. A few newspapers were scattered along the benches and among the four men that were seated in the shop. The friendly banter and laughter that ensued gave the room a rather relaxed atmosphere and it was obvious that all were acquainted with one another. I was pleased to note that Dad knew them and it wasn't long before he was included in their jovial conversation.

Finally, after Dad's haircut was completed, it was my turn. I was a bit apprehensive and although difficult, I managed to clamber up into the big chair. I quite naturally assumed that I would sit on the rich padded leather, just like Dad and the other men who had just had their hair trimmed. No such luck! Frank fitted the big cutting board right across the arms and sat me down on top of it. Although it was better than the bottom of a galvanized pail, there was certainly some disappointment. Also, it was a big downer since everyone in the shop had encouraged me to believe that I would be a real man when I got my first store bought haircut. Who did they think they were kidding? Heck, I knew that real men didn't have to sit on the cutting board.

Once in the chair, and after I was totally covered by a huge wrap around cloth, Frank asked me, in a very serious tone of voice, if I needed a shave along with the haircut. Of course everyone laughed and I was much too frightened and shy to say "yes." With hindsight, it is a shame that I was not brave enough to answer in the affirmative. It would have been lots of fun to joke back with everyone and see how Frank would have reacted to such a brazen reply.

It took Frank very little time to cut my hair. There was no pulling and for some reason, no itchy hair fell down my neck. When he was finished, he splashed a bit of the red stuff from one of the bottles right on top of my head. It smelled good and it sure slicked down my hair.

Once down from the chair, it was hard not to notice all of the clipped blonde hair as it lay on the oiled floor. I sort of hated leaving it behind. As Dad paid twenty five cents for his haircut and two dimes for mine, I couldn't help but think, how wrong it was to leave my hair clippings right next to Magnus's den of iniquity. It would have been a much better if my shorn locks had been left outside in the weeds next to our house.

Although the price was not that excessive, forty five cents was hard to come by and was only spent for a very good reason. It is difficult to know, but we must assume that the need for a special haircut preceded some very important event. While there may have been many reasons for a store bought haircut, it is certain that none could compare with a visit from the King and Queen.

****

Yes, it was true. The King and Queen came all the way from England just to see me in the spring of 1939.

Actually, it is probable that they were there for the express purpose of drumming up much needed support from their far flung British Empire colonies. This was required as dealing with Hitler and Mussolini was becoming more and more difficult. These would-be tyrants were becoming progressively more and more fiesty and were causing a lot of concern among the thinking people. If war should break out, who better than a bunch of farm boys from Western Canada to fight for the Kingdom.

Now, since I was just five years old when the visit took place, the preceding hype had a profound impact on me. No doubt, I looked forward to the visit for several weeks, with each day featuring more and more excitement. Just imagine the thrill of having a chance to see King George VI and Queen Elizabeth.

Finally the big day arrived. It was clear and sunny when we all piled into the old 1930 Chev and headed for Calgary. Uncle Carl came along since he was as usual, out of work and had been staying with Mother and Dad throughout most of the spring and preceding winter. He slept in a small granary which later became a brooder hut for small chicks. Anyway, we arrived in Calgary and learned of the King and Queen's busy schedule and predetermined travel route. We decided that the best place to view them was on the Tenth Street hill where we could sit on the grassy hillside as they passed by.

Somehow, Irene and I each got a small Union Jack flag that we could wave at the King and Queen. Carl may have bought the flags, but it was probably Dad's money that was so generously, but foolishly spent. Carl rarely had any money of his own but even during the depression, he was never too bashful to ask Dad for some of his.

When we finally arrived on the grassy slope next to Tenth Street, it was covered with people, all with flags just like ours. The huge crowd made it impossible for me to see anything but the legs and belt buckles of the many spectators. Happily, this turned out to be a short term problem, since after a long wait, Carl hoisted me up on his shoulders so that I could see the King and Queen as they were chauffeured by in an open car. There they were, the most important people in the whole world. At first it seemed that we had missed them since it only took a few seconds for them to zip by. Equally disturbing, they looked just like ordinary people - no crowns, no flashy uniforms, no nothing. What a disappointment! They didn't even look up at the flag that I was frantically waving. You would have thought that a loyal subject like me would have received a glance and a smile; but instead, nothing, absolutely nothing, no sign of recognition.

To make up for the rather rude treatment that was accorded to Carl and me, and of course Mother, Dad and Irene, (the reigning monarch didn't notice them either) it was decided that we would give them one more chance to wave at us. With a little research, it was learned that they would be leaving Calgary by train later that afternoon. With this exit, we could see them again if we hurried out to the C.P.R.tracks west of the city. Once again we piled into the car and drove several miles out of town toward Bowness. Finally, after another long wait, the train passed by. This time, the King and Queen were standing at the back of the train, waving at their loyal subjects.

More disappointment however, their train spewed black smoke and hissed white steam just like the one that had brought Grandmother to Gleichen. I had hoped it would be a really special train made of gold and silver.

Simultaneous with the Royal visit, Bedstefar and Bedstemor were vacationing in Denmark. Undaunted by the ever increasing threats of a war and much discouragement from their children, Bedsefar and Bedstemor bravely ventured off to Europe and their beloved homeland. This was to be their last ever visit with their old country friends and relatives. Apparently Bedstemor had been back for a short visit in 1921, but apart from this brief encounter neither had seen their families since 1909, when they emigrated to the United States.

Understandably they were anxious to see their brothers and sisters before the growing rumors of a war became a reality but leaving the relative safety of North America at that time was particularly disquieting for those of us who were left behind. They had scarcely left when the war rumors intensified and our concerns for their well-being became very real. At this time, there was every reason to believe that they would find themselves in a war zone, leaving them isolated and unable to return to Canada. It was a close call but happily they did get back, but not before we all suffered some very anxious moments.

Clearly, King George VI and his queen knew what they were doing, as the risk of war with Germany was growing every day. Their visit to Canada reminded everyone that we were indeed a part of the Empire and that we would be expected to help should Great Britain get involved in a conflict. We didn't have long to wait before all of this came to fruition. On September 1, Germany invaded Poland. To honor an obligation to Poland, Great Britain and Canada declared war on Germany two days later.

Although I had been terribly concerned about the possible commencement of war, my fears quickly diminished during the first few days and weeks of September. None of the fearful things that I had anticipated occurred. There was no evidence of gladiators dismembering others, nor was there any immediate activity to suggest that anything had really changed. I was much relieved.

It took several weeks, maybe even a few months before I saw men wearing the uniforms of the army, navy or air force. Finally, when I saw my first soldier, he was laughing and joking, seemingly enjoying the role of a man in uniform. This did not at all square with the serious and bloody scene shown in Bedstefar's "Book of Knowledge."

Actually, during the early weeks of September, I was much more taken up with the matter of Irene starting school. This was an immediate and local problem of great importance since for the first time in my life I would loose a playmate for most of each day.

****

Canada's entry into the European war was the fulfillment of my very worst childhood fears. Although it signaled the beginning of a long and bloody conflict, it also ushered out the worst economic interval in modern history. The Great Depression started before my birth in 1929. With an economic disaster of this magnitude, it is almost incomprehensible that Mother and Dad would have decided to get married in 1931. With virtually no money and little hope ever to have any, it took tremendous courage to begin their life together and take on the responsibility of having children. With this as a backdrop to their relationship, it is clear that they made almost unbelievable sacrifices during their early years on the farm.

There was absolutely no money for a honeymoon. Also, there was nothing but old, well used furniture for their new home. Almost everything in their possession was second hand and well used. This was typified by the kitchen set, a wooden table and four chairs which carried coats of paint that may have dated back to the nineteenth century. This was also true for the dining room furniture and the beds. Dad made the crib that Irene and I first slept in and this included the springs which were made from stripped barb wire woven over a wooden frame.

Tools for survival were without exception, previously used. Dad had collected and scrounged these items from various sources, including makeovers from junk thrown away by farmers enjoying better circumstances. Although substantially all of the farm work was done with the help of the old John Deere, most if not all of the equipment was designed for horses. The binder had a set of wheels under the pull tongue called a truck. This allowed a team of horses to pull the rig with the driver sitting at the rear so that he could also trip the bundles and manipulate the cutting bar. I don't recall Nancy and Beauty ever pulling the binder but Dad owned a long bamboo whip that in earlier years, helped to steer and maneuver horses while seated on the machine.

There were trucks on the cultivator, disk and drill, three of the more important items required for farming at that particular time and place. In my memory none of these common farm implements were pulled by horses but it is certain that Dad frequently used this mode of power during the years before my birth.

Even the hand tools were from a different era. Pitch forks, shovels, rakes, hoes, and crowbars had either been purchased at farm sales for ten cents on the dollar or received in lieu of money for work performed.

Often it took a great deal of ingenuity to keep these farm tools functioning. Dad was often obliged to repair the tractor and among other things, grind valves and replace the piston rings. When repair was beyond his own capability, a patch job could be affected by Mr. B.C. Skipper, the local blacksmith. Even the horse harness was old and Dad would frequently spend an entire evening repairing it.

In the very beginning, Mother did all her laundry in a tub with a scrub board. This back breaking, hand rubbing task was finally displaced by an old wooden, hand operated washing machine. It was only a slight improvement but it showed progress and must have provided some relief from the drudgery of the wash board. In due course, this wooden relic gave way to a larger metal washing machine. This was in reality a round bottomed tub that rocked back and forth on spring-loaded gimbals, sloshing the clothes until they were clean. This sloshing action was of course supplied by hand - back and forth, back and forth.

I was at least four or five when we were blessed with our first Aladdin lamp. This was a kerosene lamp that employed an exotic circular wick which burned upward into a delicate lace-like mantel. It worked like a toot but would invariably start to smoke if you turned your back on it. Up until the arrival of this fancy illumination, all of the light in our house was supplied by two kerosene lamps. These were a good deal better than flickering candles but one needed to be seated near the light source in order to read or sew. It was a minor catastrophe if a lamp glass should happen to break. Quick replacement was possible however, since they were readily available in several of the stores in Standard. Unfortunately they cost money, a commodity in very short supply. This was equally true for the outside kerosene lantern glass which seemed to be particularly fragile.

Mother did all of the ironing with flat irons (sad irons). This was of course fairly common in those days and wasn't a particular hardship in winter. During the summer however, it meant that the old kitchen stove was fired up to heat the irons. Mother always did a great job but I well remember the uncomfortably hot kitchen on those summer ironing days.

Today, after years of inflation and economic growth, it is hard to imagine a total society with virtually no money. It was of course a universal malaise. It would seem that the depression overlooked no one, and picked very few favorites. Even though farm prices were terrible, it was undoubtedly much worse for the city dwellers, many of whom had no work at all.

Prices of farm produce varied from year to year and for a brief interval wheat sold for as little as 19 cents per bushel. Pork was at times almost given away at $1.95 per hundred weight. Indeed, Dad once arranged for Bedstefar to take some pigs to market in Calgary. He had some other reason to take the old truck to the city and as a consequence, there was no cartage or freight charge. Even with this advantage, the gross value for three market size pigs was a paltry $12.00. Dad also recounts a circumstance when he sold a milk cow to Nick Beck for $5.00. This may well have occurred the year when our families total cash income reached the amazing sum of $13.00.

While all of this was happening, Mother was doing her share, helping out by churning cream into butter and candling eggs for sale to Leo Larsen's Red and White Store in Standard. This was a good deal for Irene and me since we enjoyed the resulting buttermilk, a favorite of ours. Also, it was fun to watch Mother run the wooden butter press which made the neatest pound-sized packages of butter. The deal was not particularly profitable, since Leo could only pay 5 cents for a pound of butter and from 5 to 10 cents for a dozen eggs. To ensure that the eggs were not too old or cracked, Leo would recandle each one before the deal was consummated. He had a real candle setup in the basement of his store which undoubtedly protected many of his customers from purchasing bad eggs.

Strangely, there were intervals when there was money enough to purchase some of the essential items and even enjoy such frivolity as our trip to Sylvan Lake. It turns out that the harvest of 1937 was particularly bountiful, and for once the price of wheat was reasonable at almost $1.00 per bushel. I am unaware of the reason for this anomaly but can only assume that Dad was able to irrigate a good crop to maturity, while for lack of rain, most of Western Canada's crops burned up in the hot sun. This would explain both the excellent prices, and this somewhat unique bumper harvest.

Whatever the reason, it turned out to be most fortuitous since Dad's appendectomy triggered some unforeseen expenses the very next spring. Happily, there was enough money left over so that even a few new farm implements could be acquired.

To the best of my knowledge, the very first new farm tool that Dad ever owned was a scythe. It wasn't a major addition, but with its curved handle, it was exactly like the one so often depicted with the Grim Reaper. Having this handy dandy grass cutter made it possible for him to trim some of the hard to reach grass and weeds in the yard and throw the cuttings to the livestock. They seemed to like it and as a side benefit, the yard took on a neat and tidy appearance. After each use, Dad would carefully stow it up in the rafters of the garage so we kids would not get into trouble with its sharp blade.

The harvest of 1937 also provided funds for the purchase of a brand new three bottom plow. The green John Deere paint was still not dry when Jim Smith delivered it to our farm. This was the first really important farm implement that Dad ever purchased. Finally he could break up part of the pasture that had never previously been farmed and was still growing the original prairie wool that had sustained the buffalo in an earlier era.

It may seem a bit strange today, but in those days each new farm implement was accompanied by one or two universal wrenches. These almost useless tools, which were somewhat similar to a cast iron Swiss Army Knife, can still be seen as a favorite exhibit in nearly every Western Canadian pioneer museum.

Perhaps the most important purchase of 1937 was an ironing board. Up until that time, all of Mother's ironing was done on the kitchen table which she padded with a few old sheets. This new special device, bought at Leo Larsen's Red and White Store was really something. The legs were designed to fold up for storage but would spring into action whenever a few steel braces were snapped into place. It was truly a fine addition to the assets of our home, and while it seems almost silly today, its purchase may have been one of Mother's most treasured conveniences on the farm.

With the depression raging during my early years, everyone had to be as frugal and resourceful as possible. Mother and Dad were no exception as they labored and struggled to make ends meet. A typical example of their ingenuity was the way they decorated the old farm house. Mother was a good housekeeper; and she always liked when things looked pristine and in order. This desire was in conflict with the kitchen floor which was for all practical purposes, worn out. It's impossible to know the age of the linoleum that covered the kitchen and pantry floor but it is likely that it was laid when the farm was first occupied, sometime between 1909 and 1919. At the very least, it had been in service for many years and the pattern was completely worn off in all of the high traffic areas. This included the spot right in front of the kitchen stove, the traffic trails that led to the parlor, the dugout cellar, the pantry, and to the outside door. The worn linoleum even revealed the exact foot position needed to crank the cream separator which squatted in front of the north wall window.

The old chrome and black iron cookstove stood up off the floor and the area under it looked unused. It was surprisingly attractive and if it hadn't been for this like- new spot, the whole floor may not have looked so shabby. The contrast was particularly unattractive and there was little that Mother could do to bring it up to her high standards. Something had to be done, but for cost reasons new linoleum was out of the question.

To fix the problem and brighten up the kitchen, Dad procured three cans of paint - one green, one light green, and one orange. To start the fix up, he painted the entire linoleum surface a light green. This included the still perfect portions of floor under and behind the stove where the old coal scuttle stood. This was allowed to dry for several days during which time everyone had to step around on one or two table leafs that were strategically located over this new paint job. Dad then built a cleverly designed paint dauber out of a feed sack and a short piece of wood. The feed sack was bunched up and nailed to the wood so that it intentionally made an uneven print or pattern each time it was loaded with paint and daubed on the floor. This was carefully done, thus leaving a unique two tone, darker green design over the entire area. At this point, Dad could have stopped but after yet another drying period, the process was repeated with orange, while using a fresh dauber design. The effect was remarkably good, showing three coordinating colors in a nearly rigorous pattern throughout.

We all liked the result which was a magnificent improvement over the old shoddy worn-out linoleum. The bad news was the distinctive taste of turpentine which lodged in almost all of the food stored in the pantry. The effects on butter was the most offensive but other foods also took on a less than pleasant taint. Even months later, some of Mother's usually excellent cooking would inadvertently be tainted through the use of some item such as chocolate which still harbored this awful turpentine flavor.

The surplus green paint was carefully saved and stored, and to this day I have a homemade tackle box painted in the color of our old farmhouse floor.

Even during hard times, Dad never allowed his beard to grow and always tried to maintain a reasonably civilized appearance. Razor blades were not terribly expensive but perhaps more notably they weren't very good. Normally one or two shaves were all that could be expected from a blade. I suppose that the best of a bad lot was the Gillette Blue Blade, but even these could inflict brutal pain after one or two shaves. To extend their life and save a few pennies, Dad would sharpen the used blade inside a wet glass. This could be accomplished by sliding it back and forth inside the curve of a glass or jar.

I never actually learned how well this technique worked since my own shaving days were still a few years off. At times, Dad would humor me with a shave of my own as he would let me lather my face with soap just like a grown up. Unbeknownst to me, he would then remove the blade and allow me to skim off the soap with the empty razor. It was several years before I discovered that I wasn't getting the real thing.

Today while thinking of the "dirty thirties", I cannot help but be reminded of the many repairs that were made to almost everything; hardly anything was thrown away. Socks were often mended several times, patches were appropriately applied to tears and rips. Pant legs were lengthened as they became too short. A lost gas cap could not easily be replaced and at least one car in ten on the streets of Standard sported a substitute rag protruding from the gasoline fill spout.

Repairs applied to some implements were often extremely creative and wire was indispensable for many such fix ups. It could be used to mend a broken wagon tongue, a snapped harness trace, secure a loose head lamp on a car and wire up a door that wouldn't otherwise stay closed.

By the end of the depression, almost all of the containers on the farm had been repaired. Few things are worse than a leaky bucket or kettle and we had our share of both. If the milk pail should happen to spring a leak, Dad would fix it with a bit of solder. This of course assumes that the leak did not come by way of Bessy the cow, who had been known to put her foot right through the bottom of a pail. If one of Mother's pots or pans required fixing, a unique washer and screw device could always be depended on to do the job. Enameled or aluminum containers could not be soldered and these leak busters were the real "sailor's pants." When things began to improve in 1940, our kitchen water pail and dipper had several such mends. Also by then, a fair number of Mother's mixing bowls, plates and a few everyday cups had been in the presence of a glue pot for major refurbishment. Even the lid for the ceramic butter churn had undergone a serious glue job and when it finally broke beyond further repair, Dad carved a wooden lid which worked just as well. Glue was also useful in keeping some of the modest ornamentation in shape. Mother's few souvenirs, mostly from her childhood, had various parts still attached courtesy of the glue pot.

Finally, I will never forget Dad's rubber gum boots which were adorned with a multitude of red tire patches. They may have looked funny but this did not deter Irene and me from using them for a hike to the outdoor toilet. After all, they were always handy and during inclement weather, we could step into them without removing our much smaller shoes. Maybe we were the problem?

The term "dirty thirties" accurately describes this interval of time perfectly. Not only was there an economic down turn that affected the entire western world, but Western

Canada, and I presume most of North America, underwent a devastating climate shift. This incredible change coincided with the financial crisis and most certainly exacerbated the problem. Rainfalls were generally much below normal and crop yields were significantly reduced as a result. This in turn provided an almost perfect environment for dust storms of a gargantuan scale. At times these squalls were so intense that day time hours became dark as night. Indeed, they were often so devastating that at high noon, the garden gate, not more than thirty feet away, was not visible from the kitchen window.

As much as I dreaded the darkness, by any measure the air was the most disagreeable aspect of these disgusting prairie gales. Each suffocating breath was filled with soil and dust which left grit in ones mouth and an aftertaste which seemingly remained for hours. I have long since lost from memory the precise flavour of Alberta's almost black, top soil but will never forget the mournful sound of the wind as it went shrieking over the naked prairie and bent its way around our unprotected house. To this day I find myself wincing whenever I see a drifting tumbleweed or hear the cry of the wind streaming past a building or into a partially opened window.

It's hard to imagine what it would have been like to be caught outside in the billowing dust and dirt of a serious summer wind storm. Without some protection from the choking winds and dust, I honestly believe these storms could have been life threatening.

The aftermath of these dastardly dirt blizzards was also quite incredible. Top soil would blow away, lodging in ditches, fence lines, and virtually anything that would disturb the wind enough to let the soil and dust remain behind. I recall seeing Uncle Edward's cultivator buried so deep that it was unrecognizable. Before using it, he was obliged to dig it free from its premature grave by moving a miniature hill of drifted soil. To make matters worse, the entire process had to be repeated a few days later when once again a storm buried it beyond recognition. Dad's harrows were completely covered and could only be found because the control levers protruding through the mounds of dust and soil betrayed their presence.

While buildings were often surrounded by dunes of drifted soil, the really distressing part was the accumulation of dust inside our house. It was sure to appear next to any crack or opening that allowed entry from the outside. During these hot dry summers, Mother was constantly cleaning the sometimes not so small ridges and piles of dust that filtered under the windows and doors or through an almost invisible crack. She could shake and beat out our bed coverings but no matter how hard she tried and until they were laundered, there was always the scent of dust as we slept in our beds.

Along with the drought and the hot dry winds, farming methods as employed in those days were not conducive to the conservation of soil. Almost all crops - wheat, oats, flax, barley, and rye were harvested with binders and threshing machines. This left the fields devoid of the straw and fiber needed to resist the erosional effects of the wind. A well cultivated field, clean and black, free of any unsightly stubble, the sign of a good farmer, was really in trouble. Such a naked field with all of its top soil laying loose was totally vulnerable to the unmerciful wind which hardly had to blow before the entire surface started to move. It took only a modest line squall to billow up and produce clouds of black soil that moved across the prairies like an advancing wall of darkness. There were some land areas that were especially susceptible to wind erosion. These were largely made up of the light soil that pending better farming methods would have been much better left as native prairie wool.

****

With the dust and grim of the dirty thirties, I took considerable comfort in knowing that our land had irrigation and that Dad knew how to use it. Our farm, more properly described as S1/2 Sec10 - Twp24 - Rge22 - W4, had all but four acres that theoretically enjoyed the benefits of irrigation.

The system, built by the Canadian Pacific Railway in 1907, was known as the Western Irrigation District. It was designed to take water from the Bow River in East Calgary. The main source point and senior irrigation canal was, and is to this day, located just above a ten to fifteen foot river weir that dams the rivers flow near St. George's Island. This main canal which leaves the river at that point feeds the water east and is the source and continued sustenance for Chestemere Lake. Today this body of water is nearly within the City of Calgary, or more specifically, its ever growing Forest Lawn suburb. Water from this man made lake was and still is distributed throughout the Strathmore and Gleichen areas. The water moves via a series of ditches, one of which cut through the southwest corner of Dad's farm and which by design was located at the highest possible elevation point on the entire half section. Other smaller ditches (tributaries in reverse) branched out from this main source, which in Dad's farming days made it possible to get irrigation water from two points of delivery. The lesser water gate was at the extreme southeast corner of the farm, very near Alfred Petersen's farmyard. This ditch and gate was most commonly used to water the pasture, the trees, the garden, and in later years, the lawn that surrounded the house.

It is probably worth mentioning that "The Canadian Pacific Railway Company's Irrigation Project" was and is the largest single source irrigation system in the world. Its four hundred and eighty miles of main canals and ditches, costing some $5,000,000, is spread over a block of 1.5 million acres.

The system, as designed in 1904, is capable of gravity feeding water to nearly half of this area (625,000 acres).

I liked the security, or more properly, the comfort of knowing that our farm had access to water from the mountains. With irrigation, Dad was capable of defeating the hot sun and the drying winds. However, I did not always enjoy the several times each summer when our trees needed water. This always produced extensive mud in our yard, and for a few days at least, reduced my play area to a small number of islands within the farmyard. In most cases, our playhouse stood in two or three inches of water.

To cope with this invasion of water, an entirely new batch of games were invented wherein one could contemplate all manner of grandiose fantasies. Frequently I would employ the small feeder ditches as the focus of my play. Here, small harbors could be built and pretend naval tactics could be practiced by floating sticks of wood into these tiny setups. This made up for the confinement of the mud but carried with it the risk of getting outrageously dirty. With notions of becoming a naval war ace, mud bombs would be deployed to sink the stick boats that filled the miniature harbor. This game may or may not have originated from the real business of sinking the Bismarck, but it was easy to emulate such a feat with an allied victory in the irrigation water. It was pretend, but all of the bombing sounds were made with each direct hit and blast from a blockbuster lump of mud. If Irene was playing with me, retaliation with carelessly tossed mud bombs quickly became the standard of battle. As things degenerated, it was certain that our clean clothes would become the final and only real casualty. Mother was not pleased.

The main water gate at the southwest corner of the farm could dump copious amounts of water into our field when it was needed. It may seem simple, but it took more than a little skill and planning to handle and navigate a large volume of water over a sloping field of grain. Dad was a master at the task.

He had an unusually well developed sense of elevations and could judge the location of each ditch without the prior benefit of a surveyor's level. Now of course, anyone can predict that water will flow downhill, but these ditches were not so simple and were designed and positioned to have little more than two to four inches of drop for every hundred yards of length. It took an incredibly good eye to see such an imperceptible change in elevation. If Dad had played golf, I am sure that he could have read the greens just as well as Jack Nicklaus or Greg Norman.

In most cases a surveyor's level was employed in locating the ditches, which from above, would have resembled contours of nearly equal elevation winding around each hill or berm. In this way the water could flow from many outlets on the downside of each trench, sweeping over and flooding the parched land lying between the almost parallel watercourses. These were plowed into the field at intervals of approximately two hundred yards.

In order to effect this style of irrigation and avoid minor soil erosion, some growth was required. Typically the grain had to be six to eight inches in height before any water could be applied. Revitalized with moisture, the dry sprouts quickly responded and in a day or two it was easy to see where the water had been. This was not immediately true however, and with the cover of the grain it was difficult, if not impossible, to see the encroachment of water and the mud that goes with it. On several occasions Mother failed to noticed or check the waters flow when delivering afternoon coffee to Dad. At these times, driving the 1930 Chev into the grain field was fraught with risk and in a few instances she inadvertently drove from solid soil into about ten inches of mud. When this happened, she and the car were solidly stuck.

Leading the water from the ditch was grueling work as it meant walking in eight to ten inches of mud for most of a day. Adding to this, the sun was hot, and can you imagine a better place for a mosquito? It didn't take them long to discover these ideal breeding grounds.

Subject to the risk of hail (not a minor concern), there were definite rewards in the fall when the harvest was gathered in. Yields could often triple and quadruple dry land crops. In fact, during the dirty thirties, there were many occasions when dry lands were not worth harvesting thus yielding absolutely nothing.

On one occasion, the benefits of irrigation came early. While slogging through the mud, Dad noticed a great deal of commotion in a small section of the grain. Upon investigation, he found a large pike flopping around in the shallow water and mud. Somehow the fish had managed to move from the river to the canal and follow the water's flow, right into the green spring wheat. What a curious and early reward for hard work.

****

The early pioneers settling in Western Canada were eager to educate their children and schools were among the first amenities provided for in each community. As a consequence the rural areas of Alberta were generously sprinkled with one room schools. Indeed, in 1939 it would be difficult if not impossible to find a farm on the prairies that was more than a few miles from a school house - an easy pony ride, if you please. In the Standard -Gleichen area there were several dozen such school centers, each with a teacher committed to the task of bringing at least some learning to children of the nearby farmers' and ranchers'.

Our school, Craigantler, was just a smidgen short of being two and one half miles west-northwest of our farm. It stood within a fenced enclosure having an aggregate area of about five acres. This yard, on the brow of a hill, was carved out of Henry Dankwerth's field and adjacent to the main road running west to Calgary. It was defined by a border of tumble weeds and Russian thistles that had been stranded in three lines of rusting barb wire that encircled the entire lot. This wire obstruction, almost invisible amongst the dry weeds and debris, was loosely supported by a series of unevenly spaced split cedar posts.

The nearby farmers, acting as custodians, had in the distant past seeded the entire tract into brome grass. Unfortunately with only a modest amount of rainfall, this normally hardy dry land plant had struggled through the 1939 summer and fresh growth was barely evident.

In preparation for the upcoming 1939-40 school year and Irene's September introduction into the halls of learning, someone had recently mowed most of the open spaces in the yard. In the absence of a good summers growth, this produced very few cuttings and these minuscule fibers were left to blow away in the hot September breezes. These same winds had dried the clumpy stubble into a brown-grey hue which more or less characterized the entire set. The only evidence of earlier growth was a few straw colored tufts, still standing at the foot of the steel swing standards, where the bashful mower blade had been unwilling to risk a closer cut.

Standing near the southern boundary of the yard, and only a stones throw from the main road was the school house. The building was more or less square with its pitched roof gabled south to the road and north to the partially haze obscured Wintering and Chimney Hills, some ten miles in the distance. Much closer, but also shimmering through the dusty mirage-like air, rested the village of Standard. This oasis of color, easily visible from the school yard, was dominated by six grain elevators and a collage of other brightly colored buildings.

The front of the school house had three concrete steps which led up to an enclosed porch. This was barely large enough to accommodate the front entry, the door of which opened inward to a second door leading directly into the single class room. Well above the porch and running almost the full length of the building was a well painted black lettered sign which read "Craigantler S.D. NO 2428."

As there was no electricity, the classroom was illuminated entirely by way of six, four paned windows, three to a side. Since the school year missed most of the hot days of summer, these were all permanently fitted with storm windows. As you would expect, each had the usual three air holes on the bottom mullion.

Over the many years since its construction (1911), a virtual army of volunteers had victimized the cedar siding with layers of poorly applied white paint. The window trim and frames were painted fire engine red, and here the gratuitous workers showed a particular carelessness as there were many paint smears on the glass panes. A close look from the inside displayed several shades of red, each one covering the miscues of earlier unsteady hands and brushes.

While the shingled roof had at one time enjoyed a black paint job, this was badly faded and now in 1939, the main features were the protruding red brick chimney and three lightening rods perched on its peak. Each of the rods was festooned with a pale blue glass ball.

Although rain was a seldom event throughout the thirties, the modest rainfalls and snow melts had over the years created small but clearly discernible grooves in the clay below the open eaves. These small depressions directly under the roof line were partially filled with small pebbles, left behind as the finer soil had been washed away by the dripping roof runoff. These perfect lines of fine gravel had the appearance of deliberately placed furrows, framing the cracked concrete foundation which hunkered on the sun scorched prairie dirt.

Squatting on the north side and just a few paces from the back of the school house was a red ochre coal shed. The black coal dust and slack surrounding the low, shovel scarred entrance betrayed its years of constant use. I was to learn later that the carelessly stacked planks and boards crammed between the coal bin and the school building were in fact, part of the stage that was erected and used for each annual, well advertised and relatively well attended Christmas concert.

Not far away were the usual his and hers outhouses, both painted white but otherwise quite ordinary.

At the northernmost part of the property stood a shanty roofed barn capable of stabling six to eight ponies. Although it was not in use during my time, its interior still harbored the pungent and unmistakable odor of horses. Also, the nearby well and small steel trough clearly hinted of days past when a pony was the most likely form of transportation from home to school. Indeed, I believe Lyle and Loraine Enevoldsen often rode their bay gelding to school in 1939 when Irene first entered Craigantler.

Now, it never made the history books, nor did it ever challenge Cambridge or Oxford, but in its day, Craigantler was an important part of the community. More importantly, it was the place where Irene and I started our formal education.

The exact date is lost forever, but it is most likely that Irene entered grade one on the Tuesday following the 1939 Labor Day. She was really excited. It was a major event for me too, since our whole family had been talking about this momentous occasion for most of the summer. When the big day finally arrived, Mother had Irene attired in a meticulously ironed pink dress and a nearly new pair of canvas running shoes. Adding to the formality, a neatly knitted tam was perched on her head. She had also obtained a pencil and scribbler for the occasion. No doubt the paper in the notebook was of the type that revealed its origin of wood chips and would most certainly soak up ink like a Kleenex if one foolishly applied pen and ink to its rough surface.

Dad did his share by punching nail holes in the lid of a honey pail that was to serve as a lunch bucket. The first day's lunch is unknown, but a tomato sandwich and an apple would be an easy guess.

We didn't always go as a family but on this special occasion everyone got into the 1930 Chev for the short ride. Upon our arrival, we met the school teacher who was as new to the school as was my sister. She was especially pleasant and even took the time and trouble to speak with me. I was terribly proud.

Miss Weir, a very young first-time teacher, had grown up in Calgary and had graduated from the Calgary Normal School. While in Craigantler, she took board and room at the Fred Dankwerth farm, just one half mile south of the school. It must have been quite a change for her since she had been raised with all the amenities available in a city. As I recall, the Dankwerth's had few creature comforts, no running water, no electricity and for sure, they were obliged to use coal for heat just like everyone else in the neighborhood. No doubt the outdoor privy provided a new experience for Miss Weir during the cold winter of 1939-40. Also teaching grades one through nine had to be something of a challenge for a young city girl.

Irene was the only new entrant in 1939 and was, as a consequence, the sole student in grade one. Henry Dam sat in the solitary grade two desk. There were no third or fourth grades, but Audrey Dankwerth and Loraine Enevoldsen made up grades five and seven respectively. The two other scholars, Lyle Enevoldsen and Lloyd Danwerth, all much bigger and older, sat in desks that were designated as grade eight.

At the time, it didn't seem to be a small enrollment since for me at least, it was seldom that I saw that many kids at once. Six pupils seated in nine possible grades represented the entire student body.

Irene quickly settled into a school routine and I promptly discovered how much I missed her for the few hours that she was away. While each day was filled with a period of unfamiliar boredom, I was able to discover a few ways to relieve the tedium that goes with being all alone.

****

Each year before snow and frost displaced the warmth of summer, Dad heaped dirt against the house foundation. This more or less covered the cracks in the concrete and provided a modicum of insulation against the inevitable cold that came with winter. This convenient pile of loose soil also became a good place to build roads for my two toy trucks. In Irene's absence, I designed and constructed a whole host of miniature highways and hauled many make-believe tons of dirt around this small but sunny patch of prairie soil.

Construction of these magnificent byways brought with it a completely new vocabulary. I learned to mimic all of the requisite truck sounds including an almost perfect double clutch for gearing down on hills. The idling purr of a well tuned gasoline engine could quickly turn into a grinding whine as one of the trucks got mired in the soft dirt. Always available, the second truck would roar into action, pushing or pulling the helpless unit out of it's sorry condition. I tried but was never able to develop an appropriate motor noise for two trucks simultaneously laboring under heavy loads.

When the toy trucks were silent on the south side of the house, it is probable that I was learning to swing on a dandy new swing that Dad had positioned on one of the arms supporting Mother's clothesline. Although the swing was probably less than six feet high, this frequently used item soon produced a well worn groove in the soil where my one button canvas shoes wore down the chickweed, knotweed and foxtails that in late summer covered much of our yard. Dad's scythe could only do so much, and for sure, no self-respecting cow or horse would touch these ubiquitous plants with their rough bearded seed pods.

Irene had hardly started her first grade when both of us contracted mumps. After a few uncomfortable days, we were almost as good as new but were still quarantined and unable to leave home. Apart from the pain in our jaws whenever we ate sour pickles, we were not suffering any real discomfort and were as a consequence quite capable of enjoying ourselves. It was great to have my sister home again and those long hours of loneliness were at least temporarily forgotten. The quarantine period lasted about two weeks and I took full advantage of the situation. On rare occasions, she could be persuaded to give up her dolls and play with me and my trucks. These were enjoyable moments but I must admit some disappointment. Girls just don't know how to make truck sounds and to make matters worse, she never knew when to shift gears. Every young boy knows that a heavy load forces a truck driver to gear down on a steep hill. Obviously that fact is not universally known to the female gender since Irene's trucks never missed a beat, up hill or down.

****

The swing setup which Dad had built was at the far end of the clothesline, very near the garage. One day while enjoying this new plaything, I noticed that one of our farm cats had made a serious error in judgment and had gotten stuck under the garage door. No doubt the cat entered the building in the hope of finding a mouse or two, and it is certain that the door was open when this misadventure started. Unfortunately, the door was now closed and the escape path under the door was much too small for a fully grown mouser. Who knows, maybe the situation had been aggravated by a successful hunt and a full stomach. In any event, the cat was trapped and had failed to use his whiskers to gauge the opening, thus warning him that the exit point was undersized. Although I was only five years old, even I knew that a smart cat would never risk entry into an opening that would not pass muster with its extended whiskers. If this well known feline fact had merit, it was clear that this long haired, mangy gray animal had screwed up and wasn't terribly bright.

Approaching the cat was easy since it was firmly held between the door and the hard clay beneath its flattened body. Gaining its confidence was another matter and it soon became clear that he was not expecting anything good from my attempts to befriend him. After a series of angry, soprano "Meows" and a great deal of hissing and clawing, this almost wild animal finally allowed me to pet and comfort him. After all of this fussing around, it is possible that he had expended most of his energy and was too tired to fight.

Happily, with my superior intellect, compared to the cat that is, it was discovered that a little digging under and near the distressed creature would increase, at least marginally, the size of the opening. This extra space, combined with the outward swing of the door, should free the cat. Sure enough, a little gouging with a stick helped, and although I could not reach the locking mechanism, the door could be pulled up and out just enough so that the pitiful animal more or less fell into the space that had been created. I was relieved when the cat crawled out from his painful situation. With freedom however, he immediately bounded off, leaving me to wonder if he had any appreciation for my scratched arms, Trojan strength and triumphant resourcefulness. Actually, he was in no shape to run very far and after a little pleading with Mother, I was able to obtain something from the kitchen as an inducement for a better relationship.

In most circumstances, Dad was the only person who had any rapport with the farm cats. They always sat around waiting for a dish of warm milk as he milked the cow. Clearly however, my efforts to free this cat improved my standing, and with the passing of a few days and a lot more food from Mother's kitchen, I finally established an enduring bond with this not particularly handsome ball of fluff. Musa, as I named him, soon became a pet that would heed my call and follow me around the yard. Each morning after breakfast I could summon Musa who would suddenly appear, purring like a noisy motor boat, and begging for more food and attention. I thoroughly enjoyed Musa and for at least one year we spent a lot of time together.

We have already established that Musa was not a mental giant, but among his peers, he was a most influential leader. With my almost daily raids on Mother's pantry, it wasn't long before the farm's entire mouse brigade was hanging around the front porch waiting for a handout. It soon became obvious that he could talk, or at least meow a feline language. Of this, there was no doubt since it was clear that he was able to communicate with all of his colleagues, now seeking favors from Mother's food larder. Who knows how many mice were saved from a rather sad fate as a result of Musa's leadership skills.

****

For as long as I can remember, Mother religiously attended the Danish Ladies Aid meetings (Kvinde Moude as it would be known in Copenhagen). These Monday afternoon engagements were church sponsored but were usually held at various members' homes. As there were no baby sitters available, both Irene and I took in many such coffee and cake get-togethers during our very young years. You may be sure that we met and played with other children who were suffering the same circumstance. Frankly, I don't recall any of the prior events but clearly remember one such meeting that occurred at Alfred and Edna Petersen's home shortly after Irene started school. With her safely in the hands of Miss Weir at Craigantler, I was obliged to attend without the usual benefit of an older and protective sister. In all probability, this ladies assembly was much the same as all previous ones except on this occasion, I had to fend for myself.

At Alfred and Edna's place, the only other child in attendance was Bernice Sandersen. She was from town (Standard, that is), so I knew that she was very learned and sophisticated. She was however my age and like me, still waiting to start school.

It was a clear warm autumn day and Bernice invited me outside to play with her and her skipping rope. I was very bashful and could hardly believe that a cute little girl from town would want to play with a dumb farm boy like me. Being surprised, frightened and shy, my brain dissolved into mush. I became absolutely tongue tied and at best, may have made a few babbling sounds. Although totally dumbstruck, I went with her only to discover that under such strained circumstances, jumping a rope was not easy. To be honest, I couldn't even swing the rope with one end tied to the gate post. It all seemed very hopeless and in the end I became so incoherent that even an excuse was beyond my abilities. In short, I was an absolute klutz.

I was totally embarrassed by my lack of ability and disgraceful performance. Damage control was completely out of the question but realizing that my first ever encounter with a previously unknown member of the opposite sex had been a total bust, something had to be done to set the record straight.

I don't know why, but in an effort to cut my losses, I turned my hat inside out and made a lot of funny faces. It wasn't very clever, but on short notice, what's a fellow suppose to do? If this was expected to prove that I was indeed a man of talent, I am afraid that my efforts failed miserably. No doubt, Bernice went home that day thinking that she had been in the company of a complete mental derelict.

****

It wasn't long after this most embarrassing experience that Bernice and I met for a second time. Sunday School started and at long last, it was agreed that in my advanced years, it was time for some real honest learning. I was ecstatic. Irene was after all on the verge of becoming a person of letters and all I could do was make truck noises and funny faces. Hopefully, all of this would soon be behind me as I could now attend class with other people eager to learn and take a serious and important role, in what for me was an expanding society.

Sunday School was of course held each Sunday just before the formal church service. This required a trip to Standard, just five and one half miles north of our farm. In those days, even this short distance was an excursion. Each visit to town was eagerly anticipated and was almost always an exciting adventure.

Standard, the village which anchored our community, was spawned by a number of families from Iowa, most of whom were of Danish extraction. It all started in 1909, when the Canadian Pacific Railway, or its agents, ran a series of advertisements in a number of Midwestern USA newspapers. These ads promised the availability of cheap land in Western

Canada and made specific reference to an anticipated rail spur that would open a new area for development. More importantly, the railroad sales pitch also made mention of a designated partial township block (twenty three thousand acres) which could provide the nucleus for a new community.

In response to this public notice, several Iowa frontiersmen immediately left their homes to check out this new area. For the most part, these adventurous Danish Americans ended their rail travel at Gleichen's depot, at which point they were obliged to take a horse and wagon to the proposed area for settlement some twenty-two miles north. Notwithstanding the endurance of considerable hardship, they liked what they saw and within the next several years, a large contingent of colonists moved north to Alberta and the Standard area.

Although Alberta was by now a province of Canada (1905), there were only trails meandering through the prairie grassland. Fortunately, the land had undergone a legal survey in 1883 when Chas E Larne, D.L.S. meticulously measured off and staked all of southern Alberta. Locations (legal descriptions) were filed into the steel corner pins that defined the northeast corner of each section (640 acres). These were coded in Roman Numerals and were probably just as hard to read then as they are today. Equally important, and apart from a few venturesome ranchers, the land was void of any civilization since by this time all of the Indians were confined to various reservations.

With the promulgation of "Treaty Number Seven," which had been signed in 1877, most of the local natives from the Blackfoot Confederacy were comfortably ensconced in modest government homes. These were located on a large reservation adjacent to, but south of the C.P.R. line running through Gleichen. Hunting and living off the land had become all but impossible since most of the buffalo were gone. To replace this previously available and vital food source, the

Indian agents were trying to promote ranching as an alternate lifestyle. Meanwhile, the Church of England had been applying a Christian ethic to the band through a mission established in 1883. To this day, some of the buildings from this effort still exist just south of the C.P.R. tracks at Gleichen.

While all of the initial investigations for settlement were carried out in 1909, it is clear that few Danes came to the area until the spring of 1910. By that time several interlopers (non-Danes) such as George Day had also taken up residence. Mr. Day founded a store which became, and for some time remained an important supply center for all of the new arrivals. This store, located on Broadway, Standard's main street, obtained all of its merchandise by way of horse and wagon from Gleichen, the nearest rail center.

In the early days prior to provincial status, Gleichen was a small metropolis having a population of nearly two thousand. As a supply center having an all important railway connection to the east, it also featured a well equipped C.P.R. demonstration farm just east of town. To ensure law and order, the town boasted a major detachment of Royal Northwest Mounted Police having a total of four to six officers and constables.

Until Standard was blessed with its own train service, Mr. Day, like the Iowa investigators who preceded him, made countless horse and wagon treks to the rail point at Gleichen.

Other adventurous colonizers made their respective contributions to the village and by the time the railroad was completed late in 1911 or the early 1912, a small but effective trading area was in existence. Also by this time, vast areas of the rich prairie soil had been broken up by large steam engines and gang plows. This equipment, unavailable in Canada, often came from suppliers as far away as Chicago or Racine, Wisconsin. One of these, a Rumley steam plowing unit, is blamed for a fire that spread and burned the prairie wool to a point near Medicine Hat, some one hundred and forty four miles to the southeast.

In truth, not everyone was happy with the arrival of new settlers and their steam plows. After the Indians agreed to live on reservations and the main C.P.R. line linked the prairies to eastern beef markets, ranches popped up in several sectors of Alberta. While some operators obtained "Federal Leases" for an annual rental of a penny per acre, most ignored the surveys and the railroad's ownership of the land. Several of these mammoth operations were established in the Standard area and the rich grass laden hills to the north. These ranchers, operating large spreads, known as the Cold Storage, CX, Bar Two, and Crescent Star were not all pleased with the arrival of barb wire. Although they finally accepted advancing civilization, there are still lingering reports of a few confrontations which could easily have exploded into a full scale range war.

While Standard settlers were not involved, it is known that a farmer claiming his land in the Hussar community, was roped and nearly dragged through his own barb wire fence. Fortunately, a handy jackknife cut the offending lariat and was sufficiently threatening to drive off the over zealous cowhand.

****

Standard is located at the foot of the southern slopes of the Wintering Hills. This anomalous ridge of hills more or less provides the high ground separating the drainage flowing north to the Red Deer River and south to the Bow River. In days past, the hills also provided a boundary defining the specific domain of various Indian tribes. It is not clear who controlled this spine of land, but it is most likely that the southern Indians (Blackfoot Confederacy), were in charge most of the time. In any event, the abundant saskatoon berries which flourish in the glacial ravines during early summer must have been a temptation for the Plains Crees and Metis to the north. Also, as the name implies, the wind swept hilltops were often void of snow in winter, thus assuring that the buffalo would seek out the exposed lush prairie wool when lower, less windy levels were covered in the deep white.

At that time, the adjacent Chimney Hills to the northwest were often dotted with smoking Indian lodges, handy to the many animals that congregated in the hills during periods of deep snow. As a further inducement, these Indian hunters were conveniently located near a constant supply of fresh water which flowed out of a sandstone bluff right in the heart of this Cornucopia. Indeed, for a short time this unique water supply, known as Rocky Springs, was being tapped by the Village of Standard. The source never faltered but proved inadequate when the town's population expanded to its present level.

It is therefore not surprising, that this choice hunting area was the scene of many Indian battles when a tribe infringed on the territory of its neighboring brethren. To this day, there is evidence of at least one such battle which was fought approximately six miles north of my home town (S E 10-26-22-W 4). Here on the crest of a large hill overlooking the Red Deer drainage basin (Rosebud Creek), there are faint but clearly discernible remnants of trenches and breastworks carved into the hillside. Looking north from this vantage point, the Blackfoot Indians had a marvelous view of the plains reaching north to the Red Deer.

We can only speculate on the number of battles that have been fought in the Wintering Hills. It is likely however, that the last deadly encounter took place during the mid-eighteen hundreds. During that period, over hunting and over grazing by vast herds of buffalo produced a severe famine for many of the plains Indians. Apparently this staple food source ate themselves into starvation to the point that during the "Palliser Expedition" (1857- 60), even a horse could not find adequate grass for survival between the Cypress Hills and the eastern edge of the foothills. In search of a fresh game filled hunting territory, it is not surprising that a number of pitched battles took place in southern Alberta with fierce warfare between the starving Blackfoot, Stony, Sarcee and Plains Cree. It is known that several hundred warriors were killed in 1870 during a major confrontation at or near present day Lethbridge. This battle was fought fully three years after Confederation, as enacted by the British North America Act in 1867. In such a tense atmosphere, you can be sure that control of the Wintering Hills was vital. Any Cree or Metis foolish enough to venture into the lush saskatoon patches, (Okonoki, in the language of the Blackfoot) or intending to poach a buffalo from its windswept slopes, did so at peril of his life.

In these dire circumstances, the bones of many fallen warriors were scattered throughout the plains. A few years later, at the turn of the century, most of these were carelessly included with the large number of buffalo bones that were shipped east. Bone pickers were paid $6.50 per ton for this charcoal and phosphorus source and were not at all particular if a few human skeletal parts were included with the vast number of animal bones, which bleached white by the sun, lay in profusion among wild rose and buck brush bramble.

The hills were always a fascination for me since Dad had ridden those windy slopes as a cowboy during some of his first years in Canada. Finding lost cattle in the alder filled gullies must have presented a challenge during early winter when a quick storm could suddenly blow in from the north. I still have the angora wool covered chaps that protected his legs from the cold and the thorny wild rose thickets that grew in most of the shallow coulees.

The village of Standard is located, and largely confined to, NE1/4-3 and SE1/4-10 - Twp 25 - Rge22 W4. I do not have personal knowledge of its early history, but how did most of the streets and avenues get mysteriously skewed, conforming to the railway which came nearly two years after the town was established? The rail bed runs in a northwest, southeasterly direction, and so do the avenues. Main street, Broadway, by name, is exactly perpendicular to the railway, the depot, and station house all of which lie at its foot . Even George Day's store was precisely lined up with the railway despite the fact that it had been in existence for two years before the rails of steel reached Standard.

Now with this scrupulously accurate detail, someone must have enjoyed some foreknowledge of the railway's direction and location. Here, it would seem, was the perfect setup for a sinister land deal involving innocent farmers, land speculators and of course a villain, probably a greedy railway magnate. I am sure that no such scoundrel existed, but it is clear that the Canadian Pacific Railway had control over the initial development of Standard.

****

It was probably late September, well after harvest, when Sunday School started. Today, it is common to begin each new season with the secular school year, but back then, harvest was a priority and delayed most activity until Harvest Festival, "Hoest Fest" if you prefer Danish. Invariably, this event was usually held on or near Canadian Thanksgiving.

By the fall of 1939, I had enjoyed many trips to town and was more or less familiar with many of its peculiarities. On this day, my first ever visit to Sunday School, it is likely that I was not particularly observant. Had I been, I would most certainly have noticed the six grain elevators of the day, lined up and adjacent to the railroad. These monsters were clearly the most prominent features of the village. They were all carefully painted either dark red or silver and featured the names of Pacific, Federal, United, Pool, National and Pioneer. Also along the track was the train depot and section foreman's house, both painted the usual dark "CPR Red." Even the Knowlton's chicken house and Gwen and Gerald's playhouse were clad in this unforgiving tuscan red color. This was in stark contrast to the dazzling white of the seldom used stockyards which were located a few blocks west but within the C.P.R. right of way.

Moving farther north from the steel rails, it would be hard not to notice the cared for appearance that proudly characterized the whole village. With the exception of Skipper's blacksmith shop, the old weather-beaten skating rink and the never painted S and S Hall, each house, store, hotel, and shop was individualized in its own unique way. Freshly painted homes varied through the entire light pastel spectrum, but for a pleasing contrast, some were finished in a very attractive Wedgwood format. The most notable exception was Leo Larsen's "Red and White Store," which built on a major intersection, was of red Chicago brick. Its sintered exterior stood out as a particularly sturdy structure amid the softer wooden framed shops that fronted on Broadway.

Unlike many small towns, the shop windows were as clean as a polished gun barrel and the back lanes were for the most part, tidy and neat. This orderly and groomed deportment never seemed to change and was a source of pride for all of the townspeople. They were quick to claim that this pristine appearance could be attributed to their strong work ethic and the Danish fetish for cleanliness.

Perhaps the most notable feature within the town was the lack of trees. In the absence of irrigation, it was impossible to grow a tree of any size. To make up for this omission, there were generous plantings of caragana which bordered virtually every lot. Also, the rather large city park located right in the center of town was filled with beds of this hardy, dark green, thorn bush. While most of the plantings were squared off into well trimmed hedges, this was not so for the growth in the city park. Here in the absence of a gardeners shears, the unfettered limbs stood well above the height of a man on horseback.

It was entirely proper and fitting that caragana hedges grew in such proliferation throughout the village. This tough dry land plant had been introduced into North America by Professor Niels Ebbeson Hansen of South Dakota who brought the original stock from Siberia and the steppes of Russia. Dr. Hansen was a brother to Mrs Jens Rasmussen, a founder and early settler of the community.

By the turn of the century, coal had been discovered in the Standard, Rosebud, and Drumheller areas. Actually its availability was rather obvious since it outcrops in various areas of the Chimney Hills. Indeed, a poor quality surface coal could be found in an old lake bottom immediately southwest of the Standard townsite. To exploit a higher quality fuel, several mine shafts were eventually sunk and just slightly beyond the northern boundary of the village stood the headworks of the Standard Coal Company. For many years this mine was a reliable source of bituminous coal, providing the entire community with fuel for stoves, furnaces and an occasional steam engine. It also supplied a tremendous amount of cinders from the huge slag pile that lay just west of the pit-head. These red cinders were used extensively to cover all of the streets and avenues. This gravel like material gave the town a totally unique appearance. Following a rain shower, the streets took on a blood red hue, that in combination with the brightly painted shops and houses, were really quite attractive.

The seldom used tennis courts within the city park also featured a cinder surface. After being packed down with a huge cement roller (which incidentally I could not move) this colorful surface reportedly produced a good bounce and a lot of action to a spinning ball.

In those days during my fledgling years, all of the cars parked on Broadway were positioned in the middle of the street and placed at ninety degrees to all of the comings and goings. In effect, the cars provided a boulevard that separated the less than busy traffic lanes. This parking arrangement left the sidewalks and curbs clear for the still present but infrequently used hitching posts, which in a few spots paralleled Standard's main drag. Also, and perhaps more importantly, each vehicle was free to be pushed if for some reason its balky engine failed to accept a normal crank startup.

During these early years, it would have been impossible to sneak up on a rock concert while walking on Standard's sidewalks. They were made of planks and the clatter of busy feet could be heard throughout the village. Over the years the cracks in these board walks must have swallowed a small fortune in lost coins. Also, who knows how many ladies spike heels were broken off and walked away from.

****

The northwest corner of town, and in some respects, the most remote, was the site of the Nazareth Danish Lutheran Church, my destination on this my first day of Sunday School. The church, an unusually attractive building, along with the adjacent manse, occupied several acres of rather barren land mostly covered with ripe fox tails and dark green knot weed. The property was fenced off with a woven wire fence at the front and the usual caragana hedge at the back.

The church's exterior was fitted with nicely painted white cedar siding. This almost blinding white was in sharp contrast with the shingled roof and metal plated steeple, both of which sported a fresh coat of black paint. The gothic arched windows of frosted glass allowed light to enter on both sides of the building. These were meticulously trimmed in black, as were the double front doors which sat under a large gothic transom window. This front entrance was positioned at the top of a wide wooden porch and stairs that complained with an array of squeaks even under my modest weight.

The front doors opened into the vestibule, which was in fact the base of the bell tower. This classic and architecturally attractive building had an extraordinarily fine and wonderfully resonating bell that rested at the top of the tower, and just below the steeple. From here it sounded its Sunday morning message out to the world through three sides of the column. Each side had two window-like portholes similar to the gothic side windows. At the very top of the steeple's spire, which seemed to reach up to the clouds, sat a beautiful golden cross. No doubt it was made of wood, but in those days I was sure that it was solid 24 karat.

Inside the vestibule, next to the front entrance, were two ropes extending down through two small holes in the ceiling. In their normal position, these were hardly noticed since a restraining hook in the corner held them captive to the wall. I of course knew that they were the ropes used to ring the bell and was always tempted to give them a good yank. I never did, but have always regretted not having this experience during my youth and early years of upbringing. It would have been worth the certain spanking.

Fixed to the south side of the building was a small shed-like protrusion which provided access to the basement below the sanctuary. Although it was rather damp and subject to an occasional influx of rain water, this basement was often used for social events such as potluck dinners, wedding receptions, pie socials and all congregational meetings.

Back upstairs in the nave, the vaulted ceiling was covered with embossed metal plates, having an off white calcimine finish. The walls, also of metal, were calcimined a darker tone reaching down to the brown wainscoting that encircled the interior. For some reason, these metal wall coverings would not permanently accept paint or calcimine and there was almost always a few bare spots where it had sloughed off. Fortunately, even these ceiling and wall blemishes did not totally detract from the alluring appeal of the sanctuary with its particularly well appointed chancel and sacristy. The most notable feature was the semicircular communion rail of varnished darkened pine. The balustrade underlying the rail was of cusped gothic arches that were set behind a kneeling pad of burgundy velvet. It centered on the altar with its vases and candlestick holders of brass and silver. These stood directly below a beautiful painting of Christ falling under the weight of the cross. The painting was in fact an excellent copy of Raphael's early sixteenth century painting entitled "Fall On the Road to Calvary." While the original painting hangs in the Prado Art Museum in Madrid, Spain, this excellent copy was painted by Mr. A. Hansen, the father of Mrs. Jens Rasmussen.

Framing and accentuating the picture was a mammoth darkened pine backdrop in a gothic motif. This was crowned with five spires, four of which would have given pleasure to the Quebec Nationalists since each was topped with a fleur-de-lis. The center spire, and the tallest, had an ornately carved cross at its peak.

Sitting to the side and behind the choir pews was an oak reed organ. This antiquated music box exposed a variety of ivory stop buttons which when manipulated produced a few variations to the windy sound. The music that escaped from the side vents required considerable physical effort to produce, since the air running through the reeds was generated by the organist, who was obliged to pump two large foot peddles under the keyboard. The volume was regulated by applying pressure to knee paddles which protruded out at ninety degrees from the double manual.

Reigning over the entire sanctuary was a pulpit in the shape of a huge wooden egg cup. This has now been shortened, but at that time it stood so high that the pastor could, if he chose, literally shout down to the cringing parishioners. Even the few balcony seats at the very back were vulnerable to this onslaught if the message should happen to be one describing the fires of Hell and its eternal punishment. With this exposure, few if any dared to sleep or even squirm on the hard pine pews that were meticulously positioned on both sides of a center aisle. This walkway was dressed with a full length twisted rope carpet.

The lectern within the pulpit had an authoritative appearance with a gold fringed burgundy velvet cloth screening its wooden frame. The gold cross stitched to the middle of the draping ornamentation added to the formality and seemed to punctuate the stern messages that emanated from this intimidating podium.

Sunday School always started one hour before church service. There was no special educational facility and as a consequence all of the classes were dispersed throughout the main sanctuary. As you would expect, the pew arrangement was less than perfect for teaching multiple classes. Fortunately, the teachers were both resourceful and innovative and this shortcoming was easily resolved by seating and confining each class to every other pew. This allowed the teachers to occupy the pew immediately ahead of their respective class. During the actual lesson the teachers could only face their eager students by kneeling on the hard bench. This probably created a few nasty cases of "house maid's knee," but I don't recall any complaints. Since there were a fair number of classes and not many pews, the entire process was a bit confusing and noisy in a funny sort of way. Even with each teacher whispering, the whole forum sounded like a bunch of cows being milked simultaneously into a giant empty pail.

I am not sure whether my first teacher was Emelia Larsen or Aksel Nielsen. Indeed, it is very likely that both were involved. In any event, I still have a small wooden plaque that Emelia gave to me during one of my earliest Sunday School classes. It depicts Jesus walking with a flock of sheep and features a small inscription reading, "The Lord is My Shepherd." On it's back a faded ink note reads "Richard Jensen from Emelia, 1939."

Irene was immediately promoted to grade two, so once again I found myself alone and in the company of a strange group of kids. Miriam Nielsen and Arthur Klemmensen were new acquaintances but to my continued embarrassment, Bernice was not. I was still wearing my hat but this time I had the good sense to keep the yellow lining on the inside where it belonged. It all turned out well however since the first lesson was about Adam and Eve. I already knew their story and had little trouble answering several questions about them and the Garden of Eden. For a few days at least, Bernice may have realized that I was slightly better than a feeble minded imbecile. Also on this occasion I had been able to entertain the whole class with my double jointed thumb. Everyone was quite impressed.

After class and roll call, which was always handled by Aksel Nielsen and Anton Myrthu, everyone received a small postage stamp sized card featuring both a picture and Bible verse. With each Sunday that followed, we were given more of these cards which could be turned back to my teacher for a bigger prize. Depending on the number of cards collected, the prizes varied from a small Testament, to a badge or plaque. As I write this, the assortment of buttons and badges which clutter one of my drawers includes a "Little Lutheran" lapel badge, a prize for consistent Sunday School attendance, and the collection of many small cards.

One of the truly memorable features of our church was "The Little Lutheran" newspaper. This diminutive tabloid, filled with short stories for children, was distributed monthly to each Sunday School attendee. The paper was delightfully styled and was a part of Sunday School in which Irene and I took genuine pride. Having our own newspaper gave us real status, and while it may seem somewhat trite, we were both thrilled with the idea of being treated like near adults.

****

The fall of 1939 was filled with change and activity. Although the war in Europe had started, there was little immediate and direct evidence of a significant change in our community. Apparently Hitler had not yet determined his next move so things were fairly quiet. There was however, growing prosperity and it was clear that the depression was nearing an end. Everyone seemed to sense this and the prospects for a better economy were altering attitudes. For the first time in years, people were making new plans and changing jobs. As an example, The Molgards, Uncle Ernie and Aunt Agnes, along with cousins Margaret, Donna, and Patsy moved to New Westminster, B.C. from Calgary. Ernie had enjoyed reliable but stagnant employment as a baker throughout most of the depression years. Now with an improving economic climate, Ernie had the courage to risk a fresh start with his own bakery and pastry shop. Ernie and Agnes, always resourceful, moved to British Columbia and a more enjoyable and bountiful lifestyle.

At the time, it was hard to understand and appreciate the motives for the move. New Westminster seemed to be an incredible distance and we were all sorry to see them go. Also their move represented the first real breakup of the otherwise very close Rasmussen family.

Those who didn't change jobs often made other plans. Uncle Chris Rasmussen went to the New York World's Fair. This also seemed to be an incredible journey as visiting its Trylon and Perisphere would certainly not have been considered a few years earlier. On the way home he made a modest detour to Detroit were he picked up a brand new Dodge coupe. It was a beautiful car and was probably one of the last ones produced before the universal war effort directed all well equipped factories to produce munitions instead of cars and other less essential items. This was truly a shame since suddenly, after the long depression, many manufactured items were in great demand and enjoyed a robust market.

The war was still more smoke than fire, but rationing of some items was introduced by the Canadian Government. Many of the staples in short supply had little if any impact on us since we produced a goodly portion of our own food requirements. There were however, a few things that showed up less often on our dinner table. For Irene and me, less sugar was the only real loss. For Mother and Dad, coffee was one item that received more than a little judicious management.

All rationing and all items embraced by this imposed shortage were monitored by a new government agency, "The War Time Prices and Trade Board." This bureaucracy distributed ration books to everyone for all items that were deemed vital to the war effort. While many of the things seemed to be plentiful, gasoline was undoubtedly the one commodity that deserved some control.

To manage gasoline, the government arbitrarily set allocations of fuel to the general population. City folks with an automobile were deemed to be the least deserving and were classified as A users. To show this Status, an "A" sticker was required on each city resident's automobile windshield. An accompanying "A" ration book, filled with five gallon coupons, went with the sticker. I don't know how many coupons were in the book or how many gallons of fuel were allowed each year, but it must have been very few since most "A" users were obliged to car pool. Moreover, because the fuel shortage was real, these "A" sticker automobiles were more or less confined to the city. Few, if any long distance country visits were possible.

If memory serves, farmers were also given the "A" sticker and the gasoline ration that went with it. However, they also qualified for a "Double A" sticker which more than doubled the available gasoline. Frankly, I have no memory of ever going short of gasoline, but it is certain that our car was used less frequently when rationing forced us to be more efficient with trips to town and Calgary.

Fuel for tractors and certain trucks deemed to have an essential function were largely exempt from rationing. Curiously farm pickup trucks were thought to be more important than a car and were given a special allotment of fuel via a special "B" sticker and ration book. In most cases a farmer having a pickup with all three stickers was over supplied and driving was virtually unrestricted for such a lucky person. Unfortunately, this rather arbitrary gasoline advantage caused some bad feelings and precipitated some truly creative and circuitous ideas designed to beat the system. For most of the war years Uncle Edward drove his old Plymouth coup without a trunk lid and a more or less permanent wooden box positioned in the back where the trunk or rumble seat should have been. With this configuration, his car became a truck and qualified for all three gasoline stickers and ration books.

****

Winter had barely started when Miss Weir, Irene's teacher, organized her rather diverse student body for the traditional annual Christmas concert. Practice went on every day and Irene came home from school with a litany of lines that required memorization. In those days it was expected that every country school present an imaginative Christmas concert, the success of which often provided the basis for grading the quality of the teacher. With the typically small country school enrollments, everyone had several parts to play. Irene was cast in several short plays and other special performances. Although still not in school, I was invited to participate and given a small recitation for this big event. In total, it is likely that less than forty people attended this gala affair but for me it was equivalent to a performance in Carnegie Hall. The poem I was obliged to learn and recite went something like this:

"When I was a little boy, just so high,
Mother used to spank me and make me cry.
Now I am a big boy, and Mother can't do it,
So Papa takes a broomstick and hops right to it."

Adding to the moment, each line was dramatized with an arm gesture showing my height past and present.

Apart from my sterling performance, which I am sure earned a standing ovation, the concert included a terrific silent silhouette play acted out behind a large white bed sheet which was positioned in front of several gas lanterns. These, the only source of light in the building, were moved from the audience side to the back of the stage where they could cast shadows of the silent but active performers on the opaque bed sheet. There may have been better and more entertaining presentations but the silhouette show is the only one that still comes to mind.

After completion of the plays, songs and poems which had been performed for a most appreciative and forgiving audience, the chairs on which they had been seated were stacked on top of the already heaped desks in preparation for a dance. At this point the stage was opened and took on an entirely new look with two adults and their musical instruments. The entire orchestra consisted of Fred Dankwerth and Roger Sheets each with a violin. A third member eventually joined the duo for a few numbers and provided a slightly different tone with his well worn button accordion. Their repertoire was rather limited, but no one seemed to mind when they played "Let Me Call You Sweetheart" for the fourth time.

The dance lasted several hours during which time the small classroom was a proliferation of talking and laughter. Also it became rather hot and the attendees were virtually assaulted by the blue haze that was spawned by all of the cigarettes, pipes and probably cigars. It seemed that all of the men smoked. Everyone had a great time and no doubt Miss Weir was much relieved to know that she had survived her first major test, a Christmas concert that was a resounding success.

Finally, before everyone left, there was a draw for a door prize and I was given the honor of picking the name out of a box that Miss Weir had prepared for the event. Can you believe it, I picked the name of Edward Rasmussen, our neighbor but more importantly, Edward was my uncle. The door prize was a small box of groceries including a can of hard to get, Nabob coffee.

****

It wasn't long after Craigantler's Christmas party that we attended yet another children's concert. This one was sponsored by the Sunday School and both Irene and I were heavily involved. We were of course bona fide members and after three months of attendance, veterans of the school.

This program was different and although it featured a much bigger and more beautifully decorated tree, it was in fact a rather somber affair. Unlike Craigantler's crepe paper streamers and no candles, the church had electricity and their tree was well lit with various colored lights. These were nicely spaced among an array of carefully placed garland and tinsel.

It is probable that the tree had been supplied by Alfred and Edna Petersen who had a beautifully robust grove of evergreens just south of their barnyard. At any rate, the tree, with its electric lights and star at its top, was absolutely radiant.

The concert, scheduled for a Sunday afternoon just before Christmas, appeared to be structured on the premise that all parents are anxious to see their child or children perform. This may or may not be the case, but after a few Christmas carols and a brief message from Pastor Christensen, each class was sequentially marched up to the front of the church where they, all in order, grades one through confirmation, offered some memorized Bible verses to the congregation.

Irene and I had been assigned a few words to memorize so that we could participate and theoretically make Mother and Dad very proud. Even at this early age, I was somewhat cynical about this public viewing, but did learn my minuscule bit which was a part of Christ's well known words as written in the Gospel of John 3:16. I had to remember and be able to utter the words "that whosoever believeth in Him." Since there were four students in my class, each member was expected to learn by rote, roughly one quarter of this Bible verse. Reciting these parts in proper sequence should then miraculously reveal the entire message to the beaming parents nervously sitting in the pews. This would have been great if it had worked - but when it was our turn to file up and appear in front of the well decorated tree, everything went wrong. We left our particular pew in correct order, but when we turned around to face our admiring audience, we had reversed the lineup and our otherwise well designed program was destined to crash in abysmal failure.

Arthur, who should have been last, was now on the right side of the line and was invited to speak first - "should not perish but have everlasting life." I followed with - "that whosoever believeth in Him," while Miriam added - "That He gave His only begotten Son." Bernice, who should have been first had little choice but to conclude with - "For God so loved the world."

I knew that we had goofed and was ashamed of the way our performance had turned out. Our team's failure was made even worse by the fact that everyone else seemed to have completed their assignments without catastrophic results. No doubt our teacher, Emelia Larsen, was disappointed and perhaps a bit embarrassed with our less than praiseworthy exhibition.

In the end, it didn't seem to matter since when we all adjourned to the basement for refreshments, I got a Jap orange and an apple along with a sack partially filled with unshelled nuts and hard candy. This surprised me since my sack was just as full and complete as that given to Irene whose grade two program was letter perfect. Clearly someone screwed up with the rewards, but I wasn't complaining.

It is hard to know how this fiasco effected my attitude toward the annual Sunday School concert but it is certain that I never liked them and in later years absolutely refused to attend.

****

Although the joyous Yule Season started early in 1939, as usual the real celebration came on the eve of December 24th at Bedstefar and Bedstemor's house. Unfortunately gasoline rationing curtailed the movements of the Fred Andersen family who were obliged to stay home in Calgary. For sure, cousins Dorothy and Betty would not be there and of course the Molgard cousins were far away in British Columbia. Irene and I were a bit disappointed with the certainty of reduced numbers, but took comfort in knowing that the Holms would be present. They lived only a few miles east near the village of Hussar and unless the weather got stormy, they were sure to take in the festivities. We always had loads of fun with the Holm cousins, Gordon, Roy, Fred and Lars. Christine could be fun too, but after all she was a bit older and didn't really need to play with us little kids.

As expected, Christmas Eve was a most pleasant and festive event. With a lesser number of cousins, linking hands and moving around the tree was a bit awkward but as compensation, we got to the presents a bit earlier.

I probably got a sac full of small toys but the items that are best remembered were a little red wagon from Mother and Dad and a pair of skis from Uncle Chris. Actually, this is not quite correct since the skis were to be shared with Irene. Apparently, we were each to have one ski.

We really had no idea how to use skis but did realize that they were employed to slide down hills and glide over snow. The pair that Irene and I got on this Christmas eve were homemade and it was obvious that Chris had gone to a great deal of trouble in crafting them. They were of fine maple and to skim over the snow, the tips were properly turned up. To accept this shape, Chris had softened the maple boards by having them in boiling water for several days.

Skiing would have to wait since there was virtually no snow during the 1939-40 winter. It didn't really matter as we were probably too young to try them anyway. Finally when snow came the following year, Irene and I experienced total failure as we tried to master the infernal things. Quite frankly, few if any would have had much success with these maple staves since the harness was simply a leather strap that slipped over the toes of our overshoes. This left our feet in a totally undisciplined position, often turning at least sixty degrees out of alignment. Adding to our problems, the underside of the boards were sanded smooth, without any groove or system to keep them pointed in the intended direction. With such a precarious setup, they were either crossed or deviating in two completely different directions. Neither Irene nor I ever considered entering the Winter Olympics as downhill contestants. Moreover, it is likely that our early ineptness kept us away from legitimate ski hills for the many years that followed.

****

I missed my sister while she was at school but there were certain advantages that went with being an only child at home. I was often alone with Dad and this gave me a special opportunity to learn new things and enjoy the one on one companionship that was not possible when the whole family was together. It can be assumed that a modern sociologist would term this "male bonding," but for me it was simply a happy time filled with new excitement and learning experiences.

Whenever Dad went to town for mail or groceries, I was always thrilled for the chance to tag along. These trips were a preliminary lesson in trade and commerce, but they also allowed me to sit in the front seat of the Chev where I could see and learn about the business of driving a car. Dad explained the reason for the gear shift, clutch, brake and gas peddle. Learning their exact function would have to wait for a few years, but at least I was able to develop some appreciation for their names.

While sharing with the chores or making trips to Standard, Dad told me about things that happened long before my birth. These fascinating yarns included a whole host of events and experiences that he had lived through when he was a little boy back in Horning, Denmark. I learned that his father died when he was only four years of age and that Grandmother was required to send her children, including Dad, out to work at a very young age. To pare down on expenses, Dad, at the age of eleven, was compelled to leave home and work on a nearby farm.

At this tender age, working for board and room was no cake walk. Although the farmer and his wife were kindly people, they could not afford to accommodate to Dad's needs without a substantial work commitment. Real labor was involved and to satisfy the school agenda and complete the chores, Dad was obliged to rise at 5 A.M. each morning. The daily work required that he feed the farm animals and keep the barn clean. This not so small task kept him busy hefting and pushing a man-sized wheelbarrow. Also, feeding the animals was far from being a snap since turnips made up much of the winters hog fodder. Apparently these frosty, nearly frozen tubers were dug and pulled from the field without the benefit of gloves or mittens, making cold fingers an everyday experience. It didn't sound like fun and hearing these stories made me feel exceedingly lucky to be a part of a farm family with two loving parents and a warm house in which to live.

We talked about lots of other things too. I learned about special people like Babe Ruth, Lou Gehrig, Ty Cobb and Jack Dempsey. I didn't become a baseball expert but did learn that Tinker, Evers To Chance, was not a Monopoly move.

Dad was always interested in sports and we often dropped in for a visit with Dr. Fletcher. He and Dad would reminisce and joke about days past when they both played soccer. Their banter was always entertaining and it was fun to hear them relive some of their past exploits on the soccer field.

Also, each trip to Standard allowed me to meet and become acquainted with a few more of the good folks who made up the community.

It is likely that one of the most unusual and perhaps intimidating features of my hometown were the names of its citizens. The townspeople and the families from the surrounding rural areas were almost entirely of Danish extraction. As such, there was an incredible duplication of last names. This had to be confusing for everyone including the local postmaster who had the unenviable task of sorting out all of the Andersens, Christensens, Hansens, Jensens, Larsens, Nielsens, Petersens, Rasmussens, and more. To make the job easier, there were a preponderance of nicknames. These varied from insulting adjectives to the more common descriptive terms often characterizing an accepted feature of some person.

In common parlance, many of Standard's residents were better known by these descriptive idioms than their actual last names. There were for example, Short, Long, Loud, Black, Dirty, Little, Big, Fast, Fat, Slim, and many others which I am too polite to mention. Some of the names were actually comical and Dad wisely warned me about those which should not be repeated in good company.

****

As already noted, there was little if any snow through the winter of 1939-40. January was cold but the fields were as black and clear as if it was a summer day in August. If

114

there was any of the white stuff, most of it had drifted into a few ditches or low spots only to be covered and discolored by the blowing soil. This was too dry to freeze and the open fields were capable of generating a fair bit of dust whenever the wind came up.

I don't know what they were eating, but for some reason there were a phenomenal number of rabbits during that winter. They were everywhere, bounding across the open fields or pretending to hide in some shallow hole or patch of dried weeds. With such an abnormal number of bunnies, shelter was at a premium. To hide from the cold wind and predatory coyotes, they dug countless numbers of shallow lairs into the soft fallow fields. No doubt, they would have preferred safer sanctuaries but perhaps the deeper soil supported enough moisture to freeze solid thus rendering more ambitious excavations impossible. In any event, the rabbits didn't seem to know that their snow white winter coats were not very good camouflage in the snowless fields. They were as obvious as a lantern in a coal mine. The dark fields were dotted with stark white patches as the rabbit's furry backs eclipsed above the edges of their shallow burrows.

Dad was never a keen hunter and did not always approve of my continuing interest in the shooting sports. This was not at all obvious during the months of January and February of 1940 when rabbit hides were worth about fifty cents each. Dad was not only diligent in his pursuit of rabbits but he was good at it.

It probably didn't go with us to church on Sundays, but we seldom made a week day trip to Standard when Dad didn't have his twenty-two caliber rifle with him. Since the rabbits were of commercial value and easy to find, he almost never left his rifle at home. Every departure from the farm became a hunting trip. I loved it and as we drove along we would keep our eyes peeled for a telltale spot of white, easily visible in a black fallow field or a clump of brush or grass. On rare occasions our efforts were temporarily deceived by a piece of paper but we both soon learned to recognize the difference between an old Calgary Herald and the soft white fur of a rabbit.

Naturally the routine varied, but typically we would both notice a likely white patch. Dad would stop the car and carefully retrieve the unload rifle from the back seat. Once outside he would slip a few cartridges into the magazine and meticulously wend his way through and across the weed filled ditch. Crossing the barb wire fence to the prospective field and quarry was always a challenge since the taunt wire almost always had a propensity to squeak as Dad lowered it to slip over. If the wary rabbit happened to notice the noise, it would often bound off leaving Dad with little more than an embarrassed smile on his face. It was during these near misses that I knew how much he was enjoying himself even though he would never admit that hunting was fun. Efforts to slide through a fence or more specifically, maneuver through the strands without touching them, were generally unsuccessful as Dad's winter jacket proved to be a bit bulky, often leading to an even greater disturbance. Also on those occasions hunting was less enjoyable since such a misadventure often resulted in a rip or tear in either Dad's pants, jacket or both.

I knew that Mother would give me the "what for" if I came home with a rip in my pants. It was however, something of a surprise to note that a wife could also scold a husband for the same misdemeanor. When that happened, Dad and I were both cast as villains and there was true male bonding in shared misery. Modern psychologists would be delighted.

Although it happened on rare occasions, Dad was seldom triumphant with his shooting once an alarmed bunny decided to move out in truly serious flight. At best, hitting a bounding jack rabbit at almost any distance would have to be considered a lucky shot. In most cases however, they were somewhat cooperative and if no shots were fired, a fleeing lagomorph would often stop for a look back. When they were so inclined, and still reasonably nearby, Dad almost always managed to bring one back to the car or wagon where I had been obliged to wait.

For me the whole episode was terrifically exciting. Moreover, in the spring Dad had a large sack full of rabbit hides that he sold to "Simpson and Lea," a fur trader in Calgary. The number of pelts collected, or the amount for which they were sold is unknown, but the enterprise was definitely a financial success as well as a great deal of sport for both of us.

Throughout the entire season I had been highly tempted to bring my pop gun whenever Dad had reason to believe that we might happen upon a rabbit. I knew that quiet and stealth was an important part of the hunt and wisely decided it would be best to leave my noisy but ineffective firearm at home. Dad of course knew that I would have liked a more active role but said little about it.

One day after the spring winds had darkened the rabbits fur and the hunting was over, Dad took the rifle down from it's place over the stairwell and asked me if I would like to try a shot. I could hardly believe my ears, but it had to be true since he handed me the rifle and invited me to carry it down to the barn. There, shooting down into the ravine at the back, I would be allowed my first ever real pull of a trigger. It was an absolutely euphoric moment.

I noticed that his rifle was much heavier than mine but had little trouble toting this real weapon to the back of the barn where this momentous event would take place. When we got there, Dad pointed out an old milk pail that was dangling from a post about thirty yards distance. He suggested that this would be the target and judging from its condition, it was clear that it had seen target service on previous occasions.

Dad took the rifle from me and carefully loaded one cartridge into the magazine. While he still had control of the weapon, I was allowed to pump the cartridge into the chamber. Wow! What an authoritative sound. Finally, but still with considerable support and assistance in pointing at the pail, I placed the stock to my shoulder. By reaching my arm to it's maximum length, I could just reach the trigger. At this point, I was to make the final alignment of the sights which more or less pointed at the post and bucket. I missed the intended target by about twenty feet. The trigger released much quicker than expected since it was significantly lighter to the touch than was the pull on my pop gun. It didn't matter since I had at last fired a real honest- to-goodness rifle with real bullets.

Some years later, Dad taught me gun safety and the business of squeezing off a well aimed shot. With this help and other less obvious and explainable factors, I have always maintained a keen interest in hunting and the shooting sports. Indeed, as I write this, it is no exaggeration to say that over time I have fired thousands of rounds of ammunition. Every shot has been enjoyable but none have surpassed the thrill of that momentous first ever squeeze of the trigger with a real live bullet in the chamber.

****

Winter finally gave way to spring and although the creek just north of the farm would normally flood, this year was an exception. There had been some late winter snow before the ducks and geese returned to their nesting grounds, but not enough to wash away our now infamous culvert. We were all happy about this but the municipal leaders decided it was time to grade up the road and deepen the ditches. This operation took several weeks and in some ways it was more confining than a spring flood.

The machine that high graded our road was fun to watch but the turmoil of its passing made access to our farm totally impossible. For a few days we were land locked.

Basically, the road improvement program deepened the side ditches and dumped the dirt on the old, well worn trail. What a mess! The clay and gumbo from the ditches left huge lumps even after a grader tried to level the new higher road bed. Moreover, our own driveway ended abruptly into a deep ditch and until this was corrected with a culvert and a level passage over the chasm, there could be no normal traffic to and from our yard. Added to this confusion, Dad decided to relocate our driveway which had been little more than parallel tire tracks through the weeds. For several weeks he drove Irene to school through our field to a west gate. Here she was able to catch a ride with Hans Dam who was taking Henry to his grade two class at Craigantler.

In the end, the new road became useable and everything returned to normal, except when it rained. When that happened, the road became totally impassable, leaving any venturesome vehicle stuck and imbedded right up to its axles in the sticky clay. This of course assumes that the hapless car or truck did not first slide off the wet gumbo into one of the deepened ditches. During the first year or so, this so called improvement to our road was in fact a hazard.

While all of this was underway, I decided that it was time to bring my new wagon outdoors. It had remained in the house since Christmas. Mother warned that once it got its wheels dirty, it would have to remain outside forever. In spite of this, I could hardly wait to unlimber my new toy. Besides, I think Mother really wanted it out of the house so that I would stop banging it into the furniture.

Although it was harder to move around in the grass and weeds, it wasn't long before I could zip around with one leg in the wagon and the other one pumping along. It was certainly not perpetual motion but it was the closest thing I had to a real truck or car. With the tongue turned back for steering, my truck noise vocabulary continued to improve. I could go through almost anything and pump ever so hard when I double clutched down to low gear.

On very rare occasions I could get Musa to come along but the bone-jarring ride was not always to his liking. Even a soft sack for a pillow failed to satisfy my feline friend. Notwithstanding this slight disappointment, there were many less complaining things that I could haul around the yard in my new "Radio Flyer."

The one thing that I could not carry was a bucket of water. I will never understand how I could leave the pump with a full bucket and arrive at the house with barely enough for a good drink. Whenever I started to pull the wagon, the water sloshed out of its container and even managed to get me wet.

I loved my new wagon and used it almost every day. It was especially pleasant to pump it around and steer it like a car. Unfortunately this did not always work out. On one such occasion, it was pumped right into a barb wire fence. I had my head down but looked up just in time to have the middle strand cut into my face and right shoulder. Boy, was I ever a mess. There were cuts on my cheek, my nose, my forehead, and right shoulder. I looked like a Donnybrook street fighter who had been bested in a broken bottle bar brawl. A few days after the incident, my scar filled face could not smile, frown or for that matter do much of anything. To this day I carry the scars from this, one of several encounters with barb wire.

Perhaps my worst ever experience with my red wagon occurred one summer day while I was busy pumping along on one of the smooth tracks of our new driveway. These were well packed and provided a dandy surface between the dandelions and fox tails. On this well worn roadway the wagon would move at a seemingly astonishing clip.

Having ventured down to the main road, I was now on my way back when suddenly and without notice a large black car crept up right behind me. While there was no danger from the almost silent vehicle, a slight toot from its horn gave me a severe start. Looking over my shoulder, I quickly pulled over into the ripe fox tails, thus allowing it to pass and drive on toward the old barn where Dad was working. As the car slowly passed by, I noticed that it was driven by an R.C.M.P. officer. When he made his exit from the car all decked out in his officious stiff brimmed hat, his yellow striped breeches and brown leather leggings, I was panic stricken.

Ditching my wagon into a hoard of ripened fox tails and weeds, I ran pell mell to the safety of the house. I was certain that the police was in our yard to arrest and send me to prison. I was terrified and could hardly babble my concerns to Mother, who had no idea why I was so incoherent and frightened. Finally, after a lot of confusion, I settled down enough to learn that the police was simply seeking Dad's help in locating a farmstead where a robbery had been reported.

While the incident was a major and unforgettable scare, it provided Mother and Dad with the opportunity to teach me that police are friends of society and that I should never be afraid of them. Moreover, the police could be expected to help should I ever need their assistance.

****

Thinking back, it is hard to imagine how "The Pelican Man" became so popular. He was a Calgary radio personality who hosted a late afternoon children's program. We kids religiously listened to the performance as it was perhaps the only thing suitable for children on any of the three Calgary radio stations, namely CJCJ, CFCN and CFAC .

Basically, "The Pelican Man" (real name forgotten) was the moderator of an amateur talent show. The thirty minute program mostly featured children performing in groups although an especially talented solo act was occasionally allowed. There were no prior auditions but each individual or group was expected to emit a unique or outstanding sound by either singing, tap dancing, or playing a musical instrument.

While the show intended to reveal talent, the major thrust and interest of each half hour were the brief conversations that "The Pelican Man" had with the various participants. Strangely, most of the performers were from the country and in fact often an entire country school was represented. In truth, the talent was nearly nonexistent, but the interviews and conversations were slightly entertaining and may have had a few redeeming features.

It is not known who spawned the idea, but near the end of June, just before Irene was due to graduate into grade two, it was decided that the student body of Craigantler should visit "The Pelican Man." To make it even better, all of the kids from another nearby country school, either Yule or Alton, were to be included in this pooling of previously unheralded talent. Just imagine the splash this would make on the airwaves of Southern Alberta.

While the entire episode may now be seen with some cynicism, it was in fact a big deal in the spring of 1940. Even though I would not be allowed to participate, I was excited for Irene.

In the end, few if any of the kids spoke to the great man as the entire studio was filled with groups of youngsters, all trying to get some radio time. They were sitting on chairs, standing in the corners and even laying on the floor out in the hall. It was a crowd well beyond anyone's expectation and it took some bold maneuvering to get the Craigantler gang inside for their performance.

With a joint choir, there had been no opportunity for a rehearsal but Miss Weir played the piano for a stirring rendition of "You Are My Sunshine." This was sung despite the fact that it had already been on the docket, courtesy of a group from out High River way.

Although some of the adults may have been less than enthusiastic with the outcome, Irene was pleased and we were all very proud to have her emerge as a bona fide radio star. Hollywood may be a long way from Standard but who could tell?

****

The war was getting progressively worse and the daily CBC news was almost entirely committed to the activities of Hitler and his Nazi renegades. I well remember the shock and concern of almost everyone when in April, German troops marched into Denmark. We were not acquainted with any of our relatives in that country but almost all of our neighbors had a friend or various family members in this now occupied territory. Bedstefar and Bedstemor were understandably upset with this turn of events since both had brothers and sisters in the direct path of this growing cancer.

Denmark's fall was soon followed by additional action, and by my sixth birthday, Hitler held sway over nearly all of Continental Europe. In fact, it was on my birthday when all of the allied troops were forced to pull back to England from France (Dunkirk). There was a colossal loss of men and equipment and it is hard to imagine the basis for Churchill's bravado when on the same day he gave his most famous of all wartime speeches -"We will fight on the beaches - We shall never surrender."

It is almost certain that this offered tremendous encouragement to the British, but France was in big trouble and totally collapsed to the German army and their despotic rule just a few weeks later.

By this time there were growing indications that Canada was at war, as many Standard boys were in uniform preparing for eventual transport to England and combat. Indeed, several of our locals had been among the first contingent of troops sent to England and had already spent a Christmas away from family and loved ones.

A trip to town almost always brought news of someone joining the ranks of the army, air force or navy. Also, it became fairly common to see someone in uniform while either he or she was home enjoying a brief leave before embarking for Europe.

Each home with a family member in the service proudly displayed a window sign or card featuring a large star in the middle. Some families had several sons and or daughters in the military and in such cases the display featured more stars, one for each family member in the service. Eventually, before the war was over, with the defeat of Hitler and his gang of ruffians, some families could boast three and even more stars shining out to the world from their living room windows. There was certainly no limit to the number, as nearly everyone fitting the age requirement went to war.

Although I was still very young, I was old enough to feel the surge of patriotism and spirit of togetherness that ran through our community. Love of country and common purpose came easy as we were all being inculcated with stories of German evil and of course, our own righteousness. The whole country was pulling in the same direction. Even the characters featured in the United States produced radio shows were favorably aligned with Canada's war effort. For example, Maw Perkins and other soap operas were embroiled in war talk even though the plot and story line of their program did not feature any legitimate involvement until the bombing of Pearl Harbor, which came a year later.

****

The Calgary Stampede has always been an important event in Southern Alberta and very deservedly is regarded as one of the world's great rodeos. Over the years, I have visited many countries and have always been amazed to discover how well the Stampede is internationally known and recognized.

At six years of age it was a particular thrill to attend, and plans were made several weeks in advance. To ensure that no one would forget, Irene and I were on our very best behavior, and helping Mother and Dad a little more than usual became part of our pre-Stampede agenda. Knowing that good behavior was most likely to be rewarded with a trip to the Stampede, our conduct was exemplary in every way.

Waiting was agony, but finally for what seemed an eternity, the big day arrived. We all got up earlier than usual and off we went to Calgary and the excitement of the Stampede. In anticipation, I had slept very poorly but this failed to dampen my enthusiasm and eagerness to get on our way for the hoopla of the parade.

In those early days, we always took in the parade which was scheduled for the first Monday following the first of July. Although the event went on for seven days, for me at least, Monday was by far the best and the proper day to attend since it was parade day. Wow! What a show. For over two hours I could sit and gawk at all manner of things going by. There were cowboys, wagons, Indians in native dress, bands, clowns, soldiers, and horses. Everyone was in a festive mood.

Excluding the suburbs of Forest Lawn and Bowness which were annexed later, Calgary was a city of about seventy thousand and it is almost certain that this population doubled on the parade Monday of 1940. Farmers and ranchers from the surrounding areas converged on the city for this fun filled western country festival. The road from Standard, now part of the TransCanada Highway, was teeming with cars and farm trucks. For the most part, this highway was little more than a country road and with all of the Stampede traffic, it was virtually shrouded in one long cloud of choking dust. It was unpleasant but I didn't mind since my thoughts were of the Stampede.

Upon our arrival, it became obvious that the parade route was already well established, leaving many of the streets and avenues blocked off to normal traffic. As you might expect, this created a good deal of confusion and a colossal parking problem. Fortunately, there were no parking meters and very few "No Parking" zones so any available parking spot would do. On this occasion, Dad parked on the C.P.R. right-of-way, leaving just enough room for a passing train. This parking spot positioned us fairly close to the parade route and since we were all in a hurry to get there, no one seemed particularly worried about the car or the risk of a passing train.

I am not sure when we first attended a Calgary Stampede but feel reasonably certain that we were all there in 1940. Not only did the parade have a large number of cowboys and Indians but on this occasion it also featured countless soldiers, airmen and sailors. Instead of wearing the traditional Tom Mix straw hat, which I always found to be uncomfortably hot, Mother and Dad had bought me a more comfortable blue peaked cap just like the ones worn by all the men in the air force. It had two brass buttons on the leading edge or prow and to make it even more official, Uncle Carl had given me a small brass airplane pin which was affixed to the left front side of the cap. I really liked this partial uniform and quickly learned to wear this mini head covering slightly tilted to one side, just the way the big fellows wore theirs. It made me feel very patriotic and was certainly in tune with the theme of that particular Stampede.

As you might expect, the parade route sidewalks were crammed with festive onlookers. Despite our initial reluctance to leave the comfort of Mother and Dad, Irene and I were encouraged by the nearby adults to sit on the curb where there was a totally unobstructed view of the proceedings. At first it was frightening to be separated from Mother and Dad and be surrounded by strangers. We felt vulnerable but soon learned that everyone was friendly and as the parade progressed, our concerns lessened. We did of course check every once in a while to make sure that we had not been orphaned and that our guardians were still in the vicinity. Happily, they were fully aware of our timidity and stayed in view even though it meant that their own vantage point was less than perfect.

I remember wishing that I was a little older so that I could have an authentic uniform and march in the parade. That marching music was terrific! I didn't get the least bit tired even though the program was lengthened by thousands of men marching by in full uniform. Some were even in full battle dress carrying full packs and assorted firearms. There were trucks, jeeps, tanks, and half trucks with cannons in tow. I had never before seen all of this military equipment but it sure looked great. I was certain that these Calgary troops could easily handle Hitler and his Nazi gang. Also, after seeing all of the paraphernalia and armament, I realized that the picture in Bedstefar's "Book of Knowledge" was not going to set the tone for this war.

Curiously all of the trucks and jeeps had the steering wheel on the wrong side. I did not understand this but assumed it had something to do with shooting. It was of course to facilitate the transition to England where all driving was done on the left side of the road instead of the right as we did in Canada. Indeed, in those days all of Europe drove on the left, the reverse of North America's right side.

Finally, the last soldier marched by and the parade ended. To my total relief, Irene and I were reunited with Mother and Dad. It was good to hold Dad's hand since we were obliged to fight our way through an incredible crowd as we made out way back to the car. We were all pleased to note that it was still intact and if a train had gone by, it had missed the 1930 Chev. Equally important, it felt ever so good to get out of the crowd and sink into the soft security of the back seat. My nearly sleepless night was beginning to catch up with me.

There was more to the Stampede than the parade but since the next act was still several hours away, it was decided that we would visit the Andersens. Uncle Fred, Aunt Karen, and cousins, Dorothy and Betty lived on top of a hill in southwest Calgary. They were only minutes away and it wasn't long before we were chugging up Sixteen "A" Street which was quite a formidable hill for the cars of that era.

We always looked forward to a visit with Dorothy and Betty, (Phyllis was not yet born) and certainly they were equally enthusiastic when we showed up. They too had seen the parade, but had returned home on a street car and were more or less settled in when we arrived. I was eager to tell everyone about the parade but since they had seen it, my enthusiasm was not appreciated.

Karen and Fred had a rather large house but throughout the depression and indeed through 1940 and beyond, they rented the upstairs to another family, the Chapmans. That was OK but unfortunately the only bathroom was upstairs and whenever I was obliged to answered one of nature's calls, it seemed to be an invasion of their privacy. That feeling was made substantially worse when Mrs. Chapman gave me a severe scolding for not lifting the seat for one of my pressing visits to their domain. Heck, how could I be expected to know about things like that? At home on the farm, going to the john was not nearly so complicated.

Actually, I was always a bit shy with all of the strange people around Uncle Fred's house. The yard was rather small and the front verandah was within easy earshot of the adjacent neighbors' porches. This made it nearly impossible to go outside without being invited to visit with someone. The next door neighbors, the Bizwangers on one side, and the Logans on the other, were very nice but I was too bashful to be much of a conversationalist. It was much easier to visit with Patsy Curtis right across the street. Patsy was about my age and since she was usually at odds with the other kids, she seemed always to be looking for a friend. I rather enjoyed her and hoped that she would invite me over to see her Dad's neat display of swords and knives which were hanging on a wall and easily visible through their front porch window. Instead, Eddie Kuhen, a neighbor boy, and I watched the almost continuous stream of yellow Harvard trainers flying overhead. Their flight path from the nearby Curry Barracks, and Station Calgary, took them directly over Uncle Fred's house. Within a very few minutes we were both able to mimic the roar of these passing military marvels.

After our brief visit at Uncle Fred and Aunt Karen's home, we ventured down to the boisterous Victoria Park Fairgrounds. The rodeo was underway but we spent all of the daylight hours visiting the midway. None of the sideshows were of particular interest but Irene and I were treated to a ride on a merry-go-round. It was a pint sized automobile that moved around in a circle. For me, it was a terrible disappointment since no matter what I did to the steering wheel, the car would not move from its set course.

Later in the afternoon, we visited the Indian Village with all of its tepees, ponies and native paraphernalia. My blonde hair was a big hit. In fact, Mother and I were invited into a huge tepee so that one of the older chiefs could view my hair. I didn't much enjoy it since the entire Blackfoot nation seemed intent on running their fingers through my nearly white locks.

I don't recall how the whole day went but have a strong recollection of the fireworks later that evening. Having never before seen such a display, they were truly spectacular. We didn't have a grandstand seat but were standing right next to the race track when the fireworks display erupted above. We were in that spot since we had watched the evening chuck wagon races from that position.

The fastest time of the day had been set by Dick Cosgrave, a rancher from Rosebud. This really pleased me since his ranch was just a few miles north of Standard, essentially making him a local talent.

The whole day had been filled with thrills and excitement and was probably the busiest and most tiring of my entire six years. I was almost asleep by the time we got back to the car which, in those days, could be parked right on the grounds next to the Royal American sideshows and merry-go-rounds. That convenience was a real blessing since I was exhausted and had hardly stumbled into the dusty back seat before sleep took over.

My next recall of events came a few hours later when I awoke to the voices of Mother and Dad who were talking in rather worried tones. Also the car was making a funny noise. I sat up to discover that we were nearly home but during our sunshine filled day in Calgary, a heavy local shower had made our new road a hopeless bog.

The old Chev made a valiant effort but finally, with less than a quarter of a mile to go, the wheels could no longer get any traction and in the gumbo they could hardly turn. We were stuck in the middle of some deep ruts and going on was hopeless. The good news was that we were less than a quarter of a mile from home. While the offending clouds had drifted away and it was no longer raining, a ghost like mist was steaming up and hovering a few feet above the mud that represented the road and its equally dark and frighteningly deep ditches. Weeds and grass had not yet taken root in this wasteland of barren nothingness. It was a unique and eerie scene under the bright moon and star filled sky.

After a very brief discussion, it was agreed that we would walk the rest of the way. It was a good idea but after about two steps, Irene and I walked right out of our light canvas shoes. They remained glued to the greasy clay and it was impossible to move without loosing our light footwear. Not only did the gooey muck take our shoes, it hid them in the dark footprints and ruts, making retrieval in the dim moonlight a dirty and almost hopeless task. After a messy search and recovery, we all carried our shoes and socks as we barefooted the last few hundred yards to our farmyard. The track was greasy and slippery and was made even more weird as we crossed the infamous culvert. This minuscule piece of real estate, which often washed out in spring, featured a nearly perpetual water hole at its base. This anomalous patch of the great wet, was always filled with frogs and other aquatic life. We were all too tired to talk but as we crossed over this minor water course, the chorus of frogs fell silent. It was indeed a strange and spooky moment. Finally we arrived in our yard and the relative comfort of some wet grass which we used to clean most of the mud from our very cold feet.

Getting cleaned up was difficult and it is a certainty that Mother and Dad had some doubts about the value of our Stampede visit. I was exhausted but by morning knew that all of the trauma and discomfort had been worth it. I could relive my fantasy of marching along with all of those blue uniformed airmen. Even better, I could dream of flying one of the yellow planes that were constantly roaring over Uncle Fred's house. Indeed, within a few weeks, these same planes were doing loops over our farm.

It was amazing what the war in Europe was doing to our small, insignificant community. In addition to the attitudes of support and patriotism, a whole host of physical changes were underway. Most notable was the construction of innumerable local air training bases. Great Britain was under a continuous air siege and "The Battle of Britain" was making the business of training pilots an absolute priority. This urgency was being dealt with in Canada where the training of new airmen could go on unmolested. This fact was evidenced by the countless number of Harvard trainers, which within weeks of the need, filled our skies, practicing aerobics and teaming up in mock dog fights. These bright yellow planes were easily distinguishable by a loud clacking sound as they passed directly overhead. Apparently this clamorous racket, which I soon learned to mimic, had something to do with a variable pitch propeller that had been developed and employed by the British Air Force. In actual fact, this innovation, tested and proven in the skies of Western Canada helped make the Spitfire and Hurricane aircraft superior to the ME 109 Messerschmitt, the major foe in the air battles over London. Who knows, the air space over our farm may have contributed to the defeat of Hitler's Luftwaffe?

****

To fuel this commotion in Alberta's skies, Canada's meager petroleum resources were being strained to the limit. Turner Valley, the largest and virtually solo source of oil in Canada was producing at capacity. Located some thirty miles south of Calgary, this giant oil field, discovered in 1914, was being called upon to produce without regard for "good production practices" and the accompanying natural gas was being flared as a waste byproduct. The myriad of fires produced a huge halo over the entire oil field. At night this incredible radiance lit up the sky and its glow was often visible from our farm some seventy miles to the east. Not only was the fire's aura visible, but during a west wind or Chinook, the smell of Turner Valley's contribution to the war effort easily extended to our farm. During the forthcoming winter, it was claimed that all of Western Canada's hobos converged on this firestorm. By locating oneself near one of the many gas flares, sleeping outdoors could apparently be quite comfortable.

Closer to home, and for some completely unknown reason, grain production was expected to increase dramatically. This gave rise to the construction of additional storage facilities throughout most of Alberta. One of Standard's six grain elevators was torn down but in it's place several huge but ugly granaries or annexes were built along the railway and next to the remaining five grain elevators.

****

Our farm was not without its war effort as Dad built a large pig barn during the early summer of 1940. Bacon was one of the staple foods used to feed the rapidly growing military force and this unprecedented demand was quickly developing into a shortage. Moreover, Denmark was now in the hands of Germany and as England was unable to source its pork requirements from this traditional supplier, Canada was expected to make up the shortfall. For bacon lovers it was all very sad, but the opportunity to benefit from this mounting shortage was irresistible. The need was real and Dad was quick to recognize it.

I thoroughly enjoyed watching a construction project so I was more than a little excited when Dad started this mammoth hog project. At first, it was a bit boring since the initial activity was directed to the matter of clearing the

133

ground and staking out the site for this new hog factory. Like the chicken house, sizable piles of sand and gravel were the first materials to make their appearance. Somehow, Dad was able to borrow a cement mixer and within a few days a neat exterior foundation was solidly but silently announcing the spot on which the new barn would be located. Within a few more days, the rather expansive floor was completed thus giving additional tenure to the building plans.

Did I ever enjoy this gargantuan surface. Me and my red wagon had not enjoyed a smooth flat surface since we were banished from the house several months earlier. Pumping around was incredibly easy but these joy rides were relatively short lived since with pen construction, the space soon became a bit cluttered.

Although not very useful, I was old enough to learn, and didn't miss a trick as Dad lifted and positioned the two by four frames into place for the long barn walls. Also, I was witness to every nail that he drove. Each part of the building was a new learning experience and by the time it was completed, building one by myself seemed possible, had I been strong enough to saw the boards.

****

The pig house was certainly not my inspiration but during the summer of 1940, I invented and single handily built a Spitshort, the best toy ever. This seemingly useless doodad had the remarkable ability to energize my movements and allowed me to run without ever becoming fatigued. It has long since been forgotten, but it is likely that the name was an embellished version of the Supermarine Spitfire, the British fighter plane and ultimate victor of the "Battle of Britain."

With all of its marvelous attributes, one might be tempted to think that a Spitshort was a medical breakthrough, universally suitable for the rejuvenation of all tired muscles. It was in fact, a collection of uncomplicated parts, assembled through the genius of a six year old. This included a worn gear wheel from an unused junk binder, a long wooden leg and back support from a broken chair, a steel treadle yoke from a derelict washing machine, a large nut and bolt and a short nail.

These parts properly assembled basically formed a wheelbarrow having only one handle and no container for carrying a load. Put in other terms, it was a simple stick with a wheel at one end. Properly held, with the old gear running on the ground, it added zip to my every step. This was especially true if airplane noises were added. To this day I cannot explain the physics or chemistry of this invention, but it did seem to generate as much energy as did a good breakfast of puffed wheat or stack of Mother's outstanding pancakes.

For at least two summers I ran all over the yard with this incredible, yet simple device. It made all of my chores easier as the energy required for each step was somehow replaced if the Spitshort was in hand. When it was not in use, it leaned against the house so that it would be within easy reach for each foray into the garden or barnyard.

If I had been truly clever, I would have obtained a patent and manufactured Spitshorts for the entire world. Unfortunately, this was not done and was more or less forgotten until my sister found and gave me a manufactured plastic version for my fifty-eighth birthday. To my disappointment, the handle was a bit short and as a consequence, awkward to operate. Even worse, this plastic imitation failed to impart additional energy to my much older body.

****

Sunday School went into recess throughout the summer and early fall. We of course continued to go to church, including a late July service which was also scheduled as the congregational Sunday School picnic. Instead of having the service in the church, everyone went off to a picnic area near the Bow River, south of Gleichen. The site for this festive event was actually on the Blackfoot Indian Reservation and I have often wondered if anyone bothered to get prior permission for the occasion. We always saw a fair number of Indians but to the best of my knowledge, none ever dropped in for a visit or bothered our group.

The site was located on a peninsula bounded on the south by the swift waters of the Bow River. The northern boundary was defined by an old oxbow which continued to obtain a fresh supply of water from a trickling stream feeding in from the river on the western edge. This made the backwaters suitable for swimming. The river itself was considered too cold and much too swift.

The land within these watery limits was filled with native willows, chokecherries and huge cottonwoods. Also there was a goodly portion of open space so that cars could park and people could congregate and enjoy a day in the sun or shade, whichever was more preferable. It was a beautiful setting and lent itself very well to the needs of our annual Sunday School gathering.

I always enjoyed the picnic, including the ride to this remote oasis. Crossing the Indian reservation from Gleichen was always a bit risky since there were no legitimate roads or signs leading to or pointing to a specific destination. The confusion of well worn trails running to any and every point on the compass were of little help and only added to the challenge. I think everyone more or less followed each other in a convoy, hoping that someone would prevail and find the picnic spot. As the cars bumped along, powdery dust boiled up from the deeply rutted trails. In the still air, this left a well defined dust cloud, marking out the trail for all late comers.

On one occasion, Dad either got lost or deliberately ventured east to avoid the dust filled air. In doing so, we happened upon an old Indian burial ground with its open graves. Here we could see the bony remains of several Indians, left to eternity, completely unprotected with exposure to the sun and rain and even an occasional marauding coyote.

At the time, I wasn't familiar with Indian culture, but have since learn that these burial pits were always left open. This allowed the spirits to rise from their mortal bodies, departing for the world beyond, where the water was always fresh and the buffalo plentiful. In leaving the earthly body, it was believed, in "Indian Lore," that the spirit would initially enter an owl which could transport the soul to the "Happy Hunting Ground." As a consequence, Indians never killed owls but would grace their attire with owl feathers and bones. Indeed, Chief Crowfoot, a most distinguished and famous Blackfoot and one of the signatories of "Treaty No. Seven," always wore an owl skull woven and stitched into his hair. This was done as a sign of honor and respect for this noble and mysterious bird of the night and spirit world.

But back to the picnic of 1940, which probably included nearly everyone from our congregation. Initially there was a bit of confusion but after gathering some of the errant children, Pastor Christensen preached a brief sermon, using both English and Danish in his delivery. He chose the shade of a huge cottonwood as his pulpit while the congregation either stood or sat on car blankets, seconded from the dusty seats of their autos.

Despite the location, most of the attendees were dressed in their Sunday best since for many, the alternative would probably be a clean pair of work overalls. There were no sport shirts, brightly colored pants or casual jackets.

Indeed, in today's world, an outside observer might have guessed it to be a somber graveside service rather than a happy carefree outing in the sun. Dark three piece suits, white shirts, ties and black polished shoes were the norm. It wasn't a uniform, but it might have been since every adult male wore a dark felt fedora with a turned down front brim. Each of these was fashionably decorated with several colorful feathers peeking over the right or left side of a wide silk encircling hat band.

The women, also in their best, were more colorful but here again, their dresses bordered on the verge of being formal. Shorts or pants were not a part of their wardrobes.

The children were the exception and most were in happy clothes, entirely proper for the occasion. I don't remember my entire getup but do recall that I wore my new air force cap with brass buttons and the airplane badge that Uncle Carl had given to me.

The sermon and short service were quickly followed by lunch whereupon all of the ladies produced and spread clean tablecloths on the dirty and uneven grass and weeds. Suddenly, as if by magic, there was food everywhere. This, for the most part, had arrived in large paper boxes of every size and shape. Few if any parishioners had the luxury of a picnic basket but the cardboard containers worked just fine.

Each family brought their own plates, knives, forks and spoons, but to be totally ecumenical, the food, when set out, was shared by all. In short, it was a mix and grab arrangement which meant that we all had choices. If you didn't like the beans prepared by Mrs. H, you could try those of Mrs. J. Similarly, if Mrs. M's fried chicken was better than Mrs. O's, you could eat from Mrs. M's supply. Unfortunately, this meant that everyone loaded up on Mrs. N's potato salad, leaving Mrs. K with the embarrassment of leftovers to take home.

In a way, the whole process was a bit cruel since children and even an occasional adult could at times be less than charitable. To make matters worse, and despite the rueful looks of some distraught mothers, words were occasionally spoken which went along the line - "This fried chicken is awful" or "Don't eat salad from that bowl, it's yucky."

In the end however, everyone's hunger was satisfied and appetites were set aside for a few hours of leisure and adventure. If there were hurt feelings, I was not aware of them and in testimony to Mother's cooking, never surprised when she had nothing but dirty dishes and cutlery to take home.

While the women of the church were cleaning up the chicken bones, soiled tablecloths and dirty dishes, often half filled with messy food, the men of the congregation were lally-gagging in the shade. Here, without the constraints of an outer jacket or vest, they could with loosened ties, enjoy some unfettered conversation and a good after meal smoke. Perhaps even more meaningful, the quiet shade provided a respite from the unfamiliar cramped and awkward business of juggling a plate of beans and potato salad while hunkering down and pretending that such a position beat the comfort of the sofa back home.

At the annual Sunday school picnic of 1940, almost all evidence of hard times was gone. As proof, nearly all of the men produced a new package of "taylor mades" for their after lunch smoke. After all, a packet of Players or Sweet Caps was certain to impress and make a statement. For those slightly less fortunate but still concerned with status, cheating was possible with nearly perfect, "roll your owns." These, meticulously placed in appropriate packages, were painstakingly lit to ensure that a proper burn would occur and that a ragged ash would not betray the fraud. Dad had given up tobacco during his appendicitis convalescence and was essentially unmindful of this drama.

It would of course be unfair to assume that every man participating in this demonstration of well being was trying to make an impression. No doubt there was a large majority who smoked as they always did.

Although I always enjoyed adult male talk, I didn't hang around to watch the smoke or hear the various views on the war in Europe. Instead, it was time to go exploring or in search of adventure with my older and trusted companions, Henry Dam who was eight or nine and Kenneth Larsen who was seven.

Our first investigation brought us south to the rushing Bow River. This was accessible via a myriad of trails through a thicket of willows and assorted brush. Once at the rivers edge, I noticed a large steel bridge which apparently crossed over to the town of Arrowwood, a few miles farther south.

Henry skipped stones on the water's surface and with a little help and instruction, I finally managed to skip a few. I learned that a flat stone was much more likely to skip than a round one, and with a little coaching, soon realized that it was also important to keep the stone horizontal as it was released. I was very pleased with what I learned that day and Henry was certainly a terrific mentor.

Kenneth already knew about skipping stones, so he focused his attention on some brightly dressed Indians near the northern foot of the bridge, some seventy to one hundred yards away. They may have been picking chokecherries but it was more fun to think otherwise. Besides, Kenneth was sure they were spies and that Canada's national security was at risk. With his urging, we gave up skipping stones and decided to do some spying of our own. It sounded scary but having been told that I could not be alone by the river, I followed Kenneth and Henry as they tried to work a little closer to these desperate and dangerous people. By this time we pretended and maybe even believed that our mission was in the vital interests of Canada's war effort.

Henry devised a plan that if successful, would lead us even closer to the quarry. This could be done while staying out of sight in the cover of the willows which flanked the rushing water. Stealth was essential and added to the thrill. Also, Henry was quick to point out that it was common for Indians to scalp white folk. With that announcement, I soon conjured up the image of war and death as depicted in Bedstefar's "Book of Knowledge." I was mighty scared!

We probably spent twenty to thirty minutes making a wide but carefully crafted approach to a new vantage point on the graveled river bed. Henry theorized that if we lived long enough to emerge from the willows on the river's edge, we would be close enough to implement some serious surveillance. This was all very well, but with our progressively creative imaginations, we were nearly half dead with fright when we finally peeked out from the cover of the underbrush. As planned, we were much closer but to our surprise and horror, our spies were no longer there. Now what would we do? Perhaps they were spying on us. Even worse, they were probably crouching down in the willows with scalping knives held in their teeth just waiting to pounce on our diminutive and defenseless bodies.

I don't think we ran but it didn't take long to get back to the comfort and safety of the congregation. With a mischievous demeanor, our sudden burst into the population center of the picnic must have raised a few questions. It was of course a private and exhilarating adventure not to be shared or understood by anyone other than we three. All queries were met with silence, which probably raised even more doubts about our activities and the suspicious meaning of our closed lips.

Deep down we knew that our afternoon quest was a fabrication, but that did not diminish the flush of excitement that came with our escape from the threatening and now fearful willows that we deemed to be filled with painted savages. Maybe the Indians had been harmlessly engaged in berry picking but with our inventiveness, we could never be absolutely sure. With that thought, we could never really know how close we came to having our scalps lifted.

The rest of the picnic was more or less uneventful but did include a few foot races and ice cream cones for everyone. The ice cream was a surprise since it had been a pleasantly warm day. I was of course delighted to share in this favorite treat which had in fact survived the dust and the warmth of the day in the trunk of Anton Myrthu's car. There it had been safely protected from the heat in a large insulated container designed for just such an event. This ugly, greasy, ice cream thermos didn't look very appetizing, but its contents were delicious.

The shadows were lengthening and we were about to go home when I noticed that my airplane pin was no longer on my cap. I was very upset and prevailed on Dad to walk with me back to the river in the hope that we would be able to find it along the trail. I could never hope to retrace all of my steps and in any event would never risk a search in the willow thicket that Henry, Kenneth and I had ventured into earlier. With the coming of darkness, Dad and I were unsuccessful and I was obliged to leave the picnic area without my favorite airplane pin. I was heartbroken.

✱✱✱✱✱✱✱✱✱✱✱

Nancy and Beauty, our faithful team of horses, were well up in years and were no longer expected to pull a wagon or perform on any work detail. For most of the past year or so, both had been allowed to loaf in the pasture, enjoying a well earned retirement. Their last major assignment had been with a dirt scraper during the building of a small water storage facility in the pasture. This earthen dam caught rain and irrigation run off thus creating a fairly large pond of water. With such a supply, Dad no longer needed to carry water from the well to the livestock. The old steel drum that had served as a pasture trough, probably since the flood of Noah, was no longer needed.

There is no question that Nancy and Beauty were deserving of the plentiful water supply and their leisure time but it was evident that things were not going well for them. Both had developed a stiffness in their legs and with their advanced age, they could hardly hobble around for grass and water. Clearly it was time to sever them from life and end their obvious suffering. It was indeed a sad day when Dad solemnly herded them out to the fallow field where they could be put down with a carefully aimed twenty-two caliber bullet.

We all missed them but Dad was most effected and was particularly sorry to lose his old faithful team. To ease the hurt, he quickly went in search of a new and younger pair of horses. It wasn't long before he located a new team that was available from his long time friend, Nick Beck.

Nick Beck and his bachelor brother, Gotfried, had known Dad back in Denmark. When Dad first came to Standard, they had all worked for Henry Larsen, one of the first pioneers to settle in the area. All three had grown up at a time when horses were vital for both work and transportation and it is certain that they knew good horse flesh when they saw it.

As an upshot of this background, Nick and Godfried along with Svend, Nick's eldest son, were in the business of buying and selling horses. More importantly, Svend, then in England serving with the Canadian Armed Forces, was an excellent horseman and had been instrumental in breaking many horses for riding and team work.

The Beck farm was approximately fifteen miles southeast of our farm. Their community had grown in much the same way that had Standard but had been settled largely by pioneers from France and Quebec. While the Becks, and a very few others, were of a Danish background, they were the exception and had little or no influence on the character of the area and the small village of Cluny that anchored the settlement. This small pioneer village originally known as "Siding No. 13" on Canadian Pacific's main line, was later named Cluny after a town in Scotland of the same name. Being some thirty years older it was markedly different from my home town.

Cluny was near the eastern edge of the Blackfoot Indian Reservation and as a consequence large numbers of Indians could usually be found nearby. Adding to it's uniqueness, the major store and principle business was owned and operated by a shrewd merchant of Chinese origin.

Louie Hong's establishment was full of surprises and during the war, when there were shortages of merchandise in other marts, Mr. Hong almost always had the items that were otherwise unavailable. Rubber boots and overshoes were big sellers as was fleece lined underwear. I doubt that any other vendor in Alberta had these items in stock, but for some curious reason, Louie Hong's store never seemed to run out.

This extraordinary stash of merchandise gave Cluny an inordinate popularity that was known for miles around. It was never said with malice but the ethnic mix of the colony, combined with it's famous Chinese businessman gave rise to it's well known nickname of "French Indochina." With Louie Hong's emporium no longer in existence, this almost libelous label has little relevance today. However during the war years, when the store was patronized and endeared by shoppers for miles around, this idiom was known throughout Southern Alberta.

It was always fun to visit the Beck's farm since they had a large family and just oodles of things to explore and fun things to do. To start with, their farm was a veritable zoo. Of course everyone might think that any farm with livestock is akin to a zoo but believe me, their's was truly different. For example, instead of having one breed of chickens like our white Leghorns, the Becks had white Leghorns, rusty Rhode Island Reds, gray Plymouth Rocks, Buff Orpingtons, Mottled Wyandottes, and every imaginable mix of these colors and breeds. In addition, they also had a flock of multicolored Bantam hens and roosters which, despite their diminutive size, were feisty enough to ensure supremacy of the chicken house pecking order.

Most likely the only bird tough enough to intimidate the Bantams was a large gander. This arrogant bird roamed around, lording it over the entire farmyard. Even the abundant white and gray turkeys, along with the ducks and other geese were uneasy in the presence of this hissing and belligerent despot. I don't know how the water fowl handled their need for rest but each evening the turkeys could at least retire to the top of the barn, where like well disciplined soldiers, they lined up well beyond the reach of this cantankerous gander.

Our farm featured white pigs with upright ears, a black and white milk cow and in past tense, a normal team of horses. In contrast, the Becks had animals of every type and description. Their pigs ranged in color from white to red. Still others were variegated with black and brown spots and floppy ears. Also meandering around the barnyard were sheep of different varieties and at least one big, bad billy goat. The billy goat was always looking for trouble and would chase us kids all over the yard.

I was never victimized by one of his bold bunts but that was only because I was particularly watchful. Also, for starters, there were an abundance of old plows, tractors and various other farm implements parked throughout the yard. An escape onto one of these rusty derelicts made a safe haven, well beyond the reach of the bad tempered goat.

Curiously, a quick retreat into a huge patch of horse radish offered an equally safe sanctuary. For some reason the billy goat was reluctant to venture into this thick green profusion of foliage.

Apart from the safety accorded to us, the horse radish was fun to romp in since the plants were essentially indestructible. In truth, I think the Becks were trying to get rid of these hot tubers so no one really cared how much we trampled on this part of the garden.

If it hadn't been for the gander and the billy goat, the Beck farm would have ranked as one of the best petting zoos in Canada. Unfortunately, these antagonists were always lurking around and were not easily avoided. For a six year old they represented the dominant, never to be forgotten, attributes of the Beck farm.

It was a social visit but it was also intended that Dad purchase a new team of horses. With this objective, Nick Beck was persuaded to lock up the billy goat so that we could view the many horses that he and his eldest son, Svend, had raised. These now mature animals had largely been acquired from the local Indians and after considerable training were harness broken. Subsequently, they had been matched up into working teams.

Dad chose a small pair made up of two mares, a gray and a white. Both horses were smaller than their predecessors, Nancy and Beauty, but appeared to have the qualities that he was looking for. In any event, a deal was made and all that remained was the matter of getting them back to our farm, some fifteen miles away.

Both horses were comfortable in harness but despite Svend and Nick's best efforts, the gray, Lady by name, would not permit anyone on her back. Diamond, the white mare, was fully broken and could be ridden bareback or with a saddle. This pleased Dad, and may well have played a big part in his selection of this fine looking pair of horses.

We had brought Nancy and Beauty's old harness with us and this was soon fitted on the newly acquired team. The collars were a bit large, (altered later with long pads designed for the purpose) and despite some mild prancing around by Lady, the harness was finally draped over the new team with a reasonable fit. Although Dad made no attempt to ride Lady, since she was not saddle broken, Diamond accepted him on her back and off they went, trailing Lady in full harness.

With Mother behind the wheel, we soon left the Beck farm, passing Dad with a smile and a wave just a few miles down the dusty road. Naturally we arrived home first but were surprised at how quickly he showed up to stable Diamond and Lady in our old weather worn barn. We were very pleased and Irene and I were assured that we would soon be given the chance to ride Diamond. Unfortunately for me, this opportunity came all too soon.

****

The garden and our rather large potato patch needed weeding and cultivating. When Nancy was still in the picture this was easy. She could pull the hand held garden cultivator straight down the rows without so much as stepping on a leaf. Dad simply tied the reins over his neck as he held on to the cultivator. Nancy knew just what to do, even without specific directions from Dad.

In spite of their smaller size and petite hooves, neither Diamond nor Lady had the good sense to walk between the rows. Instead, both seemed bent on trampling everything in sight. Dad could easily steer the horse if he had control of the reins. Unfortunately, the garden cultivator would not function by itself and required both of his hands on the protruding handles. Unlike days past with Nancy in the lead, looping the leather reins over his neck was not a solution.

147

Yeah, you guessed it; I was selected to ride and steer Diamond up and down these straight but narrow rows. As you would expect, these were flanked on both sides by potato plants or some equally vital garden crop. Since I was responsible for the steering, Dad had unhindered control of the cultivator. In theory this should have worked but it didn't. It wasn't long before Diamond figured out that I was neither a good boss nor a master horseman. At six years of age, I could hardly get her to respond to any of my commands. To make matters worse, all she really wanted to do was to get back to Lady who was tethered to a fence post some fifty yards away. While going up and down the garden rows, she always veered in that direction. With her front hooves in one row and her back legs canted over in the adjacent line of vegetables, her sideways motion managed to trample two rows at once.

I am sure that Dad could have straightened her out, but try as I might, my horsemanship was just not up to the job. As this unhappy circus was in progress, Diamond was getting heck from me. I was getting heck from Dad and when we were finished with our cultivating and trampling, we all got heck from Mother.

****

It was always clear to me that Bedstefar had only a minor interest in most of his young, dirty, runny nosed grandchildren. We were of course accepted for who we were but having a sniveling child nearby was not one of his major joys of life. Who of us could blame him for that?

When we got a bit older, that is beyond the diaper stage, he would on very rare occasions, hold one of us on his lap for very brief periods. For me, these seldom encounters were always a bit frightening. At first, I was never quite sure of his motives since he almost always referred to me as a "slobert" which is the Danish word for bad boy or delinquent. With such an introduction, how could I be sure of his intentions?

In most instances my fears vanished when he smiled and tried to lighten the moment with some form of entertainment. His notion of levity often involved some activity with his boneless little finger. This oversight of nature was inconsequential in his day to day chores but came in mighty handy whenever he felt the urge to display some affection toward a grandchild. At these times he would show it off by bending it backwards to the top of his wrist. Also, he could snap it hard in such a way that his little finger would crack like a whip. The maneuvers were obviously painless and were totally fascinating.

It was his show and if I attempted to grab or manipulate his hand and useless digit, the session was quickly over. I soon learned not to interfere but instead showed off my double jointed thumb. Maybe he thought I was trying to outdo him because this ploy was equally effective in terminating our brief periods of mutual admiration.

Notwithstanding Bedstefar's apparent disinterest in his fifteen grandchildren, he and Bedstemor made it a point to organize a family picnic each year. For this I have always been extremely grateful since these seemingly incongruous events are among my happiest childhood memories.

It's hard to know when these family affairs first began but they were always scheduled for a time between summer plowing and the second cutting of alfalfa. This timing never varied and neither did the location which was St. George's Island in Calgary.

We never really knew if this festive event was for the benefit of the adults or the kids, but it didn't much matter since we all had a blast. For Bedstefar and Bedstemor it was the main event of the summer as it provided a relaxing get-together for all of the nearby Rasmussen gang.

The timing made it easy for everyone living in Standard and Hussar and with a multiple ration of gasoline, the distance was not an insurmountable problem. It was equally easy for the Andersens from Calgary who could take a street car or squander a modest amount of gasoline in Uncle Fred's Model A Ford. Even Olga and Martin, who lived in Turner Valley some thirty miles to the south of the picnic grounds ignored the gasoline shortage and always took in the party. Perhaps Martin's employment in the Purity Ninety nine gasoline refinery had something to do with this cavalier behavior. Most years, it was much to far for the Molgards who now lived in New Westminster, British Columbia.

In those early days, admission was free and St. George's Island was only accessible from the south via a narrow steel bridge on Twelfth Street East. This nearly one way ribbon of steel and wood led to the well treed island which was otherwise isolated from the city by the swift flow of the Bow River.

The park and zoo were just beginning to take shape and there was an abundance of undeveloped space throughout. These areas included some sizable graveled parking lots that were partially oiled to keep the dust from fouling the grass and numerous flower beds. Scattered among the animal cages and native cottonwood were a goodly number of dark green wooden picnic tables.

Although the main attraction were the animals, the most celebrated and distinguishing feature was Dinny, a life size concrete Brontosaurus. This prehistoric facsimile dominated and overlooked an expansive lawn that more or less anchored the entire park. Viewed from this grassed area, there was also the hint of additional Jurassic monsters hiding in the trees, with their gaudily painted backs and heads glinting through the foliage. The zoo cages were all obscured from view but the sounds of the peacocks, monkeys and an occasional lion's roar left no doubt that a wild world was not far away.

Looking to the south, beyond a few well spaced beds of snapdragons and petunias, was an entire section devoted to swings, slides, teeter-totters and monkey bars. Here in this sector, next to the Kiwanis wading pool, one could hear the unmistakable sound of hand rungs and chains clanking against the steel standard of a Maypole. In similarity with the parking lot, grass was nowhere to be found. Countless numbers of small feet had worn the vegetation down to the dusty clay like soil that made up the island.

Squatting behind a totem pole and an old log cabin, reputed to be Calgary's first building, was a small confectionery stand where among other tidbits, one could buy ice cream, soda pop, and all day suckers.

Each of the Rasmussen fun fests lasted the best part of a day. Somehow, almost like magic, everyone arrived mid morning with each family toting at least one large box laden with food. Martin and Olga always had a Coleman camp stove and the requisite elements for making coffee, an absolute essential for such a gathering.

Selecting a picnic table large enough to accommodate a small crowd was always a first priority. They were plentiful so finding one was not particularly difficult; but getting one with the promise of afternoon shade required a modest search. Usually there were several to chose from and after a brief discussion among the adults, Bedstefar would quietly put down the box that he happened to be carrying and that would be that. I actually think he was just tired of holding the box but as I recall, there was always afternoon shade on the table. After cleaning off the bird droppings, tablecloths were quickly unfurled and put in place thus formalizing our claim to the table for the rest of the day.

We youngsters were always in a hurry to get started with our investigation of all the strange noises and sounds that emanated from the direction of the animal cages but missing the early lunch would be unthinkable. This was the big meal of the day and was most often referred to as dinner. It really should have been termed a banquet.

At this time of the year there was an abundance of garden fresh vegetables. Peas, beans and carrots were the mainstay but these came along with lettuce, cucumbers and radishes, for an absolutely terrific green salad. These garden delights, served with new potatoes and spring chicken, produced a delectable feast.

We all shared the food but since everyone had provided essentially the same items, the source was of no real consequence. Moreover, Bedstemor had been the culinary professor for Mother and all of my aunts so everything was prepared in the same scrumptious way. For example, Mother's creamed peas and carrots were always seasoned with a generous sprinkling of parsley, but so were those prepared by her sisters. It was delicious!

I don't know how the food survived the two hour ride to Calgary but for some reason this noon meal was always served "stove top hot." Maybe the pasteboard boxes and assortment of blankets that Irene and I had shared the back seat with were responsible. In any event, the food was immaculately served and no one left the picnic table hungry. Indeed, there were even a few adults who declined a slice of fresh saskatoon pie.

Our assault on the food was barely finished when those of us with hollow legs and not required to help with the dishes and cleanup, made a beeline to the confectionery where we could unload some of our allowance money. Mother and Dad had supplied Irene and me with a few pieces of change. My modest fortune was carefully stowed in a small change purse that Grandmother had sent to me for Christmas.

This small brown split leather change purse was decorated on the lower left corner with the painting of an

Indian warrior all duded up in a colorful war bonnet. The three separate pockets of this money bag were protected and closed with a snap flap that almost covered its gaudy ornamentation. I was particularly proud of my new wallet and had carefully placed all of my coins into the proper pockets. I could hardly wait to try it out with the purchase of an "all day sucker." They seemed to be everywhere.

These ten cent lumps of soluble material were huge but failed to provide the advertised full days satisfaction. Indeed, they were prone to wear through to their pine stick handles in about forty-five minutes. What a disappointment! Even worse, after about thirty minutes their zesty taste was much diminished. Since they were on the big side, a dirty face was guaranteed. By midday, nearly every kid in the park sported a mouth encircled with the gooey residue left by these ghastly lollipops.

You can be sure that in this condition, Bedstefar had lost all interest in his sticky fingered, candy-faced grandchildren. Come to think of it, I doubt that our mothers were happy to see us either. On occasion the Kiwanis wading pool was used for the gargantuan sized clean up.

With so many sticky chins and soiled cheeks, it would be logical to assume that St. George's Island's concession stand sold only the highest quality merchandise and that their marketing skills were exceptional. Actually nothing could be further from the truth.

During the summer of 1940 the war in Europe was in full swing and while candy should be sweet, sugar was rationed and in very short supply. The resulting shortages fostered some remarkable inventiveness, some of which resulted in incredibly imaginative substitutes. I am not sure of the ingredients but strongly suspect that the St. George's Island all day suckers were a combination of sawdust, soybeans and a generous amount of coal tar. The end result resembled and tasted like the handle of a screwdriver. Despite their sorry taste and in the absence of anything better they become somewhat addictive. Whether this was spawned by mass peer pressure or a dash of cocaine, I will never know for sure.

As I recall, the sweet shop was quite small with but one high window opening, to which we would all queue for our suckers and all manner of other messy delights. In truth, we should have shunned this monopolistic outlet because of the stern, totally unpleasant lady proprietor. I think she was the first person I ever met who could actually scold in silence.

This never smiling keeper of the candy, peering down from her lofty wicket, could intimidate a tractor. She was constantly scowling at her diminutive victims and showed absolutely no patience with me when I tried to make payment from my new three compartment change purse. I was unable to count out the required amount for each purchase but could easily tell that a nickel was bigger than a dime and therefore should have more value. With this apparent knowledge, I had placed my nickels in the back section, my dimes in the middle and the pennies in the front.

Since I happened to be a bit slow with my money, the face grimacing down from the wicket became particularly fearsome. During these times she would emphasize her venomous character with embarrassingly long periods of silence, punctuated with momentous and noisy exhales of air through her flared nostrils. These cavernous slots located at the base of a narrow pinched nose were filled with a forest of yellow stained hair that caused the escaping breath to vent out in turbulent eruptions.

I was never quite sure if I would survive or be struck down dead by the savage blizzards that were snorted down from this throne of terror. While I lived through the misadventure, most of my cousins shared my fear of her. Who knows why we put up with this tyrant, but in retrospect, I am sure that the promise of a candy treat overpowered our apprehension. Moreover, who of us would be prepared to acknowledge that we were being cowed by a candy vendor.

Putting the candy experience aside, St. George's Island was a most engaging spot and a dandy location for a family picnic. There were a whole host of attractions, but without a doubt, the wild animals were the most notable. Compared with the zoo of today, it would be considered mediocre but in those days there was plenty to interest me and the rest of the Rasmussens, both young and old.

The monkey cages got most of the attention, but for me, Carmichael the polar bear, was the favorite. This huge white monster looked so kind and cuddlesome. With his contrasting dark lips, eyes and nose, he always seemed to have a smile on his face. He was certainly much happier than Dynamite, the grizzly bear in the adjacent cage. Dynamite was always slobbering as he bit at the steel bars that surrounded the concrete pad on which he was obliged to live out his life. Besides he was not neat and clean like Carmichael who loved being in his small swimming pool, performing with short laps for his admiring audience.

It could never happen but I would have loved having Carmichael for a pet. My good friend, Henry Dam, had all sorts of pets - rabbits, snakes, eagles, and the like. Would he ever be impressed if I had a polar bear. Imagine what Mother would do if I allowed him in the house and let him sleep on the sofa.

About a year later when Carmichael died, I wept and left his Calgary Herald picture and obituary hanging on our living room wall until the newsprint yellowed with age.

As much as I loved to look at the animals, the truly best part of the picnic was the family. I was just a little squirt in 1940 but Gordon and Roy Holm, who were several years my senior, didn't mind having Fred, Lars and me tag along on their tour of the park. Without their care, I would have been required to stay with Mother and Dad. They would most certainly have taken me to all of the animal cages but at six year of age, there would not have been the freedom that I was accorded while in the care and custody of these older and more mature cousins.

After a complete review of the various animal cages, we all wandered into the trees behind Dinny where a trail led to other dinosaur replicas. This odyssey through a Jurassic display of psychedelic concrete and plaster monsters led us back to the main lawn. Here we took some time to examine and play with a W.W. I cannon that stood near the old Fort Calgary log cabin. Most of the gears were rusted and would not allow much movement of the barrel but we took turns at the gunners seat and aimed this awkward field piece at the Tom Campbell's Hat Shop sign perched on top of the river's north bank some five hundred yards away. At the time I thought it would be great to have Hitler and Mussolini in the sights.

While we were casting about the island, Bedstefar and many of the adults had remained seated at the picnic table, visiting and enjoying the afternoon. After exhausting a series of topics ranging from war talk to hog prices and the gasoline shortage, Bedstefar quietly disappeared. He soon returned smiling like a butcher's dog and toting a huge watermelon in his arms. Even for a watermelon it was enormous and was the first one that I had ever seen. Over the years this became a family ritual and always remained his treat. After a late afternoon lunch, nobody needed more food but for desert we were all given a huge chunk of this aqueous monster. I know it was my first ever taste of this delicious fruit and to this day I still think of Bedstefar whenever I savor its watery texture and have the juice run down my chin. Knowing of his aversion to dirty chins and faces, I wonder how he came to choose such a messy delight for his children and grandchildren.

Not all of the zoo tenants were confined to cages. Ducks, geese, bantam roosters and peafowl were favored with an unrestricted run of the island. The strutting peacocks were a real fascination and we all wanted one of their colorful and iridescent tail feathers for a souvenir. We tried to catch one but soon learned that our speed was not up to theirs which in combination with some quick maneuvers left us looking rather stupid and inept. I had given up on the idea but as we were about to leave the park for home, I spotted a large tail feather under a bush near our car. What a lucky break, not only had I enjoyed a near perfect day at the zoo, I also had a special trophy to take home.

Sadly, I must report that this fine discovery was inadvertently destroyed a few days later when I carelessly waved it into contact with a fly sticker hanging from our kitchen ceiling.

Everyone enjoyed these annual family picnics and while the festive event of 1940 is well remembered, it was followed the next day with news that a child my age, Donald Goss, had been murdered on the island. Apparently this happened while we were all having a ball with the animals and in each others company. To the best of my knowledge this murder has never been solved nor has there ever been a satisfactory explanation for this terrible crime. It is known that the child was briefly on his own viewing the animals and other exhibits while his parents were resting at a picnic table. Realizing how and when it happened, I have always been especially grateful for the care given me by my older cousins with whom I spent most of the day at St. George's Island.

****

By late August the young poplar trees that surrounded our farmyard were starting to show signs of yellow and gold. Also the caragana hedge next to the house had long since lost its small yellow blossoms. These had been replaced with green pea-like seed pods which now ripened, were crackling and snapping open in the warm sunshine hours of late summer. Of more importance, the garden that had enjoyed much tender care and survived Diamond's trampling was at its peak. It was time to store these garden treasures for the coming winter.

While lettuce, radishes and small green onions were gone, there was now an abundance of peas, green beans, beets, carrots and vegetable marrow. This cornucopia of home grown groceries kept everyone busy; and Irene and I were both conscripted into service. Although our individual contribution was minor, our collective efforts in picking peas and beans was of some help. If we missed out on the picking, we were never exempted from the essential chore of shelling the peas and cutting up the green beans. Happily this could be done on the east side of the house where there was plenty of afternoon shade.

They weren't always there, but canning season was sure to bring them into the kitchen in incredible numbers. And why shouldn't they, the mouthwatering and pungent aromas that ascended from the steaming cauldrons of fruit and vegetables simmering on the stove, attracted house flies from miles around. Screen doors and window screens helped but even these mechanical guardians could only do so much. Each exit or entry from or to the house was sure to admit a dozen or more of these pesky intruders. Once inside, they made a beeline for the kitchen, the heart of Mother's fragrant canning operation.

We always had various insecticides but these were not considered safe in the proximity of food. In reality, no totally comfortable and effective solution to the problem existed but there were a few devices that offered a modest amount of help. Firstly, there was the old standby fly swatter that allowed one to wage war on the invading hordes. This did away with a few stupid insects but at best was only a minor deterrent. It did however, feel good to make an occasion kill even though this always required a cleanup and an appropriate funeral for the victim.

Without doubt, the tool of choice for fly control was the lowly, now forgotten fly sticker. In their dormant state, these ingenious doodads, were the size and had the appearance of a twelve gauge shotgun shell. They were in fact, a cardboard capsule with a sticky coil of paper wrapped up inside. Removal of the end cover, exposed the glutinous mess which could be deployed by pulling a string attached to one end of the spooled up gooey paper. This short pull string was also fitted to a small thumb tack which allowed the gismo to be nailed to the ceiling. As the fully extended paper ringlet was about three feet in length, location was of paramount importance. To ensure general immunity from traffic patterns, positions over a stove, counter or table were the rule. Over time, the ceiling over these favorite locations took on the appearance of a dart board, evidencing the countless times that a dangling fly sticker had decorated the room.

Even with careful placement, accidents did happen and tripping into one of these glue traps was guaranteed to give the unfortunate klutz a bad hair day. This was especially so if the sticker had been in place for a few days and was ripe with dead and still buzzing but dying flies glued to its surface.

****

Mother preserved enormous amounts of food in these early years. Most of the peas and beets were preserved in large fruit jars, as were the vegetable marrow which she made into absolutely scrumptious pickles. A few green beans may have been canned but most of these garden wonders were sliced into small bits (frenched) which were then placed outside in the sun to dry. Although they looked like green

159

wood chips, with the addition of water, salt, pepper and a little butter, they were remarkably tasty in January.

There was no particular urgency in digging the root and tuber vegetables but to beat the inevitable frost, we always picked the cucumbers, pumpkins and tomatoes early. Failure to do so invariably resulted in these items spoiling in the garden. Fortunately, this seldom happened but it meant having a few weeks each fall when the old weather worn house was filled with all manner of produce waiting to ripen. This was particularly true of the abundant tomato crop which was picked while still green. They dominated every empty space, lying on the floor, covering the kitchen's limited counter space, and sitting on every window sill. To maximize exposure, our beds were occasionally employed for brief periods during the day.

When my bed was pressed into service there were no complaints since I genuinely enjoyed these marvelous autumn fruits. Truly, Mother's tomatoes were outstanding and to this day are the best I have ever tasted. I wonder why the super markets never have produce equal to that grown in the gumbo of our garden. These tomatoes could be carved into segments having a diameter larger than a slice of Mother's home baked bread. With a dash of salt and pepper, this combination made an unbelievable sandwich. Unfortunately, eating one of these monsters could make a terrific mess of an otherwise clean shirt. With all of their seedy pulp and juice, such a meal was really only fit to be eaten outdoors.

With the abundance of these farm grown goodies, using a knife became an imperative. Buttering my own bread had been going on for some time but gaining permission to wield our one and only all purpose kitchen and butcher knife was another matter. As I was not trusted with such a dangerous tool, it was usually stored well out of my reach. Now that I was six years old, it was only after a great deal of persuasion and promises to be careful that I was granted the privilege of using this king of all utensils.

Having gained Mother's confidence, I could slice cucumbers with great abandon. With care, I could even carve up tomatoes. Actually, that was only partially true since I was obliged to leave the last half uncut so that I would have something solid to hold onto. I quickly learned that less than half a tomato is hard to get a grip on. Also when the first half had been sliced off, the darn thing had a propensity to flip over, slopping seedy juice all over the kitchen. Even worse, at the very moment when the knife should be doing its magic, a serious slip would put at least five of my still complete ten fingers at risk. Using my superior intellect, I solved this problem by destroying all evidence of this major incompetence. This was accomplished by eating the uncut half as a solo treat. It was an excellent solution and was delicious with a little salt and pepper.

Although I had worked out a viable procedure for handling cucumbers and tomatoes, cutting bread had me stumped. If I was ever to master this chore, it became obvious that a whole new set of disciplines and techniques would have to be learned. I could of course easily cut through a loaf but getting an even cut was a real mystery. Usually the slice would start out nice and straight but by the time the knife traversed the seemingly short distance from crust to crust, there was almost always one thick corner of nearly three inches in width. With equal frequency, I was just as apt to pilot the knife through the front of the loaf thus creating a wedge instead of a nice even slab.

Based on the proposition that practice would eventually yield results, it was crucial that I develop some basis for a drill in bread cutting. After all, how could I go through life ignorant of the many nuances that go with such an essential skill. I recognized that my game plan could be damaging to some of Mother's mouth watering home baked

161

bread, but what's a fella supposed to do? After all, such a worthy sacrifice would certainly be worthwhile as it could be expected to impart a very important learning experience. Happily, the opportunity for such an endeavor came one sweltering day in late August.

As you might expect, the old black cook stove had been fired up for the occasion and was still radiating heat into the already hot sunny kitchen. Two freshly baked loaves had just emerged from the oven and were left steaming hot on the kitchen table. To beat the heat, Mother and Irene had decided that there was work to be done in the much cooler garden.

What a setup. There I was, all alone, knife in hand with two unblemished bread loaves just waiting to donate their virginity to my hacking and education. With my knees firmly planted on a kitchen chair next to the table, I assumed a stance of absolute control over the two loaves now resting on a wooden cutting board. Poised in this position the hapless victuals didn't have a chance. When the surgery was over, there was a not so neat pile of not so neat slices covering the cutting board.

I don't recall the immediate impact or outcome of this singularly momentous event but there is no doubt that on that hot August afternoon the world was changed and would never be the same again. It would seem that I had inadvertently stumbled upon one of the great ideas and inventions of our time - sliced bread. This I leave as a legacy of my early years.

SCHOOL AND WAR YEARS

The winter, spring, and summer of 1940 produced a profound change in my persona and character. Whether it was Irene's experiences at school, Sunday School or my many one on one sessions with Dad, my learning process went through a radical transition. During this interval, it was no longer necessary to have direct exposure to a set of facts in order to learn a new concept. For the first time I was able to assimilate ideas and learn from the knowledge of others. Although I had no direct experience with baseball, Dad's appreciation for the skill of a Chicago Cubs double play trio was generally understood and accepted. As an additional example, Irene's stories from school were real to me and Sunday School lessons were believed to be true and without question. Noah's flood was a story that I could relate to and understand. Baseball in Chicago and New York was a reality and the war in Europe was more or less within my area of understanding. As opposed to direct knowledge that I had previously gained through my senses, I could now begin the process of vicarious learning. What an exciting time!

While it is difficult to explain, there is little doubt that my emancipation was very real and probably well known to students of social behavior. Whether this is true or not, this deliverance and renaissance offered a consummate change in personality and perception of the world around me. I had already learned that water is wet, ice is cold, a stove can be hot and that barb wire can hurt. Now for the first time, I was also becoming acquainted with things and ideas that I could not hear, see, taste, touch or smell.

My exposure and acceptance of the experience and knowledge of a surrogate was in reality the end of babyhood and the beginning of childhood. Also with this breakthrough came new responsibilities to myself and others. Not only was I expected to do certain things, I could now begin to understand the purpose and reason why. Equally important, this extension of learning and understanding provided new freedoms that allowed new relationships to develop and grow.

New friends were treasured and welcomed into a life that heretofore had responded mostly to close family members. As an example, Kenneth Larsen and Henry Dam became close confidants with whom I could recount ideas and secrets. Some of these were not even shared with Mother and Dad, a previously unthinkable notion.

I think this preadolescent behavior is quite normal as it would seem to be an absolutely essential prerequisite for a formal education. Certainly in my case, I was looking forward to school and was even more excited in 1940, than had been the situation the previous year when Irene embarked on her journey of school house learning.

Now it was my turn and although I was eager to start school, there was certainly a fair bit of uneasiness. I had no fear of the teacher or the other kids but there were considerable doubts about my own ability to learn all of the new ideas that would be thrust upon me. If my failed Sunday School Christmas Concert was any example, success was far from a certainty. On this basis I had good reason for my apprehension.

As August came to a close, I was filled with trepidation but suddenly and seemingly with absolutely no warning, the big day arrived and I was in grade one. Frankly, I have no recall of going to school on my first day but can easily remember the events that followed.

Miss Weir had been replaced by Miss Nelson, a relatively inexperienced young lady, fresh out of teacher's college. The enrollment had expanded and now included Eric Selgensen in grade eight or nine and Alvin Shear who was just a few months older than me and in grade two with Irene. With Alvin's arrival, I had the very real prospect of a new friend to go along with my pal, Henry Dam, who was now in grade three.

Alvin was a friendly guy who usually sported a wide grin which went well with his freckled face and rumpled blond hair. As long as I knew him, he never took himself or anything very seriously. He was lots of fun and enjoyed doing outrageous things that usually resulted in him getting dirty. Also, I think he would have been unrecognizable if his shirt tail was properly tucked in. No matter how clean and put together he was in the morning, by noon he looked as though he had been in a train wreck. Even his dress was different as he was invariably outfitted in tough black denim trousers. These canvas like duds, reinforced with heavy white stitches and brass rivets, allowed him to roughhouse in ways that would have left my more conventional clothing in tatters.

He seemed challenged by height and was always making like a monkey. Almost every recess would find him climbing on the swing, up the steel legs right to the top. He would then crawl upside down along the top horizontal member and yell like Tarzan. After getting everyone's attention he would swing down along one of the swing chains. On one such occasion, he slipped and fell, bouncing off the swing seat onto the hard brick-like clay below. This seemingly painful crash had no apparent effect as he almost immediately scrambled back onto one of the steel standards, going hand over hand, right to the top.

One day during a particular recess, we found Alvin perched on the uppermost part of the swing. This wasn't that strange or unusual but after getting everyone's attention he let go to hang upside down by his legs. With limp arms dangling and howling like an African baboon, his now totally lose shirt hung over his shoulders and face. After a good deal of noise and expressions of concern from his limited audience, Alvin finally decided to regain a solid handhold on the upper cross member. This should have been easy but with the constraints of the lose shirt, there were a few tense moments. Success was finally achieved but the tangled shirt paid the price with a huge rip right up the back. I wonder how Alvin explained all of these misadventures to his mother?

I thoroughly enjoyed Alvin while we were classmates at Craigantler. His freewheeling devil- may- care attitude was totally foreign to me but in some ways it was also refreshing. He was a real kick and most certainly made an impression on me and my conservative, less adventurous ways. Henry and I were both in absolute awe at some of his careless antics and unbelievable tolerance for pain.

During the ensuing years, Alvin continued to defy all conventional behavior and was constantly getting banged up in various confrontations with gravity or something sharp. He almost always had a scab or two on his scared face and arms. For him, car wrecks were the norm and he seemed to enjoy them. Sadly, when he was about sixteen, Alvin had his last car accident. This time his recklessness was fatal.

✱✱✱✱✱✱✱✱✱✱✱

In what was to be Craigantler's last year as a hall of learning, the fall of 1940 saw a grand total of nine students enrolled in six grades. Preparing for each days activities would have been a formidable task for any teacher and certainly the young unseasoned Miss Nelson was thoroughly challenged. Although there were only a few students, she was obliged to prepare for each grade and simultaneously direct the cirriculum for six separate learning levels.

Through no fault of hers, this system festered with inequities and complications. Although direct and continuous attention was not required nor expected, Miss Nelson clearly had trouble balancing her time between the various grade levels. While giving instruction to one class, the others were left unattended and ignored. This was especially true of grade one which, on my first day of school, got virtually no attention or recognition. To keep me occupied, I was directed to the blackboard where I was expected to draw circles. In addition, I was told, in very stern terms, to be perfectly quiet. This strict admonition meant that there would be no talking or communication with anyone. Indeed, even the squeaky floor attracted sideways glances. This turned into a glaring scowl when I made three pieces out of one by carelessly dropping my chalk on the floor. Knowing this, I was sure that the punishment for talking was at least a public hanging or firing squad.

In any event, there I stood in front of my eight fellow students drawing circles, Heck, drawing circles was no big deal, but if Miss Nelson wanted circles, who was I to question her motives? It wasn't long before the whole board was filled with circles. In fact, to continue, I was obliged to draw small ones inside the big ones. While this seemed to be a clever innovation, I soon had the whole board filled with concentric circles.

There was no way of knowing how long I had been chalking the board but whatever the interval, it had to be quite a while, since nature was pressing. For a time, the problem could be eased by standing on one leg and when that didn't work, I would switch legs. Finally, in the end, crossing both legs was the only solution. I was in trouble but asking permission to leave the room was out of the question. After all, the last thing I needed was a public execution, especially on my first day of school.

"Maybe just a little dribble would ease the pressure - Oops! That was more than a little - now I can't shut it off. That warm feeling running down my leg is no laughing matter. Hopefully no one will notice - Oh darn, now its in my hand-me-down canvas shoe. Don't look now, but I think the floor is wet - Yep! Just as I thought. What will I do now?"

Finally and mercifully, one of the older boys, probably Eric Selgensen, asked the teacher if the school had flood insurance. This innocent comment invoked a few snickers but also got an immediate response from Miss Nelson, who quickly realized that I had been a captive of my circles for a very long time. For the first time she also became aware of my shyness and that I was too timid to seek permission to leave the room. While there may have been a few more titters from the class, her invitation for me to take an early recess was made with quiet dignity. I gratefully rushed outside, but it was much to late for any meaningful visit to the privy.

By lunch time I was more or less dry but still smarting with embarrassment. Happily when I returned to class in the afternoon, no one made reference to my misfortune, and all evidence of my work at the board and on the floor had vanished. This included my beautiful circles which were nowhere to be seen.

In hindsight, it is likely that Miss Nelson realized that her almost militant demand for complete quiet was a bit over zealous, particularly for an easily intimidated first grader. Aware of my humiliation, and in my absence, she probably requested the class to remain silent about the incident. They did and I was glad.

Apart from my crushing first day's experience and Alvin's wild escapades, I have virtually no memory of the first few weeks of school. Although there had been days loaded with excitement and great anticipation, school turned out to be a minor disappointment. Perhaps this was my own fault since I probably had unrealistic expectations. Also I had no foreknowledge of the many hours that would be filled with somewhat boring drills. Drawing circles is certainly not an enlightening adventure in learning.

In the long run, it turned out that entering grade one was simply a continuation of Irene's start up a year earlier and seemed much less important the second time around. I was however provided with a scribbler, a very large but dull pencil, and a hard rubber eraser that was hopelessly harsh on the gruesomely coarse paper in my scribbler. Despite these rather mundane items, I was also given a blue covered reader entitled "Highroads to Reading - Jerry and Jane." This primer was and is a prized possession that is still permanently displayed in my library.

****

Although my recall of school is a bit out of focus and probably warped by the distance of time, it is easy to remember the frightening BBC news broadcasts regarding Germany's continual bombardment of England. Some of the bulletins were even enriched with real sound effects, including screaming bombs and thunderous explosions. I of course soon learned to mimic these sounds.

The Battle of Britain was in full swing and to make matters even worse, there were numerous rumors proposing specific dates for Hitler's likely invasion of the British Isles. Despite Churchill's bold rhetoric - "We will fight on the beaches and we will never surrender," everyone knew that such an event would ultimately endanger Canada. At the very least, an invasion of England would put many local boys into harms way. This was particularly true since Canada had now adopted full military conscription, thus insuring that almost every single man of the right age was now or would soon be pressed into military service.

To bring the battle even closer, civil defense units were established in most of Canada's larger cities. These home front warriors, (A.R.P. Air Raid Patrol), largely made up of older men, exposed the population to certain war games that may come in handy should war break out on our side of the pond. Mock air raids were a favorite drill during which time all home owners were expected to cover their night windows. Presumably these blackouts were being practiced to ensure that any attempt to bomb Canada would be a frustrating experience for the Germans. While we were never asked to cover our farm windows, Uncle Fred's house in Calgary was set up with dark blankets that could blank out any light that might otherwise escape to the outside and help an unfriendly bomber find the city.

Fortunately by mid-October, the German Luftwaffe had suffered devastating loses and the "Battle of Britain" was essentially over. Unforeseen just a few weeks earlier, it was now evident that Hitler's invasion plans would have to wait. Even he was wise enough to know that an invasion without air support would be unthinkable.

With this apparent victory by the R.A.F., it was now for the first time, clear that England had a chance for survival. Everyone was a little less concerned, although no one really knew how things would eventually turn out. For my part, I had enhanced my war sound vocabulary with the addition of bomb noises. This was tremendously useful when our planes started to throw a few explosives on top of the German cities.

****

It doesn't come to mind, and I have been unable to find anyone who can confirm the year when telephone service finally reached our farm. It seems that no one knows for sure

170

when this momentous event came to pass. We all agree however, that it came about in either the fall of 1939 or 1940. We know it was autumn since the World Series was in progress and for the first time in my memory it was broadcast on the radio. Except for the potato harvest, Dad took time out for all of the games and it was certainly a pleasant change from the BBC war news. In any event, for a few days the telephone had to compete with the radio. Imagine, with this new fangled piece or equipment we could, at our choosing, converse with people at the site of the World Series.

It was never intended to rival AT &T or MCI but the South Standard Telephone Company was formed one fall evening in our living room. The house was absolutely filled to capacity. I more or less knew everyone since they were all neighbors but it did seem a bit strange having all of them in our house. I was told to be quiet but was allowed to listen as major decisions were being made.

When all nine or ten subscribers had committed to sign up and the company was properly constituted, the membership quickly decided how and where the single wire line would run to serve everyone. In some instances, where some extra distance was involved, the required telephone line would not necessarily follow a road allowance, but would as an economy measure, traverse a field along an existing fence line. This was the case with Uncle Edward who was a mile west of everyone else and was not in close proximity to the bulk of subscribers. To reach his farm house, the required telephone poles and wire ran along the fence line between our farm and that of Ray Green.

It was some time later, after the farmers (South Standard Telephone Company shareholders) had set the poles and strung the line that we finally received the luxury of a working telephone. This high tech equipment was essentially a varnished oak box that hung on the kitchen wall next to the Delaval cream separator. While the black mouth piece was permanently affixed to the front of the box, it was hinged to move up and down and thusly able to accommodate a variety of users of varying stature. At the very lowest point, Mother's diminutive five foot two inch frame was just right, while at its maximum extension, Dad could speak directly into the machine.

The black bakelite ear piece hung from a yoke-like hook that was fixed to one side. This hook was spring loaded in such a way that the weight of the receiver would disengage the phone.

Undoubtedly, the most striking feature of the phone was a pair of nickel plated disk bells that jutted out near the top face of the oak box. These were activated by a magnetic clapper that rattled out a clamorous ring whenever someone made a call. To make such a call, it was necessary to engage a small crank that protruded out of the box on its right side. The manual rotation of this appendage drove a magneto which charged the line thus causing all of the phones on the line to ring.

Each subscriber on the South Standard Phone Companies line had a simple but clearly identifying ring. We answered to a "long and two short" which was orchestrated by a quick few turns on the crank followed immediately by two half turns. Actually, everyone on line nine (South Standard's line number), had a slightly different style in making a call. Over time, it became possible to know and recognize who was phoning whom. Bedstefar's ring to Uncle Edward, "three short and a long," always sounded rather tired. On the other hand, Mother's technique was quite different and I am sure that the generous length of each ring unit was easy to identify as her special and unique signal.

For the truly curious and to confirm who was calling whom, it was easy to listen in on a conversation since all of the telephones were connected. The prying ears that are characteristic of a party line (rubbering in) were almost as easily identified as were the distinctive rings. Each phone receiver had a unique click, which combined with chiming mantle clocks, barking dogs, squeaky screen doors, and careless voices, made it possible to pinpoint each uninvited eavesdropper. Important confidential business could not be transacted over the phone. Also there was an unenforceable law which made it illegal to use language unbefitting a public assembly. Conversely, for anyone so inclined, a party line was a dandy almost indispensable tool for starting delightfully scandalous rumors.

Our telephone number was 912 and to reach someone other than the nine or ten members and shareholders of the South Standard Telephone Company, it was necessary to push a small button on the phone box and ring one long burst on the crank. This button allowed the ring to be monitored in the central telephone office in Standard where a telephone operator could be requested to patch our line into one of the other Standard area systems. Such a call was free, and of course opened the ensuing conversation to everyone on the other line. Wow! Could this ever be interesting.

Calling long distance was somewhat similar but this required the Standard office to make contact with yet another operator who physically hooked our line into one of the long distance circuits. For these calls, a long distance toll was extracted, the amount being determined by the length of the conversation. This was manually timed by the Standard operator who prepared the monthly bills for all of the telephone users in the general area.

****

By late fall, Dad's hog business was fully operational. His new pig barn was nearly full of sows, each with a litter of piglets. With a gestation period of only three months, three weeks and three days, it didn't take long for the pig business

173

to become an integral and important part of our farm's productivity. Bacon was still a few months away but there was a definite feeling of optimism and Dad was in a happy and generous mood.

I think it was this feeling of well being that stimulated the notion that Irene and I should be blessed with a bank account. Dad made the point that saving money is an absolutely essential skill that can only be realized by way of a genuine savings account. In his view, it was a virtual prerequisite for growing up and he insisted that every real person should have a firm relationship with a bank. He went on to say that anyone wishing to achieve anything in this world must first develop some money management skills and learn how to save. As I recall, there was also some mumbo-jumbo about self discipline, immediate denial and future gratification. No doubt about it, Dad was trying to impart a very important character building lesson to us kids. While I hardly knew what he was talking about, I quickly realized that the two nickels left over from the family picnic and safely stowed away in my split leather change purse, were not a meaningful part of the conversation.

This fact was soon confirmed when Dad opened his own wallet and produced a few paper bills. This folding green was divided equally between my sister and me. When we had recovered from the shock of seeing all of this money, it turned out that I had three dollars and so did Irene.

While we were allowed to place these treasures into our individual change purse for the night, it was clearly understood that this small fortune was destined for a savings account at the Royal Bank of Canada, Standard Branch. Here it could work for us and earn interest which we took to mean, money for our old age. That seemed to be an incredibly long way off but the very next day right after breakfast, Dad reclaimed the money.

That evening, when Irene and I returned home from school, Dad proudly presented each of us with a dark blue bank book. My book had my name carefully inscribed on a white sticker affixed to the inside cover. Also the first page in the ledger columns featured a hand written notation indicating that I had three dollars on deposit where it could earn copious amounts of interest.

Interest was paid every six months at the astonishing rate of two and one half percent per annum. Since I was apparently saving for my old age, either the interest rate would have to change or getting old would have to be put on hold. To make it even more discouraging, when finally six months had passed, my bank book showed a posting of three cents while Irene had earned four cents on her deposit. This left me mildly disappointed and wondering how such a terrible mistake could have occurred. It is my fervent hope that the bank staff did not have too many late nights looking for Irene's penny.

This original bank book was in my possession until just a few years ago when it was lost during our move to Arizona. It clearly showed the three dollar deposit and the initial interest posting of the three cents. Moreover, there was no indication that the bank had ever corrected this careless atrocity with the addition of a penny to my account.

During those early years, a visit to the bank was an intimidating, almost frightening experience. Although there were several people working, no one seemed to speak and except for a very noisy adding machine, the office was deadly quiet. Even Mr. Reese Hugh, the manager, spoke so quietly that only one person at a time could make out his hushed voice. Presumably his whispered tones were intended to keep all banking transactions confidential. It was of course a hush-hush matter that I had three dollars and three cents on deposit. There is no telling what kind of extortion threats could evolve if this information was carelessly leaked to the public at large.

Making the office even more unfriendly was the huge steel cage that dominated the entire public area. This ugly crate contained one flustered teller who was hardly visible through the steel mesh which totally enclosed his crowded and seemingly messy work station. There was even grillwork covering the roof of this teller's cage which made it totally inaccessible to all but this one lonesome employee.

Apart from the sinister appearance of the banking hall, the actual business of banking was very different in those days. There were of course no on-line facilities, A.T.M. machines and so forth. Credit cards were unheard of and I am sure that getting cash would be nearly impossible unless the bank customer was personally know to the teller.

Each transaction or at least every cheque and draft was subject to a federal tax. This levy was collected by way of a Canadian Government stamp affixed to every negotiable instrument. The greater the amount, the greater the tax exigible and number of stamps needed to make the transaction viable. In relative terms, the amount was not great but at the very least, it was inconvenient and often very awkward. The clumsiness of this tax almost always showed up when two parties putting a business deal together had to decide who would pay for the stamps. Undoubtedly there were deals left undone simply because the parties could not agree on the imposition of this modest assessment.

****

School droned on without incident and by early winter I was totally comfortable with my new Craigantler environment. Also I was learning to read and was well into the supposedly exciting life of Jerry and Jane, the characters in my first grade reader. While these prissy individuals seemed somewhat unreal, it was fun to use and enjoy my new found reading skills. Words were starting to form sentences and despite my limited vocabulary, there was progress and a few excursions could be made into other more challenging books. Even a few words in my monthly Little Lutheran newspaper were now recognizable. I was really quite pleased with myself.

In keeping with Craigantler's historical behavior, preparation for the annual Christmas concert became a big part of each day. Our school room was in shambles with all of the desks pushed to one side. This made room for the stage which now occupied nearly half of the limited space. The performing platform had been assembled by Lyle, Pete and Eric, who with some difficulty, had dragged in the various parts from what appeared to be a pile of junk lumber stacked outside and behind the school.

Bed sheets pinned and strung up to a wall to wall wire provided the stage curtain. At times when the over worked safety pins that held the sheets on the wire snagged, or the curtain was jerked a bit too hard, one of the nails holding the wire would pull out of the wall and the whole set would collapse. It would not be hard to imagine the mess and confusion this would cause during the actual concert. In an almost vain effort to find a remedy for such a catastrophic event, Miss Nelson simply hammered in more nails. By Christmas, a part of the north wall looked like the backdrop to a rifle range.

I enjoyed the preparation for the school concert, but the practices where marred by ever increasing rumors that Craigantler School would soon be shut down. As Christmas drew nearer, these rumors were finally displaced by a factual proclamation announcing the fate of our school. Despite the efforts of the Craigantler parents, the Provincial Department of Education made it clear that a school having only eight students would not be allowed to survive. Even Dad's efforts as a member of the School Board were ineffective. By Christmas Concert time it was known that our performance would be the last. Even if the nail remained fast to the wall, it was certain that the curtain would fall on the nearly famous Craigantler Christmas Concert for the last time. Our little country school would officially close on December 31, 1940.

Starting in the new year, our puny group of country hicks would be transported to Standard by way of a school bus. No one liked the idea but there was little that anyone could do.

Notwithstanding the genuinely disconsolate attitude of the audience, the Christmas Concert was a tremendous success. Irene and I were both featured in several short plays and skits. If it had mattered, which in fact it didn't, I am sure that Miss Nelson was fully satisfied with the performance. I had remembered my lines so at least there was a small reason to be happy.

Christmas came and went but with all of the excitement and anticipation of going to the big school in town, I have little recall of any festivities or celebrations.

The move to Dana School was a fearsome business but as you might expect, my trepidation was more than offset by a feeling of great exhilaration and expectancy. After all, going to such a large school would certainly be something of an adventure. Also being picked up by a genuine bus every morning conjured up some real enthusiasm which largely diminished my otherwise melancholy spirits.

Craigantler was one of the first rural schools in Alberta to terminate its teaching function. As a consequence, there was little experience to draw on and virtually no standards set for the closing procedure. As an example, the fate of Miss Nelson is unknown and it is doubtful if the Department of Education gave her job survival much thought. Of equal importance there was little if any planning given to the consolidation of the students who were literally thrown together. At my level this was not terribly important but it is probable that the higher grades found the melding process a bit awkward.

****

For my part, the daily bus ride was expected to be an exciting adventure but sadly, this turned out to be the most disappointing aspect of the whole process. I had assumed the vehicle would be a brightly painted bus with nicely padded seats flanking a center aisle. This was not to be and during the first few years, it was nothing more than a well used Nash car. To make matters worse, transporting eight kids in an ordinary car meant that I was obliged to sit on either Lyle or Loraine Enevoldsen's lap for most of the five and one half mile trip. It also required that I move my legs out of the way each time Arthur Grant, the bus driver, needed to shift gears.

It would be improper to say that the Nash was inadequate, but by today's standards, the entire rig would be condemned as unfit for public use.

During the first few years, the roads on which Arthur was obliged to travel were for the most part dirt trails running between the weeds and foxtails. In winter the only legitimate impediments were the deep drifts of snow, but during spring breakup, bridges were often washed out and of course the plain dirt road surfaces became little more than a rutted bog. Often a good spring rain or even a surprise downpour would force some of us kids to walk home from the graveled road which ran east to Calgary and adjacent to our old school house. This was no big deal for Irene and me since we were only half a mile south of this well traveled thoroughfare. Unfortunately, on such occasions, poor Henry Dam often found himself walking two very muddy miles.

There were many imponderables which made it nearly impossible to be exacting with regard to times of arrival and departure. Over the many years that we traveled to and from school with Arthur and his bus, it is likely that we were late for school at least two days out of every five. Missing a few minutes didn't matter a great deal but on occasion, when there was some serious delay, it was possible to miss the entire morning. These major problems, often weather related, were understandable and easily forgiven. Conversely, the countless, just barely but inexcusable late mornings were a real annoyance to the teachers who understandably hated to have us troop in after classes were underway. While these late arrivals were never our fault, there was always a feeling that a price was to be paid for frustrating the teacher. It's sure and certain that the interlopers from Craigantler were never serious contenders for the honor of being a teacher's pet.

With our move to the Standard school system, Mother and Dad thought it necessary that Irene and I give up our old honey pail lunch bucket. While this had served us well at Craigantler, the more sophisticated surroundings of Dana School certainly deserved a new look. This was accomplished by way of a brand new shiny black metal lunch container. Such a handy dandy item came with a genuine thermos bottle in which we could carry soup or milk if thought appropriate.

Perched on the nicely rounded top was a leather carrying strap which could barely accommodate one of my mittened hands. No doubt about it, this was a real uptown sandwich container, designed to ensure that neither Irene nor I would look like the country bumpkins which in fact we were.

For many years, we shared this sturdy lunch bucket which must have carried a ton of sandwiches during its useful existence. For some curious reason, it was always my job to carry this handsome case which over time lost its black coat of paint and became as shiny as a new nickel.

The New Year finally arrived and after all of the normal holiday hoopla, the big day came when Irene and I were scheduled to go to Standard for some cosmopolitan learning. To ensure that we would not be left behind, we were both standing by the roadside in wait of the bus long before it made its late appearance. Having anticipated something better that an old Nash, we were very upset with our first viewing of our school transport. We were all jammed in and after stopping at the Enevoldsen's, I found myself sitting on Lyle's lap. This was marginally better that having him sit on mine.

With such a dismally poor start, the whole Craigantler gang arrived well after the nine o'clock startup. Although memorable, this tardy beginning was less than spectacular and certainly wasn't very helpful with our initiation into the Standard school system. No one was waiting for us and by the time we finally got there, all of the classroom doors were closed. Since none of us had ever been there before, no one knew what to do or where to go. After a good deal of fumbling around, Henry, Alvin, Irene, and I finally found our way into the primary classroom which housed grades one through four.

After docking my new shiny black lunch bucket and winter duds in the cloakroom, Miss Smith, the teacher, assigned me to the front seat in the grade one row. Irene and Alvin sat to my left in the grade two row while Henry sat with his peers in the grade three section.

With my arrival, there were four grade one students, the others being Miriam Nielsen, Bernice Sandersen, and Kenneth Sorensen. I knew Miriam and Bernice from Sunday School but Kenneth was an entirely new acquaintance. In grade two, Irene and Alvin joined Verner Sandersen, Gerald Knowlton and Kenneth Larsen. I don't recall who was in grade three with Henry but in total, the entire class of four grades had less than twenty students.

Actually, our primary room was fairly typical of the other three which each contained approximately twenty kids.

In total, the school population was in the order of eighty to ninety students ranging from grades one through twelve. These thin ranks were directed and taught by four teachers including the fearsome Mr. Malcolm, who was also principal.

The Standard school, more properly called Dana School, was founded in 1911 right after the first pioneers from Iowa settled in the community. The original wooden structure that served the communities educational needs in that day was replaced in 1924 by a two story, four room brick building. It was this grandiose edifice that I entered in January, 1941.

My initial dismay with the ride to town was promptly revoked when I first entered the school and saw the lofty ceiling, the massive staircase, the electric lights and the huge windows. Wow! In comparison with Craigantler, this building was really something. I was impressed and thoroughly intimidated by the size and apparent quality of nearly everything.

The red brick building stood on the eastern outskirts of town on a site of approximately six acres. Access to the school was made via a wide steel gate which faced north to a cinder packed roadway running east and west. The front of the school property, or northern boundary, was defined by a woven wire fence and a neatly trimmed hedge of caragana. Starting at the gate, the property line, and running to the wide double front doors, was a comfortably wide concrete sidewalk. The front entrance itself boasted a concrete step which was at least three times as wide as was necessary. It was in reality a narrow porch, just wide enough to underline the wood and glass window panels that were fixed, one to each side of the Sherwood green double doors.

Upon entering the hallowed front hall, one would immediately be facing a center flight of stairs going up to the first level. This banistered rise of approximately four feet was flanked on either side by a slightly narrower set of stairs, each descending to a basement room of concrete floor and walls. The left side was described as the girls basement play area while the one on the right was reserved for the boys. It was here that the building was set up with a small room fitted with appropriate fixtures for nature's needs - indoor plumbing. The basement was chilly and the sinks had only cold water but during the winter months the commode sure beat the outside snow filled privy at home.

The main floor, reached by the grand stairway from the entrance door, was blessed with a wide windowless hall having a door on either side. As I was to discover on my first day, the right door opened to the primary classroom while the one on the left accessed grades five through eight.

Straight ahead but slightly beyond these side doors was another broad staircase which reached upward to the second level and the senior grades. The visible portion of these stairs ascended up to a spacious landing that featured a huge glass window which provided the major source of light for the stairs and the hallway below. The landing itself opened to both sides offering access via side stairs that reached rooms three and four.

During recess the sill below the large stair well window provided a somewhat prestigious seat for the senior girls and the occasional male student. Here they would sit in silhouette watching the commotion below as the more junior grades milled about in the hall. Being perched on this window ledge was a real honor, only available to the upper classes. We little kids relished the day when we could occupy this most eminent vantage point.

My classroom, basically like the other three, was substantially larger than the entire Craigantler school. The most notable feature was the four large windows on the north side of the room. This glass and mullioned wall was perfect for daydreaming, providing a near view of the school's caragana hedge and a distant view of Standard's coal mine and its steaming cinder pile approximately one third of a mile to the north. Beyond this were the Wintering and Chimney Hills, now snow covered, and showing their many brush filled ravines as slashes of dark, marring the otherwise pristine white.

The business walls of the room, one to the front and one to the side were covered with large blackboards which were not black but green. They were of course a dark green but even this seemed a bit strange at first.

The back wall was of plaster but painted a bilious yellow. Fortunately it was largely covered with posters and other paraphernalia including a large map of Canada with Nelson's Chocolate advertisements on each of the bottom corners.

The cloakroom was simply a space behind a partitioning wall, open at both ends. This blanked off the south side of the room, producing a narrow corridor like area filled with coat hooks. It was nearly always a mess with mixed up overshoes, lunch buckets and an array of coats and lost mittens.

We weren't late everyday so when we were on time, we could witness Mr. Malcolm starting classes by leaning over the upper banister and ringing a very loud hand bell. This clamorous event energized nearly everyone and in no time all of the students were either seated or standing by their desks.

As I recall, we stood for the Lord's Prayer and a now nearly forgotten mantra about King, Flag and Country. It went something like this: "I salute the flag, the emblem of my country, and to her, I pledge my love and loyalty. God save the King." These words were recited as we all faced a large Union Jack flag nailed to the wall, well above the front blackboard. This was of course well before Canada adopted it's own flag in 1964.

When we were seated, each day began with a short Bible reading. I have no idea who picked the readings but in most cases, taken out of context, they were about as spiritually uplifting as Genesis 36 (The descendants of Esau), or First Chronicles 4 - 9 (Genealogies of the Twelve Tribes).

****

Leaving Craigantler turned out to be far more arduous than expected. Having a nearly famous Christmas concert may have been good for my acting skills but it hadn't been much help with my reading, writing and arithmetic. I thought things had gone well at Craigantler but it was now clear that the concert had extracted its price, leaving me with a lot of catching up to do. For example, my grade one class had already finished reading "Highroads To Reading - Jerry and Jane," and were well along with other reading material. Also, they had a fairly decent appreciation for the business of printing letters and numbers. I worked very hard at home and with Mother's help, eventually brought most of these deficiencies up to a reasonable level of competence. By early spring I was more or less on an even keel with Kenneth. As you might expect, both girls, Bernice and Miriam, were much smarter and well ahead of us boys.

Now it turns out that I had been given a dandy pocket watch and chain for my birthday. It was in fact a gift that Bedstefar and Bedstemor brought back from Denmark when they were there in 1939. It was an absolutely beautiful time piece having a railway locomotive engraved on its back. I was very proud to own and wear it and its accompanying silver chain. Unfortunately, using it was beyond my comprehension. Adding to my dismay, I soon discovered that all of my grade one peers had learned to tell time early in the school term. Obviously this was another part of the ciriculum that I had missed.

While Miss Smith was aware of this omission in my country school background, nothing special was done on my behalf. Happily, an acquaintance of over a year came to my rescue. In the end Bernice, my rope skipping friend, patiently spent at least two full recesses teaching me the wonders of the little hand and the big hand. I was of course tremendously grateful to Bernice but equally pleased that clocks and time were no longer a mystery.

With this new found talent there was every reason to believe that my Danish railroad watch and chain would become useful. The watch could tick, the big and little hands could move but, now for the first time, I discovered that it could not keep time. Who knows if it ever could?

****

Recess was not always as fruitful as those spent with Bernice correcting my educational shortcomings. Most of the time I was learning the many nuances of rough and tumble play; this despite Mother's almost daily reminders that I was not to fight under any circumstances. This ill-advised admonition left me a sitting duck for any and all looking for a pushover. I was a delightful medium that was always available for someone wishing to inflate his ego or self esteem. For most of my first year I carefully obeyed Mother's instructions and made no attempt to resist any aggressive action. In short, I spent most of each recess on the floor, and on my back with someone sitting on top of me. Usually that someone was Kenneth Sorensen.

The school house was truly a fine building for its day but in the absence of an easy to care for tile, all of the floors were oiled. This uncompromising finish may have been easy to mop up but it also ensured that each wrestling match ended up with an oil covered shirt or sweater. Even the back of my blond head featured an almost perpetual oil stain. With this as evidence of my activities it became increasingly difficult to convince Mother that I was not fighting at school.

Although school enrollment was relatively small, there were some real characters interspersed among its modest population. Most assuredly one of these was Earl Erickson. Earl was probably five to six grades ahead of me but was certainly one of the better known kids in the whole school. In many ways he was the original Fonzie of T. V's "Happy Days" fame. Fonzie, I mean Earl, always wore a leather jacket with the collar turned up. His hair was slicked down and he walked around with his thumbs tucked into his tight jeans pockets. I think most of the girls thought he was really something.

Earl was probably a bit of a bully, with the result that many of his own age group ignored or avoided him. At any rate he was often doing his own thing. Equally important, he wasn't, or at least pretended that he wasn't afraid of Mr. Malcolm. We little kids really thought he was cool as he swaggered around the school house.

One recess Earl strode into view as I was in my usual supine position with someone sitting over me in total domination. Instead of criticizing my mild behavior and submission, he encouraged me to struggle free. Knowing that he was a genuine big shot, I obeyed and quickly threw off my antagonist. Even better, I reversed the situation with a take down and pin that any Saturday night tag team wrestler would have been proud of.

To my astonishment, wrestling with someone was rather easy and it felt good to be on top for once. I knew of course that my aggressive actions were in conflict with Mother's clear instructions. From that day forward but to my dismay and fear of more admonitions from home, Earl started to call me "Tough Jensen," actually "Tough Yensen." Soon everyone adopted the nickname with its Danish embellishment and pronunciation. For the next several years it

187

was even used on the streets of Standard. Here, in the presence of Mother and Dad, meeting a classmate often resulted in a greeting such as "Hi, Tough Yensen." If it happened to be Earl Eriksen, who knew that he alone had authored the moniker, the greeting was usually proceeded or punctuated with a train whistle sound that only he could produce. That was really cool and I wished that I could introduce the sound into my extensive noise repertoire.

In any event, the telltale oil stains now combined with and supported by my rather roguish label raised even more doubts about my compliance with Mother's edict of nonviolence. Even Irene's endorsement was of little value since she didn't have access to the boys basement, where a substantial portion of my supposed misdemeanors were deemed to have occurred.

By spring I was not the only Craigantler kid with a nickname. Others, even less flattering, were in common usage. In some cases these stuck and were used until junior high school, when finally we little kids had earned the right to sit on the stair well window ledge, just like all of the upper grades who had preceded us.

But back to the spring of 1941, the war in Europe was in everyone's thoughts. Almost every day there was news of more ship losses in the Atlantic. With the horrific carnage inflicted by German U boats, the Atlantic odyssey was an unbelievable risk. Understandably, there was great concern every time a Standard serviceman was sent overseas. Even though this brought him closer to eventual combat, there was a real sense of relief when it was learned that each soldier, airman or sailor had safely reached the shores of England. Running the gauntlet of the Atlantic was for many the most dangerous part of the whole war.

While at school, I was of course missing the noon time CBC and BBC news radio reports. Theoretically, this should have stopped the flow of war news but it didn't.

Miss Smith was teaching a course to grades three and four that was akin to elementary Social Studies. A goodly part of these studies required that each student report on some current event or story from the newspapers. No doubt there was the occasional reference to a local wedding or hockey score but most of the news reports narrated by the class were of the war in Europe and the Atlantic. These were treated seriously and Miss Smith and various members of the class often editorialized the stories with uninformed but alarming opinions thus, adding to the already ominous newscasts.

During these gruesome reports and the often exaggerated discussions that followed, little if any work was being done by grades one and two, co-tennants of the room. We were all listening with great and growing apprehension. In truth, there wasn't much to be happy about as the allies seemed to be losing the war on every front.

With mounting casualties of men and equipment, the only good news was coming from the United States and their continuing production of merchant ships for use on the Atlantic. The theoretically neutral President Roosevelt had persuaded his reluctant Congress to fund and provide for the construction of these cargo carriers (Liberty Ships). Although they were being sunk almost as fast as they were being launched, they did maintain a life line from America, thus keeping Britain's war effort alive.

History now clearly shows that without Roosevelt's support, England would have been forced to capitulate and the war would most certainly have been lost to the tyranny of Germany. The consequence of this is hard to imagine but it is certain that Germany's despot regime would have extended to North America after it crushed Europe.

Often at the risk of impeachment, President Roosevelt demonstrated uncanny guile in his handling of Congress. While he didn't actually persuade them into action with lies, his audacious efforts were laden with partial facts and deceptive innuendo. Churchill was fully aware of this deceitful approach and termed it "Roosevelt's terminalogical inexactitudes."

In addition to the grade three and four news reports, our participation in the war was constantly kept before us and emphasized by weekly Red Cross meetings. They were so named, but it is unlikely that the Red Cross was much involved in these motivative and patriotic events which were usually scheduled for Friday afternoons. Everyone liked them as they were a legitimate reason to goof-off and stop all normal studies. Also by then, we were all a bit weary and these spirited meetings got the weekend started a little early. Actually, they were quite interesting and were always geared to inform us of the war effort and generate support for our troops.

On rare occasions, our primary classroom was combined with that of Miss Powne, who held court right across the hall. She taught grades five through eight. These unified groups were truly exciting and usually responded to some major event. We probably celebrated with one of these festive get-togethers in the spring when Hitler's heavy and intimidating battleship, the Bismarck, was sunk and sent to the bottom of the ocean - good news at last.

During these patriotic and buoyant occasions Clara Andersen usually played the piano while the rest of us less talented patriots were expected to lift our voices in song. Invariably the repertoire included 'There'll Always Be An England," and to the tune of Edward Elgan's "Pomp and Circumstance," and everyone's favorite, "Land of Hope and Glory." By the end of the war, these and several other uplifting songs were well known to every kid in Canada. Despite their British flavor, these war time ditties always got top billing at Red Cross meetings throughout the country.

Specifics of these meetings have long since passed from memory but I well remember the pressure that was applied to each of us to buy war stamps. These twenty five cent stamps, issued by the Canadian Government in support the war effort, were purchased and affixed to a savings certificate. There were twenty stamp sized squares on the document which when filled, made it worth five dollars. Also, to make it interesting, each stamp featured various pictures of our fighting men and their armament, making each filled certificate a veritable collage of modern warfare. As I recall, the filled instruments were eventually redeemed by the government for about seven dollars, a two dollar profit.

There is no telling how much money was gleaned from the Canadian schools via this savings program. Large or small, it was a feel good idea since it was known by every student that each twenty five cent purchase was of some help in financing the allied forces. For all we knew, our support won the day for our boys in their victory over Hitler's fearsome Bismarck.

****

School was nearly out for the summer when the war took an unexpected twist with Germany invading the U.S.S.R. Suddenly we had a new ally and by his own doing, Hitler had a new enemy.

The Soviet's direct involvement in the war may have been good news, but nothing compared to my successful completion of grade one. Yes it was true, despite my floundering and having to play catch-up, I had passed out of grade one and into grade two. Having been quite prepared to flunk, this unexpected promotion made me absolutely euphoric and gave my otherwise sagging spirits an incredible lift.

As a bonus, I had also learned the train whistle sound that Earl Erickson did so well. While my whistle sound wasn't quite up to his standard, it provoked a very surprised look and a smile when I whistled back at the original Fonzie, my train whistle mentor.

It was great to be out of school for the summer. Failure would most certainly have made the summer less enjoyable but now, with grade one fully conquered, the thought of the next two months with no school and no books was something to enjoy and savor. Sleeping in on rare occasions was even a possibility.

There were no special plans but I was sure that something wonderful and exciting would happen. Actually, something had already happened which would ensure an adventurous summer and I could hardly wait to spend some time at home.

****

It was probably early May when I first saw him. The exact date is unknown but I am certain that school was still in session. It was a Saturday and Dad had reason to visit Mr. Selgensen at his nearby farmstead. His was a particularly attractive farmyard with a classy house and well painted barns. Since Irene and I were keen to visit such a fine layout, we went along for the ride. It was in one of these fine barns that we saw an absolutely captivating litter of new born puppies. They were still tiny and roly-poly, toy-like animals that squeaked as they tumbled around their mother. As a special treat, Mr. Selgensen let us each hold one of these cuddly creatures. The puppies were soft and warm, playfully biting at our fingers or anything else that happened to be handy. While their teeth were razor sharp, they were unable in inflict any damage with their small mouths and stubby little jaws.

All of the puppies were white except for a few brown markings, randomly spread around on their furry bodies. My favorite was white with a brown patch that covered one eye and both ears, one of which was always flopping down. He also had a touch of brown on his back, right over his still undocked tail.

It was obvious that Irene and I had both fallen in love with the puppies and wanted Dad to buy one. We actually doubted that Mr. Selgensen had ever thought of selling them but if he had, it was much to early for them to be weaned from their mother. While Irene and I understood this, we never let Mother and Dad forget the cute little dogs at Selgesen's farm. During the next several months, we constantly reminded them of our desire for a pet puppy.

Finally, near the end of the school term, Eric Selgensen announced that their new puppies had been weaned, and as they were now eating solid food were ready to leave home. He went on to say that we could have one if we would come and get it. Wow! We could hardly wait to tell Mother and Dad this good news. The very next Saturday we drove back to the Selgensen farm to pick out a new pet. Upon our arrival, it was Eric who escorted us back to the barn where we had first seen and held the small puppies. They were still there but had now grown much larger with a somewhat leggy appearance. To me they all looked a bit skinny and without their oversized fur coats, were not nearly as cuddly as they had been several months earlier. They were still terrific but I must admit some slight disappointment with their now grown-up appearance.

I held my thoughts to myself and since we were there to get a dog, no complaint or comment was made.

There were several to choose from but we all agreed that the one with the brown patch over one eye and both ears was the one for us. It's tail had been cut short to a few inches and my initial disappointment soon vanished when I picked him up. Now much stronger, his longer and sturdier legs were kicking and scratching my arms. Also, he was busy wagging his stumpy tail while trying to lick my face. How could I have any lingering misgivings with all of that affection?

Eric refused any money as he had been instructed to give the dogs away. Finally, after a good deal of haggling, Dad finally prevailed, and he accepted a pocketful of lose change to be used for a trip to Fletcher's ice cream parlor. A few days later, Dad announced that we had acquired our new pet for about thirty five cents. When I think of the love that was extended to our family by that little mutt, it was quite a bargain.

Tippy was the unanimous choice for a name, but his wagging tail stopped when we took him away from his familiar surroundings. En route to our farm, he was terrified and despite our best efforts, his trembling body made it clear that it would take a few days to accept us as his new family and our farm as his new home. In hindsight, his behavior was very much in keeping with his circumstance. After all, he no longer had the comfort of his mother and we were total strangers.

Tippy was never very smart but when we arrived home he immediately ran away, heading home to the Selgensen farm, some three to four miles away. Dad finally caught him but we wondered how he knew his directions so well.

In due course, after a few meals and a good deal of love and attention, Tippy accepted his new environment. Over time he virtually became a member of the family and developed a self assurance and at times an arrogance that went with it. He lived for fourteen years and during this interval he was a genuine fixture at the Jensen farm. Except for the school bus, which he hated, Tippy thoroughly enjoyed company and was always the first to greet a visitor with a wag of his tail and a bark or two. He was also the last to sound his voice as each guest drove off.

My only disappointment with Tippy was his innate fear of guns and loud noises. He clearly associated the two, as even the sight of a gun triggered an inexplicably nervous response. I always hoped that he would accompany me on a gopher shoot or a duck hunt. He never did, but instead headed for the pig house feed bin, where he took refuge until the rifle or shotgun was safely put away.

****

During the summer of 1941 and for many years that followed, Saturday nights were a not to be forgotten event for the people of the Standard community. The Great Depression was over and nearly everyone converged on the village for some shopping and a lot of festive socializing. The whole town was lit up with the stores, shops, and restaurants open until midnight. Also, the beer hall kept the pints coming and the glasses tinkling until the patrons were thrown or rolled out at the twelve o'clock curfew.

We were seldom in town late enough to see this final drama which often included a few irate and inebriated customers settling their differences outside with a few fisticuffs. For the most part, these were harmless scuffles that resulted in sober apologies the next day. There were however occasional provocations when feelings were not so easily soothed and smiles and handshakes were not forthcoming. If in these cases, the drunken protagonist had been packing a Colt Forty Five, it is possible that a few shots would have been fired. The wild west, as often depicted in the movies, may not be so far from the truth.

For the non beer drinking majority, there were equally entertaining attractions that made the evening a pleasurable experience. Doctor Fletcher's ice cream emporium always saw a good deal of activity, as did William and Betty's Cafe. Although we seldom attended, there was also a feature movie shown at the old S and S Hall. Perhaps that was just as well since in the summer of 1941 the newsreels could show nothing more than Germany winning the war in the USSR and the North Atlantic. It was a poor time to keep up with world events.

Everyone having legitimate shopping simply left a list of their needs with either Leo Larsen or Jim Madsen, the proprietors of the two general stores. With the tremendous volume of groceries being purchased, it very naturally took a while for these orders to be filled. Even Uncle Carl, who occasionally worked at Fred Christensen's Butcher Shop, was busy cutting and wrapping meat for the customers whose orders would be picked up later. No one minded the backlogs since this left lots of time to mingle on the wooden sidewalks which were teaming with people looking for some action.

With almost everyone in town, it was easy to meet a friend or for that matter a whole host of friends. For Mother and Dad, this usually resulted in a cup of coffee at William and Betty's Cafe. Indeed, I can recall when during the course of the evening, at least three coffee trips were required to handle all the chance encounters which were made on the summer streets of Standard.

At seven years of age, I was not big on coffee but usually managed one of Fletcher's delightful banana splits. These huge ice cream creations made with a whole banana and three scoops of ice cream were tantamount to a meal. Although I may have enjoyed a hollow leg in those days, one of these delicious concoctions, prepared and served by Doris or Ada Marie Fletcher, was all that I could manage to choke down.

For me the real fun and excitement came from the streets and noisy sidewalks which featured just as many kids as adults. To be truthful, I was much to shy to initiate any activity of my own but soon learned that if I hung around the seldom used hitching posts in front of Leo Larsen's Red and White Store, Henry Dam and Kenneth Larsen would usually show up. Occasionally Fabian Hugh and Carl Anton Hansen would make an appearance and when that happened, we were all in for some real adventure. While our activities were benign to the extreme, it was always exciting just to be with these older and more enterprising kids.

Actually, the most adventurous undertaking that ever occurred was peeking into the open front door of Magnus Nielsen's pool hall. That may not seem like much now but in those days it was really living on the edge. After all, Mother had warned against entering these premises and with her admonitions fixed in my mind, I was reluctant to do more than scan the interior from the sidewalk. From here we could see the smoke filled core of the building, well beyond Frank's Barber Shop. We could make out a half dozen men standing by the counter, and in the back, a few more were playing snooker or discussing the war. With their loud and often boisterous conversations, it looked and sounded interesting but wild horses could not have driven me any closer.

With the passage of time it's hard to remember if Carl or Fabian ever went inside but there was always a brace of kids who were immune to my own personal sensitivities. These, usually older boys, were lured inside with the promise of easy money for setting pins. In addition to the pool and snooker tables, Magnus also had a lone five pin bowling alley which ran almost the entire length of the building. Brunswick had yet to invent the automatic pin setter, but for a nickel a line, there were lots of boys eager to handle this chore on Saturday nights.

Each Saturday night was pretty much a duplication of the one that preceded it. On one occasion however, Henry, Kenneth and I became fascinated with the spitting that was going on in the pool hall. We of course remained well out on the sidewalk but had little trouble watching the spectacle inside. You have no idea how those guys could spit. They made it seem effortless as they spurted a stream of saliva through almost closed lips. With few exceptions, a simple turn of the head and these guys could unload an ungodly stream of sputum or whatever, right into one of the strategically located brass buckets that graced Magnus's oiled floor. Direction or distance was hardly a concern since they never seemed to miss their intended target.

We were really impressed and wished to emulate the men in the pool hall. Despite our best efforts, we couldn't come close to matching this fine art. Our initial attempts simply left a disappointing mess on our lower lip. We were almost prepared to concede that the magic of this seemingly simple maneuver was beyond our capability when Henry found the solution. This remarkable discovery came when he realized that the true masters of the art were all chewing tobacco or snuff. With this revelation, it became clear that success at this game could only be achieved with the help of some basic chemistry. Clearly this required some real inventiveness since we didn't have any tobacco or snuff and weren't likely to get any. Finally after considerable experimentation, we settled on licorice. This turned out to be a truly fine substitute.

In those days licorice was usually available at Rigmor's Candy Shop next door to the pool hall. There, for a few pennies, one could buy a whole sack full of licorice lumps all in the shape of small curved smoking pipes - you know, the chin warmer version used by Sherlock Holmes of Scotland Yard fame. To create more realism, the tobacco bowl was sprinkled with small fire red bead-like candy. For our purposes, the configuration and ornamentation was of little use but I suppose we had the option of pretending to smoke and spit at the same time.

Henry caught on very quickly but even with the help of uptown chemistry, it took Kenneth and me a fair bit of practice and a number of licorice pipes to master the right technique and not end up with a disastrous mess. Finally however, we could gush forth in a way that would have made any Boston Braves ball player jealous. While distance and accuracy were still wanting, we were now ready to face the world and show off this new found skill to any interested party. Even if they weren't interested, we could swagger around, turn or heads ever so slightly and almost without warning spew forth a truly remarkable adult spit.

No one can dignify a spit and of course our precocious behavior earned absolutely no acclaim for either of my comrades or for me. We weren't really surprised as we always knew that spitting was in most cases an uncalled-for disgusting act. To the best of my knowledge none of us retained a desire to spit. While no one ever spoke of it, I think at the time, we were secretly pleased to know that if we wanted to, we could equal or outperform the worst that Standard had to offer.

****

Summers came and went but they were almost always punctuated by visits to Calgary and at least one brief stay with Uncle Fred and Aunt Karen. The summer of 1941 was no exception and these interludes were filled with adventures not available on the farm. Also, they gave Irene and me a chance to play with Dorothy, Betty and some of their neighborhood friends. More importantly, with exposure to a whole host of new ideas and viewpoints, we both did a lot of growing up. Indeed, I still carry with me some of the concepts learned during these summer visits.

For example, it is unlikely that I will ever forget my shock at seeing Calgary's Synagogue with its shattered windows. These large voids in the front of the building were only guarded by the remaining skeletal cross members and a few shards of the broken window panes. This vandalism had been created by stone throwing anti-Semites seeking to dislodge or at least discourage the small Calgary Jewish community.

I knew that the war raging in Europe was in part being fought over differing political views and religious convictions. Despite this knowledge, it was very disquieting to know that some of the people living in Calgary were prepared to hurt each other simply because of a different philosophy or religion. To this day, I wonder if these hateful misadventures had been spawned by attitudes coming from Germany, where Hitler was spewing forth his anti Jewish rhetoric or if some local prattle was responsible. Whatever the reason, I have never forgotten my youthful disillusionment and disgust at the sight of these broken windows. Jesus was, after all, a Jew.

While at Dorothy and Betty's house, we often went swimming. Uncle Fred had a night job at the Yale Hotel so he was free during the day for swimming excursions, picnics, and bird sanctuary trips. He was extremely skilled in the water and a small park on the banks of the Elbow River in the Roxboro area was a favorite of his. For some curious reason, he had no obvious sensitivity to the fact that the flow in this water course had been ice just a few days earlier. For me it was much too cold even for wading. On the other hand, Fred had no apparent difficulty in walking directly into this frigid stream. After splashing a little water on his upper body, he would plunge forward into the current only to reemerge upstream as he masterfully performed a variety of swimming strokes.

Actually, the point of this narration has nothing to do with swimming except that with gasoline rationing in full swing, we always walked to the river. This led us through the heart of Mt. Royal, the most opulent of the city's residential areas. The homes in this prestigious section of the city were huge and for the most part, very expensive. The residents had little reason to expect transients of our ilk to walk by. No doubt we looked like a rag tag bunch with our picnic lunch stuffed into a cardboard box and our clothing more suited for swimming than walking. Returning from the river, and after having ventured into the wet, we looked even worse. No doubt about it, our disheveled hair, rumpled clothing, and grungy picnic box were out of character with the Mount Royal mansions which bordered our path home.

No one ever stopped us on our journey to and from the river but we almost always attracted a few stares and an occasional less than kind remark. Perhaps the most telling comment was made by a child playing on her front verandah who called for her mother to come and see the refugees passing by. With the war in progress there were of course a few unfortunate victims, who with refugee status, had migrated to Canada. Happily, we were not among this group but obviously the child saw us as a tribe of displaced persons, (D. P's.) from Europe.

While this innocent remark made us all laugh, it also had a lasting and profound effect on me. To this day, the child, now an adult, probably believes that she saw a pack of disenfranchised casualties from one of Hitler's felonious expeditions. Considering our appearance and the circumstances, this was not an unreasonable assumption. It does however show that things are not always as they are presented. Moreover, people cannot be depended on to reveal their true identities by their dress or behavior. I just wish that I could always remember that.

Other remembered impressions of these visits were the frequent confinements that were imposed on us kids. The Andersens were terrific hosts but by happenstance, our visits were often coincident with the annual maintenance of Sixteen

A Street. This didn't mean a repair to the pavement, it was in fact a simple re-oiling of the gravel surface in front of their house. What a mess! We were not allowed out on the street to play. The black tar and oil surface could easily be tracked into the house and who could blame Aunt Karen and Uncle Fred for their firm resolve to keep us kids away from this potentially destructive tar-like muck.

Patsy Curtis across the street was clearly out of bounds and Delores Lavoy who lived a few houses up the hill, but also across the oily gulf was equally persona-non-grata. With the road maintenance underway, the only kid on our side of the street was Eddie Kuhen and during these intervals he was about as popular as a summer cold. His idea of fun was to run out onto the oiled surface where he could load up his shoes so that he could make messy footprints on the sidewalk.

In truth, Eddie's shenanigans were not the only hazards for the neighborhood. Both the milkman and iceman made their deliveries from the back of horse drawn wagons. Despite their best efforts, oil was easily dragged onto the otherwise pristine sidewalks. Even worse, direct delivery to a porch or doorway was sure to result in some difficult cleanups.

We couldn't cross the street but with careful navigation, we could slip a few blocks east to the Kinema Theater. During the summer the local flick ran an afternoon matinee which almost always featured Lassie. "Lassie Comes Home, Lassie Goes to War, Lassie Gets Lost," this dog must have made a million movies and for the grand sum of fifteen cents each, I think the Kinema showed all of them.

In hindsight, it is somewhat surprising that we were not only constrained by the street maintenance but quarantined as well. During most of the late summers there was a much more fearsome menace lurking about than were the oily streets. It has long since been forgotten but many of our visits with Dorothy and Betty were haunted by the threat of Polio. Our visits to the city or their junkets to the farm were not illegal but were certainly not encouraged or recommended. Polio or Infantile Paralysis, as it was known in those days, was nearly always running at epidemic levels during late summer.

No one really knew how this plague was spread but there were countless cases of this crippling malaise and isolation from it's victims was the only known defense. Mother always wondered if the fresh fruit from British Columbia's Okanagan Valley was the villain. Others were convinced that the pollen from the grain fields was responsible. Whatever it was, it was a major concern and we were all carefully watched for any sign of illness.

When Dorothy and Betty made their annual sojourn to the farm, contagion always seemed to be at its peak. For this reason, Mother and Dad were particularly vigilant for any signs of a health disorder. Unfortunately this attentiveness was not made easy by our well water which could easily mask or simulate an affliction of some kind. Put in other terms, our well was not always kind to those unaccustomed to its therapeutically cleansing behavior.

By any measure, our farm well produced an absolutely delicious drink of cold refreshing water. Technically, it was totally potable and during the hot days of July and August, when the scorching sun was at its highest, nothing could beat a chilled swig from our well. In those early days, I was convinced that a drink from this source would rank with anything as a thirst quencher and that any perceived problem was pure nonsense. For me there was no problem, but for any visitor accustomed to other sources, our farm water was absolutely diabolical.

Mother and Dad knew of the water's villainous attributes but could do little about it. It was hard to make it taste better but on occasion they would purchase a lemon juice extract, which when added to the water, made a most delectable drink. In most cases this was acquired from the touring "Watkins man." This drone of our society showed up every month or so selling his wares for an exhorbitant price. His total inventory could be carried in one large imitation leather display case. His stock of merchandise was limited to soap, liniment, spices, and juice extracts. They were of an adequate quality but the price was always more than that charged at Leo's Red and White Store. I think Mother and Dad felt sorry for him and usually bought a few items including the juice extract. In point of fact, it was not too bad, and in quality it was good enough to make our well water taste almost as good as commercial soda pop.

Regrettably, all the lemon juice in the world could not change the residual impact of a drink from our well. Those of us who lived on the farm were of course immune to its cleansing and most remembered quality but it had the potential of upsetting a vacation for Dorothy and Betty. To that I can say - "Don't Drink the Water."

As I recall, Dorothy and Betty invariably split their summer visits between our house, Bedstefar and Bedstemor's and the Holms. Irene and I always enjoyed their stay although it was hard to find things to do that pleased everyone. Irene, Dorothy and Betty enjoyed playing paper dolls and games like hopscotch. Hopscotch wasn't too bad but I would much rather have played catch or gone across the road to Alfred Petersen's pasture to snare gophers.

In some ways, Betty seemed to prefer my ideas to the dolls and on at least one occasion she joined with me on a gopher safari. We had serious goals with high expectations and although there was lots of so called game, our adventure was a complete bust. We worked at it for an hour or so but whenever we found a likely gopher hole, Tippy decided that he could dig the little varmints out, or failing that, scare them to death with a lot of barking. Seeing him with his head stuffed in the dirt while trying to make like a badger was funny but not very productive. Time has marred the facts, but with Tippy as a hunting partner it is unlikely that we ever caught anything. It is certain that he didn't.

Perhaps the most memorable and demoralizing moment of our summer get-togethers occurred when Betty felt compelled to instruct me in the science of dish drying. Whether this happened in Calgary or at the farm doesn't come to mind, but I know that as a group, we kids were always assigned the task of doing the supper cleanup.

My pitiful dish wiping style was one dish at a time. Apparently this incompetent approach didn't satisfy my dish wiping partner and her idea of a division of labor. In contrast, Betty would take a whole stack of similar dishes. With this handful, she would wipe dry both the top dish and the bottom dish of the stack. She would then shuffle the top dish to the bottom and repeat the process. What a revelation, why didn't I think of it myself. Woe is me, now I have to live out my life in embarrassment, giving credit for this clever little knack to my cousin, Betty.

****

With the passing of summer the green display of growth was quietly being pushed aside by the golden hues of maturity. Also the ever present grain fields, were now cast in ever changing variegations as the early autumn breezes swirled through their ripening stalks. These were the unmistakable signs that the fun of visiting cousins and lazy vacations were over and it was time to go back to school for some real honest book learning.

As I recall, school started right on cue and once again Irene and I found ourselves meeting the school bus each week day morning. This was still the overcrowded Nash and as in the previous year, we were late a good part of the time.

There were some changes however as Miss Smith had found a better life and had been replaced by Miss White who was now responsible for our room (grades one through four). My classmates and I were moved up one row to slightly larger desks. Our old set of smaller desks were now occupied by a small group of bewildered grade ones.

There was nothing particularly special about Miss White except that she tried desperately to make everyone a musician. She played the piano and at least once every week, all four grades were set up for assembly which went on for at least a full hour of songs and music. Sometimes we would all sing as she played the piano. At other times she distributed all of the rhythm band toys for a well meaning but generally hopeless session of "learn the beat." When this happened we were in for a lot of noise and criticism.

The rhythm band experience made it very clear that the often late Craigantler gang were no favorites in Room 1. To the best of my knowledge, not one student from our bus load ever graduated from the bang sticks or sand blocks. I tried both but despite my most sincere efforts, the more sophisticated instruments such as the cymbals, tambourines, rattles and the delicate triangle eluded me forever. These classic tune intensifiers were reserved for the teacher's pets.

In fairness, my musical talents were hardly deserving of better treatment, although to this day I can still work a power sander with considerable musical dexterity.

It was well into the year when Miss White all but gave up on my musical ineptness. As I recall, our class had been assigned the task of memorizing the first verse of a long since forgotten song. The canticle to be learned had several verses, the lyrics of which were properly chronicled between the musical staves that were filled with the melodic notes of the ditty. Up to that time I had never seen written music, or at least if I had, my feeble musical mind had failed to take note of its construction. With my apparently unforgivable ignorance, I carefully memorized the first line of all five verses. The words didn't rhyme or make much sense but after all, the first verse should logically be the words in the first box. Shouldn't it? How was I expected to know that the words skip along to the bottom of the page and then repeat to the top with each additional stanza.

It would seem that while I knew all of the first lines by heart, this did not satisfy Miss White and she was not impressed. Even worse, it revealed my true knowledge of music, or lack of it.

The fiasco forever dashed any hope of being promoted from the sanding blocks or bang sticks. Indeed, my already poor situation degenerated even more and as a consequence of this terrible misdemeanor, I found myself relegated to broken or at least unmatched bang sticks. From that day on, matching colored sticks were a rarity and when I played the sand blocks it no longer mattered that the sand paper was torn or worn out. In short, I was permitted to remain in the rhythm band but my musical future was very bleak indeed.

On reflection, it is fair to say that my second year in school was not a joyous time. To this day, I believe that my musical debacle set the tone for the balance of the year with Miss White. It certainly tainted my relationship with her. In point of fact, I was probably not the only one in her room exposed to such indifference. Her strong emphasis on music could only be appreciated by a very few and she showed a certain disdain for anyone who did not share her passion for it. Happily, there were many other events outside of school that made the year notable and memorable.

****

No doubt the most important event of 1941 occurred on the seventh of December when Japanese aircraft bombed and strafed the United States Navel Yards at Pearl Harbor on the island of Oahu. I don't specifically remember this momentous Hawaiian incident but a few days later I became fully aware of its significance insofar as the war was concerned.

Within hours of the episode, Canada declared war on Japan and within a very few days later, Hitler very stupidly declared war on the United States. This of course brought the United States into lockstep with the allies and their hostilities with Germany and Italy. What had been a conflict that was more or less confined to the Atlantic Ocean and Europe had with this sudden and momentous event, expanded the fighting to the Pacific and Asia. It was now a global affair.

Although the entry of Japan virtually doubled the size of the enemy, the entry of the United States as a direct combatant, more than offset this disadvantage and changed the balance of power dramatically. With their direct involvement everyone could truly believe that the war would end soon with victory for the allied forces. It didn't make the job easier but it made the outcome more certain. Even Dad's pessimism changed and I remember him saying, "We will now win the war."

Japan was really never a viable threat to the people of North America. In those days, the vast Pacific Ocean presented an almost impossible barrier for any meaningful attack on our continent by the enemy. If however, it was their intention to win the war that they had started, a disruption of America's war effort would be absolutely essential. From this premise, it followed that Japan would require a beachhead somewhere on American soil, both to upset munitions production and to demoralize the population.

Knowing these facts, the United States almost immediately started preparations for a land link to Alaska, a part of North America with considerable vulnerability. Although the official start on the construction for this tie up is recorded to be February 14, 1942, there was at least one preliminary foray into northern British Columbia within days of the Pearl Harbor attack. Indeed, I have since met one of the American surveyors (Captain Herman Ingle), who with Canada's knowledge but without official permission, spent the Christmas of 1941 at a point near the Liard River, one of the most formidable rivers which had to be crossed by the Alaskan Highway. He and his hardy crew were assigned the task of blazing a trail out of these northern woods by the spring of 1942.

While the building of the Alaskan Highway does not rank with the China Wall or the Egyptian pyramids, it is without question one of the truly gargantuan construction projects of this century. Moreover, from my perspective, it was a manifestation of the war that could almost be felt by those of us who were noncombatants and were isolated in the relative security of Western Canada.

Canadians and Americans alike pooled their efforts and equipment in order to complete its construction in record time. With the help of farm trucks and local labor, some of which came from Standard (Gordon Rasmussen and Stuart Rasmussen) the USA Army Corp. of Engineers concluded their work on this sixteen hundred mile thoroughfare from Dawson Creek, British Columbia to Fairbanks, Alaska by October of 1942.

With the war going full tilt in the Pacific no one ever questioned the value of the highway. In fact during the summer of 1942, the Japanese attacked North America and for a time occupied various islands in the Aleutian chain.

To this day I have never driven one mile on this famous winding trail through British Columbia, the Yukon, and Alaska. Apart from the beautiful scenery, which is assured, such a trip would be a tribute to those who helped with its construction. It would certainly be of interest since I can still recall some of the stories brought back by the men from Standard who participated in the building of this vital war time link to the north.

****

Canada's patriotism was never in doubt but a little allied propaganda never hurt. After all, it helped to know that rationing and shortages of almost every item was necessary and for our own good. When the war time paper automobile license plates wouldn't stick to the windshield no one complained. Eaton's catalogue substitute orders became the norm and were accepted without a whimper. Indeed some of these catalog choices, made by an obscure but heroic clerk in Winnipeg, were not bad and the item could usually be worn with nationalistic pride, knowing that being "less than perfect" was for the war effort. To accommodate the need for various items required by the military, clothing styles were changing and were accepted with zealous support from nearly everyone. For example, nylon was yet to be invented and ladies silk stockings were nearly impossible to find. All of the material normally available for this market was being directed into the important business of making parachutes. To save wool and cotton, women's skirts were made shorter and it suddenly became fashionable for mens trousers to be made without cuffs. If you could find a suit or jacket to buy, the collars and lapels were narrower and nearly all zippers were being replaced by buttons.

Kids my age were totally immersed in a wide array of systems and mediums that were employed to develop and sustain loyalty and commitment to the war. The Red Cross meetings at school were supplemented by weekly newsreels that featured clips from the battlefront. Also, there were countless drives for material useful to the munitions industry. Irene and I found a few old aluminum pots and kettles which no doubt ended up in the air frame of a Spitfire or Lancaster.

In addition, we were able to deliver a sizable stack of animal bones, a source of bone black or animal charcoal, which with some refinement, became a major component in the filter material of a gas mask. More importantly, these skeletal remains, some of which may have dated back to the days of the buffalo, were used for their phosphorus content, a major ingredient for explosives.

The United States entry into the war brought with it a whole new set of innovations that were used to develop a sense of patriotism. Within weeks, all of the radio programs produced in Hollywood or New York featured war related scripts. Important characters in the soap operas began their enlistment into various branches of the military. Much of the usual trauma that was woven into these daytime radio serials was suddenly transfixed by the war. Even Pepper of "Pepper Young's Family" was sent off to do battle. In short, the promise of "Whiter than white," as advertised by a soap, was often less important than the patriotism portrayed by the drama which was interjected between the commercials.

Some of the most popular comedian shows on radio, "Amos and Andy, Bob Hope, Fibber Magee and Molly, The Great Gildersleave" and others, each in its own way, accommodated to the conflict with jokes and humor about men in the service. This was also true of the funny papers which now emphasized personalities like Steve Canyon, an air force major, who was busily shooting down Japanese Zero fighters. Terry and the Pirates, also a team of military personal, were liberating Pacific islands on a weekly basis. Even the old standbys like "Joe Palooka" and "Dick Tracy" either joined the army or were engaged in espionage. The more expensive comic books, which I couldn't afford, "Batman, Superman and Captain Marvel," now found themselves fighting German and Japanese villains.

All of this subtle ballyhoo played well and as intended, made me and all other noncombantants feel good. Whether we were winning on the battlefield mattered little since it was certain that we would be triumphant in the funny papers. As such, these fictional but highly patriotic epics were enormously effective in propping up the spirits of the home front.

The comic strips may have been a bit nonsensical but the stuff that came with Cracker Jack was not. This delectable candy coated popcorn, packaged in a little white box with red lettering always came with a small prize of some sort. Typically, the surprise doodads could, in prewar days, include such items as a whistle, a small mirror, a pair of dice or for that matter, almost anything small enough to hide in the popcorn. Suddenly with America's entry into the war, these prizes were patriotically replaced by a small multicolored card portraying a war plane. Detailed statistics and specifications such as weight, speed, bomb load, and armament were featured on the reverse side of each card. This series of picture cards depicted fighters and bombers from every nation, both friend and foe.

It is likely that every kid in Western Canada had at least some curiosity about these tools of war and placing an airplane card in each box of Cracker Jack was indeed a masterful marketing ploy. For my part, they were a most cherished item and to facilitate trades, almost every boy in school had his shirt pocket bulging with a pack of Cracker Jack cards. Having two B-24 Liberators would not do if someone else had none and was willing to trade one of his two P-51 Mustang cards. Recess became a trading session of incredible magnitude.

Henry Dam must have eaten most of the popcorn as he had a card showing every airplane that flew and fought in the Second World War. As I recall, he was the only guy who managed to collect the almost nonexistent Northrop P-61 Black Widow. This most difficult collectable was worth at least fifty of the more easily obtainable cards. Henry never traded it off and was the envy of every other collector. Hoping to get one myself, I was always disappointed to open a fresh box of Cracker Jack only to find another run of the mill Arro Lancaster or equally familiar Junker Ju 87 (Stuka). Luck was with me however, as I was one of the few at school with a Lockheed P-38 Lightning.

With the help of Cracker Jack candied popcorn, nearly every kid became somewhat of an airplane expert and could identify almost anything that could fly. We of course had little opportunity to see the true combat fighters and bombers, but starting in the spring of 1942 the Soviet Union was accepting a considerable number of aircraft from the United States.

For reasons of a limited range, a goodly number of these lend lease aircraft en route to the USSR, flew directly over our farm. Using my Cracker Jack cards, I was able to identify them as P-39 Bell Aircobras. To the best of my knowledge these fighter planes, bristling with guns and painted in dark camouflage, were ferried from Maelmstrom Airforce Base in Montana to Cold Lake or Nanimo and beyond. They came in waves of thirty to fifty, usually at a very low altitude. As they thundered north to their destiny, Tippy would run for cover in the safety of the feed bin. Our chickens became so flustered that their egg production stopped for a few days.

At times I thought the roar of the passing armada would rattle a few bricks from our chimney. It was all terrifically exciting and although the solo pilots were easily visible, none ever seemed to notice or pay any attention to my frantic waving. With all their noise and deadly appearance, I was always glad that they were on our side but never knew if it was Americans or Soviets at the controls.

****

During late winter Irene and I attended our first of many ice carnivals. This highly acclaimed social event, held each year at the Standard skating rink, was a real Mardi Gras for all of the locals. Many dressed up in strange and often funny costumes, so the evening was a regular potpourri of color and sound. All of the vibrant hues of the ragtag costumes moving and skating to the tempo of the music made a grand impression. For me, it was almost intoxicating and made the business of getting on the ice particularly intimidating.

To be sure there was music, but if memory serves, this element of the merrymaking came from two very scratchy phonograph records played on an archaic, barely functioning gramophone. As the evening wore on, the repetitious playing of "Life in the Finland Woods" and "The Skater's Waltz" became a bit taxing. Even worse, to the exclusion of all else, these melodies were ringing in my head for the next week or so.

Notwithstanding the monotony of the music, the festive atmosphere was enhanced with lights, sound and color which did much to hide the shabby appearance of the skating rink. While it was far from being the oldest structure in the otherwise pristine village, it certainly looked the part.

For starters, the entire facility squatted in a particularly low spot (actually a hole) which meant that the winter ice and snow made the approach to the main structure and its front door a scarcely navigable down hill slippery hazard. Despite generous volumes of coal ash spread daily on this approach, many a visitor arrived at the front door sliding on his or her backside.

For some curious reason, and out of character for Standard, not one drop of paint had ever been applied to either the interior or exterior. As a consequence, the cedar shingles that encased the exterior walls of the heated change room had aged to an uneven rusty brown. While the roof, also of cedar, had weathered to an ugly gray, its worst feature was the significant sag at its midsection. If it was not for the interior heat, perpetually venting through the uninsulated ceiling and shingles, a snow load would surely have accumulated and finished the entire mess with a giant collapse.

The interior of the change house was almost as bleak as the outside. Here the walls and low ceiling showed dark water stains randomly marking the unpainted spruce boards. This public area featured a huge pot bellied heater which when tended with large coal lumps, produced an enormous amount of heat. Indeed, the benches adjacent to this source of unrelenting heat showed little use. In contrast, those nailed to the outside walls and less exposed to the conflagration were heavily splintered through years of jambing skate blades into the soft wood and boot jacking stiff skates off nearly frozen feet.

If the benches were splintered, you should have seen the floor. There was no basement and the planks nailed to the floor joists were, in some spots, almost chewed through to the dirt below. As you might expect, this was especially true near the exit. Here, with the passage of time, the skates of many would be athletes walking to the outdoor ice surface had carved an obvious and very discernible trail into the wooden deck. This was especially noticeable right at the exit where the door sill was almost worn away, thus creating a drafty crack directly under the heavy plank door which was intended to fill the void when closed. For the door, this was an impossible task, but it did automatically close after each use. This self actuation was accomplished by way of an ingenious weighted rope and pulley mechanism which guaranteed a noisy slam each time the opening to the outdoor chill was closed.

Our gala carnival night was not a propitious time to focus on the sorry appearance of the rink. It can however best be described as an organization of unpainted boards surrounding a patch of rough ice. I took little notice of this since I was there to skate. Actually, Mother and Dad had fitted both my sister and me with ice skates the previous year. During the earlier winter, all or at least most of our activities on ice had been confined to the small frozen stock pond immediately south of our house.

This shallow pasture pool usually started to freeze in late October or early November. When that occurred, a significant portion of the unfrozen liquid which remained under the frozen surface soaked away into the mud beneath or through the earthen dam which gave origin to the pond in the first place. As the still unfrozen water disappeared, the ice layer sagged to fill the void, thus forming a solid saucer with sloping sides. Skating on this slanted surface was a bit unusual but with the snow removed, it was still slippery. It was in fact both dangerous and hard. During my first few years on ice it wasn't at all unusual to have one's legs suddenly lose footing and slip away. When that happened a good crack on the back of the head quickly followed. As I write this, there are few things that come to mind that are quite as shockingly painful as falling over backwards and bonking ones coconut on ice. There aren't that many stars in the entire universe.

For someone of a tender age, learning to skate is a time consuming but worthwhile venture. Despite spending a considerable portion of my early skating years on my posterior, time and practice brought some modest improvement and remaining upright was becoming more and more commonplace. With this transition, there was also some slight change in locomotion and, sagging ankles notwithstanding, I eventually acquired some skill at propelling myself forward.

The late winter carnival was my first opportunity to make comparisons with my peers. I had assumed that they would be much better than me but to my astonishment, my problems were their problems too. In some respects learning to skate on a stock pond was an advantage since there wasn't a wooden fence to hang onto for support. Some of my friends from town were in constant contact with the surrounding boards, while in the absence of this comfort, I had learned to be more independent. Weak ankles were the norm and falling down was a common occurrence for all of us. Thankfully by this time, almost everyone had learned how to fall and a cracked noggin was a seldom consequence.

At this stage in my development, competition was of absolutely no interest. While I suspect that others felt as I did, beaming and proud parents working in cahoots with the organizing committee eventually cajoled five or six of my age group to line up along one of the faded blue lines. It was of course intended that we race to the other blue line some sixty feet away. Sure enough, at the very start, some of us fell down. Getting up simply meant that we would trip each other and fall down again. For those who may have missed this tangle, there was the matter of going in a straight line toward the designated finish. Our individual dexterity was such that no one could predict direction with any certainty. Oh sure, we could generally go west or east and know the difference but having a primary compass point was of little real use in this situation. Here the narrow path to success was bounded on one side by a weathered board fence sheltering a jumble of cheering parents. The opposite border was made up of a line of snickering kids, older and much more proficient on their skates.

The scramble to the finish line was pandemonium as we banged, fell, crawled and stumbled down the ice. The outcome was of no consequence, but it must have been entertaining since everyone was laughing.

****

Winter could never really be winter without the affliction of cod liver oil. During the cold and darkness of short days, it was the universally accepted liquid source of Vitamin D and every Canadian child could expect some exposure to this particularly foul source of artificial sunshine.

I suppose it was an inadvertent invention of the Arctic Eskimos who, in bequeathing it to the rest of the world should, at the very least, have been honored with the "Order of Canada." After all, many who have done much less are to this day wearing their enameled petunia lapel pins with much pride and dignity. Indeed, we can never know how many children have been saved from the ravages of crooked bones and poor health were it not for this wonder wintertime elixir. With its repulsive taste and equally unforgiving smell, it was certainly a far cry from a winter vacation in Arizona or Florida, but it was just as good. Thankfully, parents will be parents and we were never given a choice between rickets or this vile potion. Were it not for caring adults, I think it likely that most youngsters would have accepted the risk of a bent femur or warped tail bone rather than the cod liver oil. I am grateful that the choice was never mine to make since Mother and Dad prescribed the repugnant treatment and filled their parental role with commendable diligence and consistency. To be sure, even during the peak of the Depression, Irene and I received a proper allocation of this disgusting cure-all. While there wasn't always money for sugar or coffee, we never went short of this poor man's substitute for the sunny beaches of Waikiki.

To ensure that the entire house did not take on the fragrance of a Nova Scotia fishing trawler, both the spoon with which it was dispensed and the clear bottle in which it was contained, were carefully stowed in the adjacent shanty. Here, in partial isolation, its odoriferous perfume could be quaffed away by the cold breezes that found their way into and through this lean-to building.

I didn't like it but managed to handle this fishy concoction with reasonable aplomb. Poor Sister Irene gagged with every swallow. Suggesting that its fragrant flavor resembled that of the finest and most expensive Black Sea caviar did little to make the daily dose a pleasant experience.

It would be inappropriate to lavish Irene with accolades but there is little doubt that her complaints interspersed among the many upchucks fit in well with a chorus of other Canadian adolescents who suffered the same grievance. In any event, with the passing of time, some clever pharmacist must have heard this outcry and fit the daily dosage into a gelatin capsule. While this made the stuff easier to swallow, it still left each victim with the breath of a viper. One could of course mask this halitosis with the ingestion of a few garlic cloves, but is that an improvement? Moreover, any careless flatulence would be in disharmony with even a horse barn and betray all attempts to hide the equally nasty exhalations.

Our school teachers were the true heroes of the day as having a morning class filled with reeking children is well beyond the call of duty and almost defies comprehension. They too deserved the "Order of Canada."

****

Finally, the snow was gone and the spring of 1942 was in sight. To my surprise school was becoming marginally interesting. That is to say, there was less class work and more time for fun, or at least so it seemed. Almost every class ended early so that we could have time off to go outside for exercise. We were in fact practicing for a field day, whatever that was. It all sounded very exciting but I had no idea why we were making such a fuss about it. The word field implied tilling the soil, planting or harvesting. I quickly surmised that none of my notions of a field day applied so I kept my mouth shut. Everyone else seemed totally familiar with the program so I thought it wise not to make any inquiries. Asking Miss White for details was out of the question since she already had me pegged as a stupid and hopeless blockhead. She may have been right but at least I was smart enough not to throw any more fuel on that fire.

As time progressed, training for the field day gained momentum and more and more of the school day was spent outdoors. By this time sand pits were positioned behind the high jump bar and parallel binder twine lanes were staked out to keep everyone lined up for the practice races. Also by now it was clear that planting crops was another story and that this junket was shaping up to be a battle of strength, endurance and physical ability.

For me the whole thing was another disaster. The only competitor and fellow participant in my age group was Kenneth Sorensen. It turned out that he was an absolutely marvelous athlete. It was just my luck to have the top athlete in the entire school as my only rival. He was in a class by himself. Even as a nearly eight year old, grade two student, he could easily best all of the boys in our room which included grades three and four. Indeed, while he was never given the opportunity, I suspect that the grade five boys would have had trouble beating Kenneth's running and jumping abilities. In the face of this incredible prowess, I was once again destined to be last.

Happily, with all of this activity, Irene got a new pair of canvas running shoes. This allowed me to inherit her old ones which were still in reasonably good condition. It was a boost for my morale and I was pleased with their lightness. In the end however, they proved to be of little benefit against Kenneth's outstanding athletic skills. Also, I would have liked them much more if they had laces like Kenneth's instead of a strap and a button.

****

I have never known if the 1942 spring sports day was a first for Standard or the entire Wheatland School District. In any event, it triggered the need for official school colors. This generated a great debate among the older kids, many of whom had very specific ideas on the matter. With each passing day the color issue became more and more intense. Finally, it became clear that the argument was becoming divisive and nasty. For final resolution, Mr. Malcolm mandated that each student would have the right to vote on a favorite set of colors.

While no specific directions were given, this democratic event saw a considerable amount of lobbying, some of which trickled down to us little kids. For the most part we were oblivious to the business of coordinating colors. We were however, enjoying the attention showered on us by the more senior students. They all wanted us to vote for their particular color scheme.

. Like most of my colleagues, I was totally blind to the business of coordinating colors, but had equal disregard for the organized lobby groups seeking my support and vote. In the end, I voted for my own choice of John Deere green and yellow. After all, if you can believe the advertising - "Nothing runs like a Deere."

The ballot box may have been stuffed but I think it more likely that the high school students coordinated their votes. In any event, Dana School now had school colors which would be revealed just before the forthcoming field day.

The color issue had been disruptive but finally the big day arrived. At first it was a bit disappointing since the sky was overcast and it had been raining throughout the night.

Fortunately, the rain had stopped and despite the less than perfect weather, I was full of enthusiasm as Arthur's old Nash delivered Irene and me, along with the rest of the Craigantler gang, to Rockyford. This small town some eighteen miles northwest of Standard was our host for this important athletic competition.

To fill the ranks of this sporting extravaganza, each participating school was allowed to enter two athletes in each age group. We were only two so despite my abysmal showing, both Kenneth and I were thrust into the heat of battle. Here at Rockyford, we would test our mettle against the best of Wheatland. In doing so, we represented Dana's contingent of nearly eight year old boys. As proof, we both proudly showed our new school colors which were represented by a pair of small ribbons pinned to our shirts. Apparently my John Deere choice had been overwhelmed by the more original and enduring, "Mauve and Gold."

It seems that Rockyford had two elementary schools, one of which was a parochial Catholic unit, run by a teaching order of nuns. Two of these black cloaked ladies had been assigned the unlikely and unforgiving task of directing the track and field events in my age group. This being my first ever exposure to these ladies in black, I was more than a little surprised when nearly everyone called them "Mother." When they weren't being addressed directly, the kids from Rockyford also referred to them as "Sisters." I was confused, and since they were neither my mother nor my sister, I tried to avoid any meaningful conversation with them.

Their dress seemed totally inappropriate for the occasion but I soon learned that those long flowing black robes were not an impediment. Indeed, were it not for Kenneth, I think it likely that Sister Marie was the best athlete of the bunch.

Most of the days events have faded from memory but I have not forgotten the last contest of the day which was the softball throw. Kenneth had easily won all of the previous events but here at last was everyone's big chance. Kenneth was average size but several of the fellows in our group were much larger and I think they logically assumed that size would enjoy the advantage in a throwing contest.

For this event, each contestant was credited with the longest of three throws, made one at a time but in strict rotation. The ball, a now obsolete "out- seam softball" had either been left out in the preceding nights rain or had soaked up a good deal of moisture from the wet grass. In any case, it seemed to weigh a ton. It was certainly much heavier than the ball that Dad had made for me. His carefully crafted denim covered, rag filled sphere was about the size and weight of a tennis ball. I could get a good grip on it and throw it a reasonable distance. Unfortunately, I was hopeless with this heavy out-seam, soggy monster. After my first toss, it became obvious that my throwing skills would not win a ribbon. Heck, I could hardly get a hold of the water saturated lump, much less throw the darn thing.

Kenneth was to follow me but politely declined his turn. To the dismay of Sister Marie, but the joy of everyone else, he also refused his turn on the second rotation. Finally however, when we got to the third and last chance, Kenneth took the ball and promptly threw it out of the yard, well beyond anyone else's best effort. It was certainly a grandstand play but left no doubt that Kenneth was the best athlete of the day. Also when Sister Marie vaulted the fence to retrieve the ball, it was clear that she was not far behind.

When the final count was in, I had won two seconds and one third place ribbon. There is no telling how many ribbons Kenneth had won, but he had taken first in every event. For me the whole day was an unforgettable experience. For the first time, my own inept athletic skills could be compared with a relatively large group of boys my own age.

While my efforts did not produce a stack of ribbons, it was pleasing to discover that I was more or less normal.

My few ribbons mattered little to the overall athletic success of Dana, but my age group was most assuredly an important contributor to the school ethos. Bernice Sanderson, also a superb athlete, took first in all of the girl events. For all of the years that Bernice and Kenneth participated, no kid in their class or age group, male or female, had a chance.

Beating Dana School at track and field became even more difficult when the Chimney Hill School was closed and their kids were bussed to Standard. This school closing introduced Nadine Mellsen and her cousins Stanley and Kenneth into our already stalwart group of athletes. They were outstanding in their age groups and over the few years that followed, garnered an incredible number of first place ribbons for Dana.

****

The summer of 1942 was more or less commonplace but I did learn how to fish for minnows. A bent pin, a house fly, and a few feet of thread from the bobbin of Mother's sewing machine was the perfect setup. Also, Vernon and Glenn Petersen, both a few years my senior, were most helpful in finding me a willow stick so that I could better position my bait directly over and into the schools of minnows that were visible from the banks of the small creek that meandered its way through the gopher mounds and ancient buffalo trails of Alfred Petersen's pasture.

Fishing for minnows was lots of fun but was totally without the prospect of profit. In most cases, those that took the bait and hook were immediately dumped into a bucket of water which was later emptied into the big stock trough in our barn yard. They seemed to enjoy that environment but never grew to more that a few inches in length. Even after a few years of this luxurious lifestyle, they were still only minnows. My dream of having them develop into edible trout like morsels was never realized.

It turned out that my fishing venture was a commercial failure but a recreational success. As such it served to dampen the pervasive gloom and frustration that was being fostered and perpetuated by the war in Europe and the Pacific.

Earlier in the spring (April 27), Canada's Parliament initiated full and absolute conscription. This proclamation ensured that virtually every able bodied man of fighting age was drafted into military service. While there were a few exceptions, largely based on essential job functions, almost every young man in our community was now in uniform. Even Mr. Malcolm, our stern and fearsome school principal, was seen wearing an air force uniform.

Adding to the pain of having an ever increasing number of Standard boys recruited into service, the war was not going well. German forces in the Soviet Union were chalking up victory after victory as they advanced toward Moscow. The allied campaign in North Africa was going nowhere and the war in the Pacific was heating up with almost daily reports of our American associates losing more ships and men.

In an attempt to blunt the almost incredible success of Hitler's ruffians, a large amphibious raid on occupied France was attempted. This mid-August fiasco at Dieppe was undertaken largely by Canadian troops who suffered terrible losses. While I can't recall if there were hometown casualties incurred during this misadventure, there were by this time a number of young men from Standard who were lost or killed in other venues of the war in Europe and North Africa. All in all, there was little to be happy about.

****

Maybe it was the war or maybe it was just me, but going back to school for my third grade seemed particularly difficult. After the pleasantly lazy days of summer, returning to school was never much fun. Perhaps it was the knowledge that sandwich lunches packed in wax paper would be the norm for the next ten months.

More likely it was the new school bus, which with the addition of students from Yule School (closed during that summer), was even more crowded than the old Nash. To accommodate this larger group, Arthur Grant had acquired an old windowless, black, hearse-like bread truck, and fitted it with wooden benches. These were arranged along each side so that the crammed-in kids at the back faced each other with their backs to the outside walls. This put their feet on the spare tire and snow shovel, both of which lay lose on the floor. As Irene and I were among the last to board, we always found ourselves sitting on someone's lap in the front jump seat.

These negatives were not helped by the messy school yard which was equally distressing. During summer, the entire area had grown over with matured chick weed and foxtails. Even the worn spots directly under the swings were almost filled in with weeds and grass.

Although little more than two months had passed, there was still evidence of the "School's Over For The Summer" celebrations of late June. These joyous moments, from the term just past, were manifested by several black but now faded splashes on the east brick wall. The partially filled ink bottles that had been hurled by some happy student were now mostly evidenced by the dangerous shards of glass scattered on and along the base path of the east softball diamond. A closer examination revealed many older but similar splinters and rusting ink well caps, suggesting that the celebration of last June was not a random incident, but a tradition of long standing. With time, these annual graffiti-like splotches faded away but the glass splinters became a lasting characteristic of the school yard. A fall or serious stumble almost always resulted in a cut hand or knee. It was a school yard but this section was not an ideal place for fun and games.

Curiously, and notwithstanding the trash, this area always seemed to be the first place to lose its snow cover in the spring. In spite of its hazards, this seriously defiled and insignificant patch of dirt attracted all of the marble players who, without prior notice, always seemed to know just when they should bring their agate shooters. Even a brief winter chinook often saw the diehards converge on this diminutive shred of terra ferma. I was never much of a marble player but Alvin Shear, Rex Green, Verner Sanderson, and Gerald Knowlton could probably have become world champions.

Notwithstanding my unorthodox musical abilities, Miss White's second grade had been conquered and I now found myself in grade three. While there was a sadness in coming back from summer vacation, there was also a bit of excitement in moving up one row of desks. Also it was fun to see my school friends, most of whom had much to tell about their summer activities.

Few of us had really enjoyed a noteworthy summer but between ourselves, we could always exaggerate enough to make a few mundane events seem interesting. Blarney of this type always played well at recess but could never really make it in the classroom. Supposedly it was an attempt to become better acquainted, but in the course of breaking in a new schoolmarm, we were almost always expected to tell something about our summer vacation. There wasn't much to tell and since I never knew what to say, this introduction to a new year was always an embarrassment. After all, how could one spice up and make an adventure out of picking saskatoons in Anton Sorensen's coulee. Even worse, what would the teacher think if my most exciting event of the past summer was going with Dad to the Rockyford Hutterite colony to buy a new boar?

True to form, Miss Pitcher, my grade three teacher, initiated the new year by requesting that each student provide a narration covering a special summer incident or activity. Wow! I could hardly wait to hear all the humbug that was sure to ensue. For my part, there were only a few choices that would pass muster as a suitable recital. Telling about the sleep over with the Holm kids or my first ever visit to a dentist would have been true but neither seemed appropriate.

The stories started with the grade one class and by the time the grade twos were spinning their yarns, you would have thought that everyone was either a millionaire or Hitler's most fearsome enemy. The embellishments were incredible but more importantly, these stories of grandeur and false heroics gave me time to think and to develop a few ideas.

In the end, I decided to tell about our victory garden. It was mostly about our almost famous strawberry patch which as far as anyone could tell had nothing to do with victory. It had been an astonishing source of strawberries during the summer just past and as testimony, countless friends and neighbors had been invited to participate in its bountiful harvest.

Actually, the idea of calling our plot of berries a victory garden was just a lucky last minute thought. Adding this patriotic touch gave my otherwise blah chronicle a lot of needed hoopla. It was the only liberty that I took with an otherwise totally true story, but giving it this popular characterization pushed it into the acceptable column. Indeed when I had completed my turn, it was almost possible to believed that our strawberries would help defeat Hitler.

We will never know who popularized the idea of a victory garden but it suddenly became very fashionable to have one. Country gardens like ours would have existed with or without a war but that was not the case for cities, towns and villages. Here in the shadow of skyscrapers and crowds, empty lots were pressed into service as growing fields for fruits and vegetables. In England, some of the most heavily bombarded areas sported gardens amongst and between the piles of rubble left by the German bombs. Here in our country, many narrow strips of soil between fences and gravel lanes were filled with a row or two of potatoes or carrots. Also, the eager gardeners frequently planted and harvested vegetable crops on empty city lots. In most cases the rightful owner never complained since growing garden crops anywhere and everywhere was considered an assist to the war effort. Also, a well cared for row of beans beat a weed patch any day. Whether the gardens were of any real use in our fight with Germany and Japan is of some doubt but they certainly provided the home front with a feeling of worthwhile participation.

Referring to our strawberry patch as a Victory Garden turned out to be a political coup that only lasted until Miss Pitcher got to the grade fours. As it happened, Gerald Knowlton had enjoyed a summer which included a lengthy trip to Nova Scotia. His story about the venturesome train ride and the truly delightful sights of Annapolis Valley was easily the best yarn of the day and took all of the steam out of my berries.

Here, some three thousand miles away, were countless apple orchards, capable of feeding hundreds of hungry sailors and soldiers. Furthermore, the land described by Gerald had a history dating back to 1497 and John Cabot. When the teacher started talking about that, my story had no chance of journalistic survival. How could it, the strawberry plants on our farm were only three years old.

****

It turned out that grade three was filled with a whole host of interesting experiences and unlike grade two, I actually found myself enjoying school. Miss Pitcher was most pleasant and was much more forgiving whenever we were late, which was still quite often. Also Mr. Malcolm had joined the Air force and our new principal was Mr. Bragg. He was much less severe and meeting him in the hall was no longer a fearsome trauma.

While Miss Pitcher had a music program, it was less emphasized and was more or less confined to our Friday afternoon Red Cross meetings. By this time everyone thought that we were winning the war and these less formal programs usually degenerated into a rousing singsong during which time we learned and sang a whole litany of popular and patriotic tunes.

Occasionally we would revert to the old standbys, "There'll Always Be An England" and "Land of Hope and Glory," but more often than not, we were learning and singing new wartime ditties.

Shortages were becoming a part of everyday life and even Louie Hong in Cluny was running out of hard to get merchandise. The one exception was music, which in the spirit of patriotism, seemed to be growing in importance. Musicians and composers never had it so good and our Red Cross meetings enjoyed a tremendous repertoire to work with. Almost every week saw a new tune on the radio hit parade and if we missed it there, we were sure to get it during a Friday meeting. Only a few names come to mind but these were most assuredly catchy tunes and to this day I can still recall the spirited, feel good melodies of our nationalistic war songs.

"We'll Meet Again"
"Keep the Home Fires Burning"
"I'll Be Seeing You"

"White Cliffs of Dover"
"When the Nightingale Sang in Barkley Square"
"Praise the Lord and Pass the Ammunition"
"When Johnny Comes Marching Home"
"Coming In On a Wing and a Prayer"

New compositions were the favorites but several tunes were reinvented from a past era and given new life in Miss Pitcher's music program." We're Gonna Hang Out Our Washing On The Siegfried Line" and "It's A Long Way To Tipperary" are two old tunes that were first heard during World War I.

Red Cross meetings were intended to engender a sense of patriotism and national pride. With this as the primary motive, we didn't often have the opportunity to sing songs that were without a spirited wartime mood. Happily, after a good deal of begging, Miss Pitcher frequently allowed some freedom and the class would be permitted to vocalize a few of the many popular but politically benign hits that were filtering into the airwaves. They must not have been too bad since to this day I can still recall some of the words and melodies of these popular hits.

"Don't Fence Me In"
"Chattanooga Choo Choo"
"Don't Get Around Much Anymore"
"Taking a Chance On Love"
"Chickery Chick"
"I've Got a Gal in Kalamazoo"
"Paper Doll"
"Accentuate the Positive
"As Time Goes By"
"Sentimental Journey"
"Pistol Pakin' Mama"
"Stormy Weather"

"Mairzy Doats"

On reflection, it is likely that Miss Pitcher worked the secular non military hits into the program so that she could listen to Verner Sanderson sing. Verner, who was then in grade four, had developed a particularly fine singing voice. No doubt it was a gift from birth but these patriotic Red Cross meetings provided an excellent forum in which to employ and refine his talent .

We all enjoyed Verner's singing but when everyone's favorite, "Roll Out the Barrel" was on the agenda, our rollicking rendition could easily drowned out the magnificence of his clear young voice.

****

In 1859 John Palliser, a British explorer, was sent to Western Canada to determine the economic potential of its prairie land. His report back to London was most discouraging, making the claim that the treeless grasslands were an "arid plain, unfit for agriculture." While there have been intervals when Palliser's description was correct, Alberta and the Canadian west have continuously prospered from a substantial agricultural economy.

With completion of the coast to coast national railroad in 1882, cattle ranching quickly became the first of many viable enterprises which blossomed forth from these largely flat grass lands. Late in the nineteenth century original stock was driven north from the United States. These cattle drives gave impetuous to ranching for a few hardy but scattered entrepreneurs who could tolerate the harsh and primitive existence that those early years demanded.

Later, with the arrival of countless settlers from Europe and the United States, wheat farming took over as the principal revenue producer. Indeed, when the railroad first reached Standard, Western Canada's annual wheat production had already exploded to nearly a quarter of a billion bushels, well up from less than thirty five million, some twelve years earlier at the turn of the century.

By any definition, the Standard community was a typical grain economy and certainly Dad's modest spread of 320 acres was no exception. Wheat was the cash crop and until 1940 when the pig barn was built and a lively hog operation was initiated, our well being had been determined by wheat yields and wheat prices. Happily, Dad's pork business provided a diversity that offered protection from both inclement weather and the general vagaries of the grain market.

The pig business changed all of that and to satisfy their ravenous appetites, a sizable portion of each years field crop was fed to the squealing swine herd. Feeding them was not easy and demanded a tremendous effort on Dad's part as he spent hours each day tending to this continuously expanding enterprise. If he wasn't grinding feed, he was cleaning pens. And if he wasn't cleaning pens he was busy repairing them. In short, raising pigs for the market was a strenuous and time consuming job. It would have been much easier if Dad had taken the easy path and confined his farming to the less complicated business of grain production. Had he not accepted the extra work and worry of hog production, our circumstances would certainly have been more tenuous and definitely much less pleasant. As a beneficiary, I will forever be grateful to him for his resourcefulness, diligence, and steadfast commitment to the well-being of our family. His effort and hard work were a priceless act of love, which Mother , Irene, and I can never begin to repay.

Our family owes much to all of the sausages, bacon and pork tenderloin that was produced during those years. To this day I feel compelled to genuflect whenever I pass by the bacon rack at Safeways.

****

During the winter and spring of 1943, the pig barn was full and there was hardly a week when Aage Nielsen and his truck were not hired to haul a load of two hundred pound porkers to Calgary's Burns abattoir and packing plant. There still wasn't a lot of money but it is certain that there was some improvement in the family finances. This was evidenced when Mother and Dad initiated plans to replace the old house with something bigger and better. Planning a new home was not an unreasonable idea since the old habitation was either waiting to burn down in winter, or collapse into its caving wall dugout basement during the summer.

Its exact age was unknown, but it is likely that it had stood on its crumbling foundation for at least thirty years, making it one of the truly early homes of the Standard area. The outside cedar lap-siding had never seen a drop of paint and its grainy, sliver infested surface was weathered to a dark brown. The front lean-to shanty had fallen away from its original position, leaving an inch wide gap through which both rain and snow could enter. In this condition it offered little protection to the front door which opened directly into the kitchen and its sloping floor.

The shifting foundation and underpinnings had twisted and warped the entire building, leaving the door jambs askew and making it all but impossible to properly close any of the interior doors. It was truly an eyesore but equally important, Irene and I were growing up, making the need for more space a major priority. Nobody ever complained but a new house would sure be nice.

Throughout the winter evenings Mother and Dad could often be found at the kitchen table, busily planning and drawing the setup for our new home. With but a single kerosene lamp, a carpenter's square and some almost white wrapping paper from Fred Christensen's meat market, they scaled off plan after plan. Changes were made on a daily basis, only to be changed back to the original design a week or so later. Even Irene and I got into the act with suggestions and designs of our own. Our architectural skills were not very well developed but we had a lot of fun pretending to help.

Finally by spring, after the snow had turned to mud and the mud had turned to dust, Mother and Dad had agreed on a floor plan. The drawings were complete and both Irene and I were thrilled to see our very own rooms featured on the blueprint. Construction would take several months but this mattered little as the coming summer promised new learning experiences and some adventurous living for the whole family. We were all looking forward to it.

As time was of the essence, every warm day was important and used to full advantage. Well before school was out for the summer, the old house had been knocked down, a proper basement had been dug and the new foundation was set. Also our yard had taken on the appearance of a small campus with temporary living and storage facilities randomly scattered along the length of the corral fence.

During the construction phase, all of the furniture, clothes, dishes, bric-a-brac and for that matter, everything that had been in the old house was moved into an empty granary for storage. Our beds were in an adjacent granary which would serve as our bedroom for the summer.

Next to the granaries was Bedstefar's old cook car which would substitute as a kitchen and dining room. Dad had borrowed this rather grandiose chuckwagon which had in years past, been used to prepare and serve meals to crews of men that had worked for Bedstefar during harvest. In its heyday, it had been mounted on a steel wheeled running gear, thus allowing it to be hauled from harvest field to harvest field. Its long narrow length was now set on wooden skids which made it possible for Dad and his old John Deere to skid its exquisite but aging form into our yard where it could find a new life for the summer. In a way, it had been rescued from Bedstefar's south land spread where it had been abandoned. Its low interior was divided into two rooms, the smallest of which was a pantry with sufficient space for a large antiquated cook stove. The front, and largest room, was the dining area which came equipped with a large rough table and side benches that could accommodate a dozen workers at meal time. Also, next to the front entrance was a low counter that served as a washstand for cleaning up dirty faces and soiled hands.

In these less than elegant surroundings, we didn't anticipate many guests and since there was considerable space, Dad took the big battery radio out of storage and moved it into the cook car. Reception wasn't great but we could enjoy the soaps and Dad could tune into the daily CBC news.

Our quarters were adequate but became somewhat incommodious during the chill of a three day rain, or for that matter, a sudden afternoon shower. Undoubtedly, our situation would become downright uncomfortable if for some reason the building project was extended into late fall. Winter living in our temporary lodgings would be virtually impossible and doubtless this was of no small concern for Mother and Dad who were fully aware of the many potential problems that could slow construction. Fortunately, with the early start and the help of Chris Petersen, a qualified and experienced carpenter, there was every reason to believe that a late summer or early fall completion was a realistic target.

With surrender of the remaining German and Italian troops in North Africa and barring Hitler's development and introduction of a miraculous secret weapon, it was becoming clear that we had a reasonable chance of winning the war in Europe. Unfortunately, this only seemed to intensify the shortages of material in our part of the world. It was hard to imagine how a war on the other side of the globe could effect the availability of home grown lumber and Canadian manufactured building supplies. Cement had been difficult to obtain but somehow Dad managed to scrounge enough for the house foundation. With the exception of two prewar pallets still at Anton Rasmussen's Atlas Lumber Yard in Standard, new bricks were out of the question. To fill the need for the new chimney, those from the old house were carefully cleaned and salvaged. Irene and I volunteered to help with the task but as we were a bit careless with our banging and scraping our tenure was short lived. These fragile blocks were incredibly precious and each one that shattered during the cleaning process brought the whole building project dangerously close to a formal shut down and catastrophe. How could the new house be completed without a chimney?

As ordinary dimensional lumber was in short supply, most of the structural material and flint hard two by fours from the old house were saved and reused. Saving the lumber and rendering it reusable also provided a modest source for hard to get nails. Wanting to help, Irene and I banged thousands of ten penny nails into reasonably straight and useful construction connectors. Most turned out more or less like new but if they happened to have a slight bend, Chris Petersen didn't seem to mind. He had the unique ability of being able to steer even bent nails into place with but a few unerring blows from his hammer.

Throughout the summer Dad spent countless hours looking for and buying hard to get building materials. Having in mind the need for certain strategic items, there were certain shortages that made sense. As an example, all of Canada's plywood was being used in the production of the much heralded Mosquito Bomber. While this was the fastest airplane in the British Royal Air Force, it was made in Canada and built almost entirely of laminated wooden beams and plywood.

Mother would have liked a little plywood for her new kitchen cabinets but the war and Mosquito Bombers took precedence. In the end, she had to settle for improvised cupboards made of boxwood. Even these were a big improvement over the raw shelves that had graced her old pantry.

In defiance of the war and its imposed shortages, the house was nearing completion by harvest time. Finishing touches were still underway but by moving into the basement, Dad could redeploy our temporary storage and sleeping quarters for their intended purpose of grain storage.

Before the winter snows arrived, Mother was able to move all of her cooking utensils into her new kitchen and give up the not so luxurious pantry of Bedstefar's old threshing cook car. We were all thrilled with our new house. Irene and I were especially excited with our own rooms, where for the first time, we could enjoy the convenience of having our own space and storage for clothing and special paraphernalia.

While I reveled in having my own private domain, the hidden and truly unexpected legacy of the summer was the building knowledge that I acquired by watching Chris Petersen. Under my watchful but probably bothersome eye, he had fashioned a livable building from little more than a pile of wood, paper, bricks, glass, and some nails. In many ways it was like watching a birth and it had been a most fascinating experience. There were even brief moments when I seriously considered following in his footsteps with carpentry as a life long career. Although this did not come to pass, to this day I am seldom intimidated by the need to renovate or build some needed item. Working with wood is always enjoyable and there is little doubt that my keen interest in carpentry was spawned or at least titillated during the summer of 1943.

****

Returning to school in the fall was not a momentously happy event. Summer vacations were always more interesting and it was with great reluctance that I gave up my front row seat at the Chris Petersen construction show. There was of course a new teacher, so I had some hope of starting out without any nasty impressions that may have been held over from the year just past. Unfortunately, it didn't take long to develop a poor rapport with my new teacher since as usual, we were late almost every morning.

Indeed, fourth grade was worse than ever, since Arthur's bus route had been lengthened to accommodate the addition of Alton school, which like Craigantler, was now closed forever. This school closing added about eight kids to our bus load and everyone hoped that we would finally get a proper school bus. Presumably the war was responsible, but our transportation was even worse than had been the case during the previous year. With the first day of school we were all dismayed to see that the old bread wagon had simply undergone an augmentation. With what seemed to be the tail end of a similar bread wagon, a six foot section had been welded onto the back end. This added additional space but made the whole contraption look ridiculously unstable. The extended section protruded at least eight feet beyond the back wheels and gave one the impression that it could easily tip back, lifting the front wheels right off the road. To accommodate the growing numbers, the two long wooden slatted seats had simply been lengthened to fill the extended addition.

In the end, grade four was different and was made somewhat interesting by the fact that we were all introduced to pen and ink. Yes, it was true, we had finally arrived, and for the first time in our lives, we were each entrusted with a bottle of "Quink Blue Black Ink". Equally important, each student was provided with a wooden pen holder which held a nib that was as sharp as the edges of a Japanese toy. Working this setup took a fair bit of dexterity since the sharp nib was particularly delicate and if treated badly had a propensity to chatter and grind as it moved across the paper.

Speaking of paper, our class was no longer expected to scribble on the coarse gray paper with lines spaced three quarters of an inch apart. We fourth graders (the big kids in the room) were really "uptown" and were provided with narrow lined, slick, ink tolerant, paper scribblers.

No doubt about it, things were looking up. We had given up playing with multicolored plasticine during the year just passed, and now even the wax crayons were gone. As an alternative we graduated to a genuine eight color "Reeves" paint and brush set. With all of this new equipment things were bound to be different and they were.

First of all Miss McIvor, our new teacher, announced that we would no longer print our words but would write everything longhand. What a break. Maybe if my scrawl was bad enough, she wouldn't notice my poor spelling.

My reasoning may have been a bit muddy but I had noticed that the letters received from some folks like Uncle John M, were virtually unreadable. With a garbled handwriting, who could check the spelling for errors? There probably weren't any, but Uncle John's letters could easily have had spelling mistakes and no one would be the wiser. With luck, my penmanship could develop into a nearly unreadable hieroglyphic and Miss McIvor would never learn of my spelling deficiency.

Unfortunately, my carefully contrived strategy did not work out. For starters, "longhand writing" was a key subject and the quality of my work was severely graded. A sloppy effort always guaranteed a rewrite. Even an occasional ink splatter made my writing exercises unacceptable and it soon became clear that poor penmanship couldn't hide my sorry spelling.

Exacerbating the problem, Miss McIvor decided that we would have frequent spelling bees. These horrific episodes involved most of the students and took the form of a competition. Two captains were selected, who in strict rotation, chose their respective team players from the ranks of grade two, three and four. As you would expect, the captains were looking for good spellers and the first pick was always Miriam Nielsen. To my great embarrassment I was usually the last pick, often chosen after the grade two and three classes were depleted.

I absolutely hated these humiliating competitions but got some satisfaction when I was often the first selected for a game of recess softball. As I recall, this was not Miriam's strong suit and if she found these softball matches a bit distressing, she will appreciate my attitude toward the spelling bees.

****

Having survived the indignity of the spelling bees and word games it was once again winter carnival time and an opportunity to dress up in some absurd way. Actually few if any of the boys my age wore a costume. Most of my friends wore sweaters featuring the colors and logos of their favorite N.H.L. club. An everyday school jacket did it for me.

Although I would have given my eye teeth for a hockey sweater, Mother and Dad made it clear that anything resembling a uniform needed to be earned. This could only come about by learning the nuances of hockey and making a team. That wasn't likely to happen soon but my skating skills were showing a modicum of improvement with each passing year. Dad had flooded a section of our yard, making a small but very useful skating rink on which Irene and I could practice. We skated almost every day and our skills were improving with every week of winter. Unlike our first winter carnival, when we could barely skate beyond the smell of the coffee brewing in the rink's skate shack, we were now very comfortable on the ice. No doubt about it, having our own ice on which to practice gave Irene and me a tremendous lift, and allowed us to catch up with our village friends who had daily access to the ice rink in town.

Our own personal rink was not large and this may have been an advantage in developing a knack for negotiating a spin or a short turn. Equally important, there were no boards to hang onto and we quickly learned to skate without the benefit of such a crutch.

No one will ever deny the importance of practice as a vital element in learning to skate or play hockey, but so is equipment. In anticipation of growth, most kids of my era were stuck with skates that fit improperly and were often several sizes too large. It didn't cost a great deal to trade skates, but whatever the price, it was always cheaper to wear them for several years if possible. To fill the void of a boot several sizes too large, two or three pairs of socks were often required. This sloppy fit guaranteed a bad case of ankle bends and often left me wondering if I was skating or simply walking on my ankles.

Happily, by the time I was in grade four my skates fit rather well and moving around the ice was no longer a particular problem. Adding to the fun, I had a stick which allowed me to practice ragging a puck around our small rink. While still in my formative years with a lot to learn and a long way to go, it was easy to fantasize about becoming a great hockey star. Really, the whole business of chasing a puck and shooting it into a snow bank was amazingly simple when there was no one there to oppose my efforts.

As a regular listener to Saturday night's "Hockey Night In Canada," my interest in the game was flourishing. This radio broadcast, sponsored by Imperial Oil Company, featured Foster Hewett as the play-by-play commentator and his between period colleague, Wes McNight. Both were experts at their craft and gave tremendous zest and color to the Maple Leaf games. With such a diet of hockey from Toronto, it is not surprising that I became an avid Maple Leaf fan, making them my favorite of the six teams then in the National Hockey League.

I took pride in knowing the entire Toronto team and their individual statistics. For me the voice of Foster Hewett was terribly important as it brought my heroes activities right into our living room. There was great sorrow when they lost and tremendous elation when they won.

Adding to this radio excitement, Quaker Oats box tops were carefully saved as each one could be returned to the company and was good for one scribbler sized picture of a National Hockey League player. Although the bottoms were identical to the tops, I scrupulously discarded them as counterfeit, assuming that I would most certainly be arrested if any attempt was made to use them for hockey pictures.

My diligence at honesty may have been commendable but eating and encouraging the whole family to eat oatmeal just so I could get pictures of my hockey heroes was in itself a criminal act. I was never so charged and in the end managed to collect three of these prized photos. For a good number of years pictures of Babe Pratt, Gay Stewart, and Syl Apps graced the wall over my bed. If you listened to Foster Hewett, for even a short time, you were sure to become familiar with these giants of the game.

Years later in my adult life, I was given the choice of watching the Maple Leafs with Foster Hewitt from his private broadcast booth or attend a play at Toronto's O'Keefe Centre. I carelessly chose the play. As I write this, I can only plead temporary insanity.

****

Finally, and apparently after months of planning and subterfuge, the Allies landed on the beaches of Normandy. Just two days before "D Day," I had celebrated my tenth birthday and while that was exciting, it was nothing compared to the fearful expectations that went with this new theater of war. These beach landings and their early triumphs were an elixir for the entire school and within a few days even we grade fours were familiar with the French names of Cherbourg, Caen and the Cotentin Peninsula.

Everyone was happy with what seemed to be the beginning of the end for the vicious Nazi Regime, but the threat of a secret German weapon was a growing and nagging concern. Imagination knows no bounds and before classes were finished for the summer, some of the kids claimed to have knowledge of invisible killer rays or exotic toxins, that with a single blast, could destroy all of the invading force. Others, even more pessimistic,were asserting that German forces were falling back and allowing an allied beachhead simply to ensure a maximum kill. This was scary stuff and certainly left me with an uneasy feeling.

Giving credence to my own suspicions and youthful concerns about these horrific killer rays and invisible weapons of mass destruction were Henry Dam's collection of comic books. Henry had a tremendous number of these ten cent masters of adolescent authority whose authors had unparalleled creativity for the bizarre.

In Henry's comics "Captain Marvel," the fearless hero of many nearly believable epics, was forever risking life and limb as he discovered and destroyed these gruesome exterminators and their loathsome captains of death. With his strength and daring he could easily outwit the Germans and their spine chilling tools of destruction. We of course knew that there was no Captain Marvel but had every reason to believe that some of these unspeakable killers of mankind could in fact be invented, thus leaving us with the fear that the allied success on the battlefield could be reversed with one giant swish. While I always enjoyed the patriotism of Henry's comic books, they failed to answer the real question of how to deal with an Axis secret weapon should one come along.

Fortunately, by midsummer the Allied beachhead had expanded to embrace the entire Cotentin Peninsula and the troops were well on their way to the Seine Valley and Paris. With these advances against the enemy, my concerns about a doomsday device quickly diminished. In point of fact, I was much too involved with my new bicycle to be fussed with the war in Europe.

****

Shortages on the home front had become more and more a part of everyday living and bicycles were no exception. Although Dad and I had made a thorough and detailed search of every store in Calgary, there was not one bike for sale in the whole city. Even the dilapidated second hand stores along Ninth Avenue East produced negative results. Here, one sleazy proprietor claimed that for a small advance payment, he would have one for delivery the next day. That seemed to be a good idea but Dad wisely knew that any such deal would involve stolen merchandise. We left that tatty store and it's unscrupulous manager in a hurry.

Both Irene and I wanted a bicycle in the worst way. Peer pressure was mounting and at the very least we were anxious to have one available so that we could learn how to ride before having children of our own. Balancing on two wheels was an unsolved mystery that needed resolution before we grew much older.

Happily, Vernon Petersen, our next door neighbor, came to our rescue. For fifteen dollars we were able to buy a bike that he no longer needed and had more or less out grown. This priestly sum provided us with a truly terrific, freshly painted coaster brake two wheeler.

We were both pleased but since our new bicycle was styled for a boy, Irene found it a bit awkward. With this in mind, Dad continued his search for a ladies model. We were all delighted when by late summer, another used two wheeler was found and purchased from Lily Laursen. It was not in particularly good condition but for eleven dollars who could complain? More importantly, it allowed Irene and me to ride around without one of us having to ride on the cross bar.

We toured all over our yard and when the trail to the field was dry and packed down by tractor and car traffic we often ventured out to the potato patch, nearly a mile from home. Because freshly plowed soil is not bike friendly, it didn't happen often, but occasionally we made like Gunga Din, riding our bikes into the field with Dad's afternoon coffee. The half mile trip to the "Calgary Herald" newspaper drop at the five mile corner was almost a daily excursion. We used our bikes constantly and soon forgot our earlier embarrassment of not being able to pedal and balance a two wheeler.

With the passage of time, Irene and I used and took pleasure with our bikes in many different ways. I think it fair to say however that we both, more than any other, enjoyed the road south toward Alfred Petersen's farmstead. This rutted but dirt packed trail ventured past our pasture and a row of large poplars bordering the road on the opposite side. Going south against a slight grade required continuous pumping on the pedals. It was however, well worth the effort as coming back we could coast the entire half mile. If we didn't land a bee or gnat in one of our eyes, this long effortless slope going home was great fun. The ride was particularly agreeable in the twilight of evening as we passed through pockets of warm air mixed with the cool chill of the coming night.

The trip south was occasionally enhanced by a brief visit with our Petersen neighbors. In season, Edna almost always allowed us to fill our pockets with crab apples from their orchard. Also it seemed that she often had a cold drink of milk for us. Neither Irene nor I were big on milk but somehow a drink poured from Edna's pitcher with multicolored spots always seemed especially tasty. Best of all, it was invariably cold, a clear tribute to Alfred's ice shed in which he kept large blocks of the stuff. These huge lumps were cut from a frozen pond in winter and housed in the shed under a large mound of sawdust. In this environment the large blocks would stay frozen and tolerate even the warmest of summers.

We didn't have an ice shed and while we could chill milk and other things in a tub of freshly pumped water, it was never quite as cold as that made possible by an honest lump of ice. In actual fact, our single cow was usually dry during the summer leaving us with little more than canned "Carnation Milk," a very poor substitute. Irene and I hated the taste and never used it but Mother and Dad always spiked their coffee with a few drops of this incredibly vile counterfeit. To this day I will never understand how anyone can enjoy a cup of coffee that has been messed up with canned milk.

A few years ago the memory of the ice and milk was given new life when Edna presented me with the milk pitcher having the multicolored spots. In years past it had rested over the Petersen's kitchen table on a narrow clock ledge. Today this memento of pleasant childhood interludes graces a shelf in my library.

****

With each passing year, personal hygiene became more and more awkward and even at times, just plain hazardous. To be sure, soap and water were in good supply and always available but growing bigger made the old galvanized tub less and less comfortable. Happily, summer irrigation brought on an all too brief period of relief from the brutal and crippling position required for a bath in a laundry tub. No, it wasn't the muddy canal that provided the ambiance of a cleansing dip. In fact, a visit to a regular irrigation canal was certain to leave one worse off in a "before and after" comparison. Fortunately, such was not the case for the irrigation spillway, which was a mere seventy yards from our house. This summer respite from the tub, being almost directly across the road in Deschamps's field, was truly a delight. Having access to a healthy flow of clear water during the irrigation months allowed me to dispense with the tub for most of the summer.

This irrigation channel, designed to carry off excess water, ran exactly parallel to the municipal roadway which passed by our farm. In doing so, there were several portions of the ditch which traversed a rather steep grade. To avoid disastrous erosion, the sections which traversed a steep grade or high slope were lined with wooden planks. Even better, all of the severe elevation changes were taken up with large box-like structures which allowed the water to cascade down onto a wooden deck. These man-made waterfalls not only prevented erosion in the ditch, they allowed the water to flow in such a way that almost all of the suspended solids could settle out, thus leaving a pristine stream almost clear enough to drink. More importantly, these erosion controlling sluice boxes offered a most inviting spot to scrub off some of the grime that inevitably came with a day at play or work.

As much as I enjoyed the small waterfalls for a good cleansing shower, nothing compared to the wooden flume that carried the water down the last hill immediately north of our farmstead. Here, one could sit on a two by four cross member and allow the rushing stream to hit with such a force that a single foot in the torrent could splash shining drops to a height of several feet.

Dangling a foot or two into the rushing water was a supreme summer sport but doing so was fraught with considerable risk. This fact was painfully learned one hot July afternoon when after a robust game of cops and robbers, Cousins Fred and Lars Holm and I decided that we needed to cool off. The fix was a simple matter and it wasn't long before we were each sitting on a cross member, comfortably positioned over the rushing water of the flume. Having rolled up our pant legs, we quickly removed our shoes and socks and plopped our feet into the violently flowing stream some twenty inches below. Not only did the speeding current feel good on our feet, the ensuing spray soon dampened and cooled our cotton shirts.

While the stream was probably less than four inches deep, the planks on which it flowed were as slippery as an August watermelon seed. This combined with the speed and force of the water made it absolutely essential that one should not try to stand up or attempt to enhance the splash zone with fancy footwork. I tried, but in less than a heartbeat, a seemingly simple foot maneuver made me a full partner of the rampaging stream en route to a small four foot waterfall some thirty to forty feet downstream. To this day, I have no idea where the blow to my nose occurred but it could have been any of several cross members which made solid contact with my schnozzle as I hurtled past. Bang! Did I ever see stars. Even the chill of the water did little to ease the pain and although I was momentarily knocked senseless, I was able to scramble out of the pounding water at the end of the flume where my banged up body had been unceremoniously dumped into a small wooden decked sluice box.

No doubt I went back to retrieve my shoes and socks but by the time I staggered back to the house for some sympathy and much needed TLC, I could hardly see. My bleeding nose had swollen to such a width that it eclipsed all but my most extreme side vision.

As expected, I lived and the swelling eventually subsided. In a week or so my two blackened eyes returned to normal but my broken and forever bent snout remains as a constant reminder that a laundry tub bath isn't all bad.

****

The war in Europe was nearing a crescendo and if the push to victory was to be maintained, it was absolutely essential that production of food stuffs and munitions be intensified. Almost every segment of the economy was involved and to optimize output, some people were virtually conscripted into specialized services. Less essential jobs were frequently discontinued with their freed up employees being redirected to new areas of activity that were related and essential to the war effort. Uncle Fred Andersen typified such a move as he changed employment from the quiet comfort of the Yale Hotel for the dirty, and noisy but more crucial C.P.R. repair shop in Southeast Calgary. Here in the clamor of a large foundry and machine shop, large deck guns were being built for the Canadian Navy.

Paradoxically, these home front efforts made it possible to get almost anything if it was deemed necessary for the production of essential war materials such as food and munitions. For this reason tractors were thought to be important and by claiming a need, Bedstefar had managed to get a new one in 1942. Unfortunately, the availability was not without limits and he had been obliged to accept one that was designed for row crops. The business of growing corn and cotton was well removed from the plains of Western Canada so it seemed a bit strange to have a tractor that looked like a giant tricycle.

Dad's twenty year old John Deere was due for retirement and after a good deal of persuasive documentation, a new Massey Harris was ordered. I had just started to help him with some of his field work but despite my best efforts, steering the old steel lugged John Deere, was beyond my abilities. This left me with less interesting tasks such as riding the binder and tripping the bundle rack at appropriate intervals. There was considerable hope that the new tractor would be a little more forgiving thus allowing me to graduate to the more interesting business of driving.

With the promise of such a promotion, I could hardly wait for our new tractor to arrive at Mons Hansen's Massey Harris agency in Standard. Rubber tires had been requested but with an almost critical rubber shortage, many farmers needing new equipment had been obliged to accept tractors with steel lugged wheels. While this was a worry, rear fenders were of equal concern. With steel needed for munitions production, domestic tractor factories were easily tempted to minimize its use and fenders were a good place to cut back. I was particularly anxious that our new tractor have proper full sized fenders.

When the big day finally came, the yard at Mons Hansen's agency sported three brand new bright red tractors. Two of these had steel wheels and one of those had modified fenders barely shielding the operator from the large rear wheels. Was I ever happy to learn that the one with rubber tires and proper fenders was scheduled to go to our farm.

With a bit of instruction from Dad, the intricacies of driving this new power source were quickly mastered. Steering was easy and with my leg fully extended I could adequately depress the clutch and shift gears. More importantly, the start up didn't require a crank or a spin of the fly wheel so by summers end, I was quite able to take Dad's place in the field, tilling the soil and occasionally hauling in a small load of straw for the pigs. I was quite proud of myself and found that driving a tractor was a new and interesting experience that within a few years, was sure to be an important asset in learning the nuances of handling an automobile. From Dad's perspective, the convenience of this new power source totally removed Diamond and Lady from the work force and their harness was seldom if ever used again.

****

Grade five proved to be somewhat of a bore even though there were a few things that contrasted from previous years. I had after all, graduated away from the little kids including their sand table and the ever present smell of plasticine and cheap glue. In my new room for the bigger kids, grades five to eight, the desks were not only larger, they were different. There was a book storage drawer under the seat instead of a small shelf under the desk top. Also, there was an armrest forcing everyone to enter the desk from the left side. This standardized arrangement leaves one to wonder if it was illegal to be a south paw. In most classes these larger desktops had an array of initials carved into their varnished surfaces. This made writing a bit difficult but encouraged me to certify my tenure in the class with a similar notation. It would certainly be embarrassing if these carved relics are still in use.

More importantly, this year saw the last of the country schools with the result that almost all classes at Dana showed some modest expansion. With the closing of South Valley School, Arthur Klemmensen, my friend from Sunday School, joined my class as did Wayne Willson, who had previously attended Long Beach School. I don't ever recall visiting this latter institution but the name has always intrigued me. Presumably a native from the unlikely village of Summit Saskatchewan provided the label. Certainly it took a sense of humor since there isn't a drop of water for miles and for sure there are no nearby beaches.

While not a school closing casualty, I also gained a new grade four friend with the arrival of Philip Jorgensen. Philip, a real preacher's kid, was the son of Reverand Marius Jorgenssen who in late summer took over the pastoral duties of our church. Prior to this Standard assignment, the Jorgensen family had lived in Brooklyn, New York and Brush, Colorado. With such a prestigious background, Philip was encyclopedic with his knowledge of the Brooklyn Dodgers, a National League baseball team. We got together a fair bit and when we weren't looking for some leftover sacramental wine, we could usually be found playing catch and talking baseball.

****

By late winter it become more and more obvious that Germany was getting thrashed and that the war in Europe would soon be over. This of course assumed that the bad boys didn't suddenly come forth with a doomsday device capable of reversing the entire direction of battle. At school there was unabated patriotism and Red Cross meetings were diligently held each Friday. Miss Tricker, our teacher, insisted that we view most of the news reels that were being shown to the High School classes. With the help of these nearly weekly showings everyone was fully aware of the situation. Curiously, in spite of these telling picture reels, there were still a few skeptics who truly feared that the Krauts would miraculously find a way to throwback the allied advances and avoid defeat.

At the time of President Roosevelt's death in April, all doubts had vanished and even the most worried of the pessimistic were obliged to concede that victory was at hand, and that Germany's Third Reich was kaput. There were still a few dangerous lose ends to tidy up but the USSR armies were closing in on Berlin from the east while troops from the United States, Canada and Great Britain were well into Germany on the west. With each passing day the allied forces were moving ever closer to the domain of the Reichstag.

Everyone was pleased, including most of the German prisoners of war that were scattered throughout our community. Like everyone else, they could easily anticipate the outcome and even with defeat, they knew that they would soon be sent home to their loved ones.

For the most part, these young Germans were a total surprise to me. They were not at all like the cruel and ugly cutthroats depicted in Henry's Dam's comic books. Most were from an agricultural background, and seeking to alleviate the tedium of a prison camp, they had volunteered to work on selected farms throughout Western Canada. In total, there were probably ten to fifteen such POWs in the Standard area.

They were easily identified by their blue denim clothes and the large red dinner plate sized patch located on the back of their outer garments. Technically, it was illegal for any prisoner to cover this patch with unauthorized clothing. Some did when their thin jackets proved inadequate for the biting cold of winter. Also on occasion, a host farmer would bring his prison worker to church in a borrowed sports coat. In these rare situations the red target identification was totally obscured.

While some of the prisoners remained on various farms for many months, I am unaware of any escape attempts. There were however a few young men who were quickly returned to their camps when they became a bit over zealous about their German heritage. At the time, they didn't have much to brag about.

Almost without exception the prisoners were skilled at various crafts. Some could paint, some could build toys, others would make ornamentation and jewelry out of everyday items such as toothbrush handles, coins, nails and strips of cardboard. Almost all were enamored with ships in bottles. It is probable that every farmer who enjoyed the service of a POW had a shelf somewhere in his home, displaying a three masted schooner in a wine flask.

While we had no need for a prisoner at our farm, Leo Larsen's German captive shared with me the mystery of corking a boat inside a bottle. For a time nearly every narrow necked flask around our house contained a small galleon with enormous sails.

As a final legacy, it is likely that the POWs interaction with the good people of Canada helped Germany at least partially restore its shattered image and reputation. There was certainly no love lost on any Kraut but with time, nearly everyone accepted the detainees as normal humans of good character. Certainly from my perspective, their presence in our community was incredibly worthwhile. It became very clear to me that these young men were not the real enemy and were simply trying to make the best of a bad situation. No doubt their fears and frustrations varied little from the Canadian troops who were fighting in their homeland.

****

The war in Europe finally started to moderate with the German troops in Italy formalizing a surrender on the second day of May. The following day, enemy field commanders sought truces in Holland, Denmark and northern Germany. Axis forces soon capitulated in other sections and by the seventh of May, all hostilities ceased. No one knew it then, but Adolph Hitler had taken his own life a few days earlier and was nowhere to be found.

Even though the outcome had been expected for several weeks, the final victory brought relief and tumultuous jubilation throughout the western world. Dad virtually wore down the battery in the old radio as he listened to all of the commentary and hoopla. To celebrate this momentous and historical event, plans were quickly put in place to ensure that the very next day (VE Day) would be a day to remember. Irene and I expected something special and were more than a little disappointed to learn that as usual, we were expected to board the bus and go to school. Upon our arrival, we quickly learned that regular classes were not contemplated and trying to accomplish anything in the classroom would be hopeless. There were in fact big plans for merrymaking.

Time has robbed the memory of every event but it is known and well remembered that the whole school gathered together for what seemed to be the equivalent of a giant Red Cross meeting. Clara Andersen played the piano as we sang a whole host of patriotic songs. The program finished with "Land of Hope and Glory" and a thunderous applause which was further enhanced by a whole lot of shouting and gleeful screams. In normal circumstances, such clamorous behavior would have triggered an immediate disciplinary response but on this happy occasion, none was forthcoming.

After lunch and free ice cream, we all marched off to the old S and S Hall, where for free, we saw a movie starring Alan Ladd. It was not a great movie but on short notice no one complained.

En route to the hall everyone carried a flag representing one of the victorious nations. There were Stars and Stripes, Union Jacks, Red Ensigns along with many other hastily gathered banners. As we marched through the center of town toward the hall, I proudly carried the red and yellow Soviet Hammer and Sickle. It was hand made and only ornamented on one side but silhouetted in the bright midday sunshine, there was no doubt that it was the standard of the USSR. I sure hope that no one took my picture with what has now come to be the symbol of a despicable and immensely cruel society.

****

As you might expect, absolutely everyone was thrilled with the armistice but it is hard to imagine the feeling of deliverance that must have come over the kids whose dads were overseas. It was probably a bit unusual but our school bus served no less than four families whose fathers were in the military and all of whom had been in harms way. There were Gordon and Collin Grant, Hugh and Dean Stickle, George and Fay Collins and Charlie Dankwerth, each of whom could now look forward to their dad's safe return. What a relief!

Although Canada actually declared war on Japan several hours ahead of the United States, there were not large numbers of Canadians in the Pacific. To be sure there were a few troops involved, but as there were none from our community, World War II was for me, essentially over. Besides, the Americans were pushing the Japs back and the outcome of this conflict was no longer in serious doubt. There was however, the certainty that a stubborn Japanese campaign could still result in thousands of casualties.

Paradoxically, it was the Japanese that brought the war directly to our community. While there is some uncertainty with the exact date, the spring of 1944 saw a desperate attempt by the Japanese to turn the tide of the war and establish a semblance of victory. To achieve this, they set lose a large number of balloon bombs which were allowed to drift across the Pacific by way of the prevailing winds. It is hard to imagine the intent of these devices but it is generally assumed that they were expected to ignite the forests of North America into a giant fire storm. Each one had an incendiary bomb that dangled below the gas filled carrier. To my knowledge no such conflagration ever occurred but one of the disarmed and deflated balloons found itself tangled in a telephone line some dozen miles east of our farm. For purposes of national security, the local Mounties tried to retrieve it but with nearly everyone seeking a souvenir from its heavy rice paper hide, the cops hardly got to see it. In actual fact, it is known that at least one farmer lined a grain storage bin and covered a chicken house roof with this tough, seemingly indestructible paper. Had they known, the Japs would most certainly have been unhappy with such an outcome.

It was early August when finally the world became aware of a real honest to goodness doomsday device. I doubt that I will ever forget the news bulletin which announced the bomb attack on Hiroshima.

Two days later we were with the Lars Rasmussen gang, enjoying the annual family picnic at St. George's Island. There was the usual midsummer Infantile Paralysis scare but this got little attention compared to the atomic bomb. Uncle Edward was particularly intrigued with the reports of devastation but like everyone else, he knew very little about nuclear energy. While we were prattling and enjoying the ambiance of a sunny day at the park, it was already August the ninth in Japan. Unbeknown to us, a second and equally destructive bomb was dropped on Nagasaki. This last and final demolition of a Japanese city brought the otherwise unrelenting and stiff necked antagonists to their knees. A few days later they reluctantly accepted the terms of an unconditional surrender. A formal armistice was signed on the second of September, 1945.

Some aspects of the Hitler, Mussolini, Hirohito menace predated my birth. I had endured their threats and had been alarmed by their intimidation's for most of my life but now at last they were out of action. The wars were over and the unfamiliar peace made for a very pleasant change. For some stupid reason, my first thoughts were of concern for the news commentators. How would Lorne Greene and other radio luminaries fill the time allotted for the news? How on earth could they talk about noteworthy events without a war to report on?

As it happened, it almost seemed that the war was still underway when the allied occupation forces began the formidable task of bringing vast numbers of war criminals to justice. The Nuremberg trials began in late November and in some cases carried on until 1948. In the end it was determined that there were twenty two surviving officers of the Third Reich that were required to answer for their sins. The drama of these trials revealed the many atrocities that had been inflicted on innocent people, both in Germany and occupied territories. Upon completion of the trials, it was concluded that nearly six million Jews, Gypsies and revolutionaries had been exterminated in death camps scattered throughout Germany, Poland, Czechoslovakia, and France. In addition some six million dissident Germans had met a similar fate for failing to comply with Hitler's directives.

As you would expect, these stories of the Holocaust filled the radio news bulletins but if that wasn't enough, the home front offered equal billing. Almost everything was in short supply and with a growing number of returning service men seeking new homes, cars, clothes and all manner of consumer goods, these shortages were exacerbated to the point of becoming a national disaster. The government was beset with complaints which took up as much space in the news as had the war itself. Adding to the problem, every auto worker in Canada and The United States decided that it would be a good time to ask for higher wages. News of labor strife and strikes filled the airwaves and for a brief period, normalizing our society seemed nearly impossible. Now with all of that, why was I feeling sorry for the news commentators?

With the war won, it should have been easy to regain some semblance of regularity, but with our overall economy in such turmoil that didn't come easy. Indeed, even the speed of change accelerated from a comfortably slow walk to a hectic unprecedented gallop. This was certainly evident in Calgary where a rapid transformation was underway with hundreds of new homes being built for returning military personnel. To this day, the city center and the surrounding environs are easily discernible by the layout of these distinctive post war homes that donut-like, encircle and define the urban area as it existed in 1945.

I had the sense that nothing would ever be the same again and in many ways that was a very pleasant thought. For starters, almost everyone believed that the world would never again be at war. However, should that ever happen, there were scores of inventions and innovations that would forever mutate the way wars of the future would be fought. Apart from the atomic bomb, which was totally awesome, there was radar, aircraft carriers, jet airplanes, rockets, automatic rifles, armor piercing ammunition, and deep water submarines, to name but a few of the new gadgets designed to kill people with more efficiency. With these newfangled tools of annihilation, who in their right mind would ever again risk a war? Moreover, having just seen some fifty five million people killed from 1939 to 1945, almost everyone was praying that the horror and memory of it all would be a lasting deterrent. Finally, with most of the perpetrators in Nuremberg being tried and convicted for their war crimes, it was expected that all future conflicts would be ironed out over a conference table at the new United Nations. I was very smug and felt good about the peaceful society which I now shared with all Canadians.

****

The legacy of the war manifested itself in many ways. There were of course inventions of mass destruction but there were also a large number of developments and ideas that played a beneficial role to all of humanity.

Everyone hated the shortages but there is little doubt that the deficiencies brought on by the war generated much of the inventiveness and social modifications that transpired during those years. Labor shortages brought women into the work force. Fuel shortages promoted many conservation practices including the need and acceptance of daylight saving time. To save a few inches of hard to get fabric, cuffs on men's trousers fell out of favor as did the wasteful notion of annual motor vehicle registration with two brand new steel license plates.

There were of course genuine inventions such as penicillin, synthetic rubber, and nylon. With the possible exception of plastic, which could be molded into an incredible number of affordable shapes, nothing compared to the ball point pen. This clever little stylus was the genius of a Nazi Hungarian inventor, Ladislao Biro, who designed and created it as a commendation for members of the Gestapo and S.S. It was to be their reward for loyal services to the Fuhrer. Apparently Hitler was delighted as the pen promised a perpetual ink supply, supposedly lasting for the lifetime of each recipient. That of course proved to be a false pledge for members of the Gestapo and S.S. who were in fact, special police and Nazi party members having their origins in the "Reichssicherheitshoauptamt, Sturmabteilunger and Sicherheitsdierst. Wow! Those names certainly explain the need for an acronym but should one of their members have need to write the whole mess, a lifetime ink supply would most assuredly be a necessity.

During the war, thousands of these pens were handed out, but with the allied victory, hundreds were thrown away by their owners. They were of course all trying to obscure their association and wartime identity with these cruel and tyrannical organizations. For many who were not smart enough to rid themselves of the evidence, they may in fact have been given a life time supply of ink.

In Standard, ball points became available sometime in late 1946. And as you might expect, they were advertised as life long, with the claim that each could role a line from Vancouver to Halifax. As I recall they were very expensive, each being approximately twenty dollars. Harold Larsen, who having traded his farm for his brother Leo's store, used one to write out grocery bills and was undoubtedly one of the first persons in our community to have one.

Everyone was fascinated with this new writing tool but when the Standard community honored the returning servicemen, at the old S and S Hall, each was given a Parker fountain pen. Parker pens and pencils are still expensive but befitting the defunct Gestapo, the much improved ball point can now be purchased for about nineteen cents.

In addition to the many innovations and useful inventions, there were also an assortment of entrepreneurial endeavors, some of which grew into lasting concerns. Even our own community saw one of the returning veterans start a daily bus service from Standard to Calgary. It didn't survive but clearly illustrates the many admirable attempts at new ventures.

While not a veteran of combat, Uncle Fred gave up his noisy position at the Calgary Ogden Shops for a run down coffee shop in Claresholm. Within weeks he and Aunt Karen had restructured it into a thriving business and one of the favorite restaurants between Calgary and the U.S. Border.

****

No one will deny that the war helped rid the world of the worst economic depression of modern times. Everyone prospered during the years of conflict and there was a general feeling of well being. Even I had an allowance of two dollars a month and felt relatively rich. With chocolate bars a dime and Pepsi Cola still a nickel, two bucks was a small fortune.

Although Magnus's Pool Hall and his ice water chilled Pepsi Cola was no longer off limits, I was as tight as a bullfighter's pants and seldom bought candy or pop. Instead, I decided to save my modest fortune. Even better, my entrepreneurial spirit had been kindled and felt certain that my allowance could be parlayed into even greater wealth. With such grandiose expectations, I sent off to Winnipeg for twelve dollars worth of carrot seed. This heady amount bought four pounds and thats a lot of carrot seed.

Having thoroughly mixed these almost invisible specks with about fifty pounds of dry sand, the resulting dry mix and its diminutive carrot seed hitchhikers were carefully spread into five long rows next to Mother's potato and vegetable garden.

I was delighted when my cash crop popped out of the ground but soon realized that my four pounds of seed could easily have covered an entire acre. No doubt, the good people at Great Western Seed Company in Winnipeg are still wondering why anyone would want four pounds of carrot seed. Despite my efforts to dilute and spread these minuscule kernels in a sand mix, my crop had the appearance of a young but robust hedge.

I thinned and weeded throughout the summer and in the end a reasonable crop ensued. Unfortunately, the need for carrots was somewhat limited and my notion of flooding the Calgary market with fresh produce fizzled. As it turned out, my only market was Harold and Margaret's Red and White Store in Standard. Clearly they felt sorry for me and bought several large sacs of these delightful garden fresh roots.

My carrots looked terrific until they were on display next to some nice clean veggies that probably came from the

Okanagan. My little Vitamin A dandies had been harvested during a rather wet fall and a fair bit of Dad's farm traveled with them to the market in Harold's store.

Memory fails on the exact profit but the twelve dollars were easily recovered and there was probably enough left over for a trip to the pool hall for a refreshing ice cold Pepsi.

THE INTERMEDIATE YEARS

The community of Standard was steeped in sports and has always enjoyed better than average athletic events and venues. Before my birth, Dad had been a member of the soccer team and reveled in many local triumphs. With the likes of Andy Hansen and Red Henry living in the area, even horse shoes was played to near perfection. All of this success isn't easy to explain but there is little doubt that the coal miners provided a core of athletes that made perpetual winners of the many local sports clubs.

With the war won and behind us, not only did we regain the potential for strong athletics, but many of the war's local veterans founded a new branch of the Canadian Legion. This quickly burgeoned into an important local organization which among other activities provided support for what might have been Standard's first ever junior hockey club.

To staff this new experiment and adventure in hockey, players were chosen from a group of eager but unskilled kids ranging in age from eleven to their late teens. As such it was not truly a junior club as the ages ranged through a whole spectrum of hockey levels. While I owned a hockey stick and had a keen interest in the game, my prowess as a player was sadly lacking. It is likely that my most important attribute was my age which happened to be eleven. In truth, it was my good luck that there weren't enough older and bigger kids who played the game. Put in simple terms, they needed me to fill a hockey sweater even if I was a sorry player.

It turned out that Dad had nearly been right when he insisted that one could earn a hockey uniform by learning a few skating and hockey skills. I say nearly, because he probably never thought that one could make a team simply because there weren't enough kids to fill the set. Anyway, after "try outs" which went on for several weeks, I was selected to join the team and given assurances that a uniform would be forthcoming when one became available. Making the team had been a total surprise but with this modest victory to gloat over, I could hardly wait for my first and very own team sweater.

A few weeks later, our school principal and hockey coach, Mr. Bragg, told us that the uniforms had arrived and would be distributed in his home room during the last recess of the day. I rarely had occasion to visit the second floor, but nothing could have kept me from this important meeting.

When I arrived upstairs the cloakroom was filled with team members, all unceremoniously bent over a large cardboard box that was standing on the floor right in the middle of the room. It contained several sizes of pullovers and after a good deal of trading and switching around, everyone found one that more or less fit. In due course I was handed what must have been the smallest one available. At first I was a bit disappointed as the supposed uniform was a very plain navy blue jersey. It looked like any other sweater since there wasn't a team logo or number to be seen. Later, when Mr. Bragg produced some saucer sized Canadian Legion emblems that were to be stitched on the front of each jersey, it became obvious that the sweaters were in fact, true uniforms. That helped a lot but the real "piece de resistance" came when he announced the numbers and handed them out to each team member.

Everyone received a number that was to be stitched to the back of his sweater. I was handed number nine, or was it a six? Surely the nine had to be a mistake as everyone knew the history of this number and it was certain that this, the "Holy Grail" of all hockey numbers, would be assigned to someone much more deserving. But yes, it must be true, because someone else was claiming the six. Finally, Mr. Bragg confirmed that I was to be number nine. Wow! Getting that number was akin to having a New York Yankee uniform with a three or four emblazoned on its back. Nine had been worn by so many great hockey players that most of the older National League teams had by then retired it from use. At the time Syl Apps, my favorite Toronto Maple Leaf, had the number on his jersey and to the best of my knowledge, it retired with him when he made his exit from the game.

At this writing, I suspect that Wayne Gretzky also knew the history of number nine but decided to better it with two nines giving that number momentum for an even greater legacy.

I certainly didn't deserve the nine but was ever so thrilled to have it and could hardly wait for Mother to sew it and the Legion emblem on my sweater. I made sure that she didn't get the number upside down.

****

Our team, still without a name, scheduled two hour practice sessions, three time a week. Missing a practice was a seldom event, but if it did happen, it was never Dad's fault. Throughout the winter he and the old 1930 Chev faithfully carried me to and from these late evening training and workout sessions. There was never a complaint from him but there was a lot of useful advice. Mr. Bragg coached and drilled the team on the ice for two hours, after which Dad offered his sometimes painful suggestions on the way home. If things hadn't gone well, he was sure to make things better with a few useful recommendations for the next practice.

It didn't take long to realize that my homemade shin pads were less than adequate and without any shoulder or elbow pads, I learned not to mix it up too much. Besides, being the smallest member of the team, agility often proved to be the better part of valor. The rudiments of the game such as shooting and stick handling were showing only modest improvement but by Christmas my skating was much stronger. More importantly, my Christmas presents included shin pads and some much needed hockey gloves for my banged up and bleeding hands. Also by this time I had learned how to avoid an intentional offside and knew enough to stay on my wing most of the time.

Our ragtag team didn't have a league affiliation so our games were sporadic events, announced with very little advance notice. There weren't a lot of so called junior hockey clubs nearby and as a consequence most of our games were with the Cluny Dormitory High School and on rare occasions, the Cluny Indian Mission. Whenever we played the Indians on their turf and with their referees, I knew how Custer must have felt at the Little Big Horn. Playing by the rules wasn't part of their agenda and curiously, they would never come to Standard where we could repay the favor.

It was several years before Strathmore and Rockyford offered a team for competition and Gleichen was out of the question as they had a truly outstanding hockey program with midget and junior teams. Their clubs were all of the proper age and to the best of my knowledge, fully occupied in a Southern Alberta B Class League. Over the years, the "Gleichen Gunners" always played superbly and have placed several players into the professional ranks, including the National Hockey League.

During this first year, I was a terrible hockey player and although our line failed to score a single goal, it was easy to fantasize that my day would come and that I would someday score the winning goal for the Toronto Maple Leafs during a Stanley Cup final. Believe me, if that was ever to happen, I had a lot to learn.

When spring finally arrived and the warm sun turned the ice rink into mush, we were all ready for it. Three weekly practice sessions mixed with a few sporadic games was becoming a drag. Hockey was fun but the almost inflexible routine that came with it was no longer enjoyable. It was having an adverse impact on my other social outlets such as missed birthday parties, family affairs and so on. The worst of these omissions was missing even a minuscule part of Dad's birthday party which always seemed to be in conflict with a hockey game.

****

Dad was born on January 8, 1899. His very good friend, Mons Hansen, claimed to be two days older, which led to a lot of good natured bantering between the two of them. Mons always pretended that Dad did not have enough respect for his elders, namely Mons. Who knows when it started but for years they both celebrated their birthdays with tremendous gusto.

Mons, who lived in town, was initially a grain buyer but eventually moved into the machinery and automobile business. Although known to be an excellent business man, Mons was equally well known as a trencherman extraordinary. To satisfy this discerning and well honed appetite, Mrs. Hansen, Marie, would prepare a birthday party food spread that would have done justice to a sultan. Mother and Dad always attended and knowing that many of the same people would be at our house within two days, Mother always prepared an equally sumptuous party for Dad.

Although my memory of these parties extends back to my very early years and the old house, time did little to change the many customs that went with this annual event. The Christmas tree always remained up until after the party and the cakes, cookies, and special sandwiches were always the best that Mother could provide. For the most part, the guests never varied and neither did the smoke that seemed to enter the house with them.

While in the hospital in 1938 for an appendectomy, Dad either couldn't or wouldn't smoke. After this lengthy hospital stay it seemed a good time to give up the habit. Although he had previously smoked like a train yard tender, Dad threw away his tobacco, matches, and roll your own paper during his convalescence. In spite of this, he was not at all critical of his many friends who smoked. Quite to the contrary, for along with Mother's wonderful baking and coffee, Dad supplied all of his birthday friends with cigarettes and cigars. You can't imagine what this did to our relatively small, tightly sealed and poorly vented house during a cold night in January.

While most smoked cigarettes, to this day I still harbor memories of Alfred Petersen, Gunnar Nortoft, Mouritz Castella and Willie Myrthu among others sitting cheek by jowl, simultaneously but unmindfully destroying the atmosphere with Dad's give away Cuban rolled White Owls. As if that wasn't enough, Uncle Chris, John Larsen and Jorgen Laursen were sure to fire up a few pipe fulls of Prince Albert or Old Chum.

Despite this invasion of blue air, and the serious risk of stunting my growth, I always enjoyed these gluttonous affairs. Missing one for a hockey game or practice would have been a major disappointment. Happily, my sports obligations were of a relatively short duration and invaded only a fractional part of Dad's extended parties. Missing a few hours still allowed for much celebration as it was always well after midnight when the last of the guests ventured out into the dark for departure in a frigid car with frozen tires thumping over the squeaking snow.

But back to hockey, which by spring, was beginning to conflict with everything, including my less frivolous agenda. There is no doubt about it, even my school work was suffering as the demands of the game were making homework a troublesome chore.

Being in grade six, homework had suddenly emerged as a major part of my school year. Mr. Shaw, my first ever male teacher was terrific. He worked very hard with his class but expected much in return. No one liked it at the time but with all of his homework assignments, learning and mastering the required courses virtually became a cake walk. When school was let out in late June everyone appreciated his efforts and his commitment to us kids. I think it fair to say that all who were lucky enough to have him as a teacher started the summer with a feeling of solid accomplishment.

****

Uncle John, Aunt Ragnhild, Grandmother and cousins Fred and Margaret arrived right on schedule in Uncle John's 1940 maroon Plymouth. They had come a long way and after having driven for several days, all were a bit road weary, but one would never have known it from the joyous greetings and clamorous commotion that took place almost before they stepped out of the car. It was mid July when these American relatives showed up at our house right before sunset but just in time for supper.

Everything was ready and the house was squeaky clean. Irene and I had spent part of the afternoon skating with woolen socks on the waxed linoleum dining room floor. It was polished to perfection. The dinner table was set with Mother's best linen table cloth and a center piece of sweet peas, just picked from the front garden. The silver had been polished and was gracing a never before used china set that had been bought for the occasion. In an effort to be fully ready, some of the delicious food that Mother had carefully prepared was being kept hot in the warming shelf that was fixed directly above the coal burners of the kitchen stove.

It wasn't dark when we all sat down to eat but in the short interval since their arrival, our visitors were no longer strangers. Cousins Fred and Margaret didn't seem to mind that Irene and I were still in grade school while they were both nearing college age. Uncle John and Dad who hadn't seen each other for many years were conversing as though they had been at the same party the night before. Grandmother, Ragnhild and Mother immediately found lots to talk about, sharing and laughing at the days events. Mother would normally have been embarrassed by lumps in the gravy, but this simply became another reason for a few chuckles when John mistakenly assumed it to be a dressing and slopped some on his fresh lettuce salad. Even Tippy was enjoying the ambiance of the moment and especially so when Grandmother slipped him a few morsels of chicken under the table.

We were after all, kin, looking forward to a two week visit with Dad's oldest brother and his family. Grandmother, whom we had seen some nine years earlier, had hitched a ride from Minneapolis while the rest of the gang came from Spencer, Iowa where Uncle John was a Lutheran pastor.

The visit had been in the planning stages for several months and as you would expect Dad was thrilled with the prospect of a visit with his mother and brother. The word got out and Marius Jorgensen, the pastor at our church in Standard, planned a whole series of revival meetings and made arrangements for Uncle John to do some of the preaching. This was understandable since Pastor Jorgensen and Uncle John knew each other as kids back in Denmark. Also Reverend John M. Jensen was well known throughout the "United Evangelical Lutheran Church" as the editor of the church paper, "The Ansgar Lutheran."

In contemplation of the visit, I had visions of spending the best part of two weeks sitting still in a church pew while Uncle John and Pastor Jorgensen were busy revitalizing me and the rest of the congregation. Going to church wasn't bad but two solid weeks of news from the pulpit didn't sound like a pep rally to me.

In the end, it worked out very well. As expected there was a package of church services but there were also an incredible number of memorable social activities. Listening to Uncle John's preaching was not at all boring and in most instances, a learning experience. His candor and relaxed manner was a hit with everyone and this precipitated numerous coffee invites that included our whole family. It turned out to be a lot of fun.

I have long since forgotten Uncle John's sermons and his revival message but will never forget the attention that Cousin Fred lavished on me. Upon his arrival he gave me a small child's baseball glove. It was much too small and I already had several that were bigger and better. While he may have underestimated my size, he was bang on with my interest in baseball.

My affection for the game probably started at a very young age when Dad told me about the likes of Babe Ruth and Lou Gehrig. More importantly, this interest was further enhanced when he gave me my first ever baseball. Actually, this introductory orb was homemade and was stuffed with rags, string and all manner of things. The cover was fashioned from two pieces of denim, each carefully cut like those used on the real thing. To complete the job, these barbell shaped patches were meticulously stitched together with grocery string from Leo's Red and White Store. The result was a nearly perfect baseball sized sphere that was heavy enough to throw and catch but soft enough not to hurt whenever I missed a pitch.

Dad and I played a lot of catch and over time the denim ball gave way to regular equipment and bona fide baseballs. By the time Fred showed up, I could pitch and catch with reasonable dexterity and thoroughly enjoyed having someone to play catch with. Fred became my willing victim and when we weren't at church or some social event, we could be found out by the barn blazing fast balls at each other. By the end of the first week our throwing arms were a wreck. Each day started with a sore arm and when Fred finally headed home to Iowa neither one of us could lift our throwing arm to wave good bye.

Seeing Grandmother again and making the acquaintance of a previously unknown uncle, aunt and some cousins had been great. In the end it had been a very active and a most memorable two weeks.

Like a January chinook, their visit was much too short. We enjoyed each other immensely and with a nearly daily diet of picnics in our poplar grove and other social events, it is small wonder that time ran out so quickly. Apart from my learning how to throw a curve ball, Cousin Fred and I discovered a multitude of other similar interests. Indeed, the two weeks had been a tremendously happy time which I will forever cherish.

****

It had been a great summer but even this was improved with a trip to Calgary for the Labor Day "Model T" Races. Uncle Edward and Dad had decided to take in this Fall Classic and with a modest amount of begging I somehow managed to join with them.

This annual affair was a genuine auto race and a real treat to see. Viewed from the Calgary Exhibition and Stampede grandstand, one could easily follow the cars as they sped around the half mile oval. They didn't rival the Indy 500 but on such a short track, their speeds seemed almost unreal.

The overall format has long since been forgotten but I do recall that there were several heats run during the warm sunshine of the afternoon. The winners of these preliminary races of about twenty laps advanced to the final event in which the grand champion was determined. By this time the sun was almost setting but the excitement was at a virtual crescendo. In some respects the whole thing was similar to a demolition derby since mechanical difficulties often intervened, leaving these Ford relics of the past stalled at various points along the raceway.

Adding to the interest, two of the combatants in the race were from Standard. Tommy Frazer and Gordon Rasmussen each had a car entered and as I recall, both drove their way into the championship event.

****

The usual fall outbreak of Infantile Paralysis (Poliomyelitis) was subdued that year and as scheduled, school started on the Tuesday immediately following Labor Day.

Rumors of a new and bigger school bus were quickly quashed when on Tuesday morning the same old hearse-like bread wagon stopped at our farm to pick up Irene and me. We were both disappointed and as usual, obliged to sit on someone's lap in what was left of the front seat. To make it even worse, Arthur Grant had made a deal to pick up Eleanor Rasmussen en route and in order to make room, she was obliged to sit on my lap for her nearly three mile trip to school. We were in fact three deep.

As it happened, we had hardly gotten into this routine when on September 18, this terrible excuse for a bus took matters into its own hands. Suddenly, and with absolutely no

275

prior hint of trouble, it veered into a ditch where it rolled over a couple of times. Like everyone else on board, Irene and I found ourselves upside down in a pile of screaming kids. In some respects we were better off than the gang in the back where they shared their crowded space with a large spare tire and wheel, a heavy square cornered tool box, a large hydraulic jack, some tire chains, and a snow shovel. These items, along with the tumbling kids and their flying lunch buckets, made kindling out of the wooden benches that ran down each side of the extended bread wagon's interior.

What probably took less than two seconds seemed an eternity as the bus tumbled over and through the ditch. It seemed that the darn thing would never stop rolling. When finally it did, the back doors had popped open and those who could, quickly evacuated through that gapping breach.

What a mess! There had been twenty four kids crammed into that lengthened delivery bus which ended up lying on its bent top in Bedstefar's grain field.

As it turned out, Irene and I were thoroughly shaken but generally unhurt. As you might expect, that fact was not immediately apparent to me and I was worried. We had been seated next to each other in the front jump seat, but when the bus finally came to rest, Irene was nowhere to be found. I was unhurt and managed to scramble out of the broken glass and debris through the passenger side door which had either been opened by Gordon Grant on whose lap I had been seated, or had by itself flipped open during the last roll. Fearing for Irene's well being, I stumbled out and quickly ran around to the driver's side door, which was jammed in a slightly ajar position.

At this point, my frantic concern for Irene triggered one of the most bizarre events of my life. I can't explain it but well remember grabbing the door's protruding edge and bending it back. I had a strange sense of knowing that I shouldn't be able to reshape a car door, but reshape it I did.

For some unknown reason, this brief moment of super human strength allowed me to pull away and kink back a corner of the jammed door. As I peered inside, it immediately became apparent that Irene was safely out of the wreckage and my curious burst and release of strength left as quickly as it had come.

Later when everything had more or less settled down, I went back to examine the door and the havoc that I had inflicted. It was not at all surprising to note that I was unable to budge or bend the door which was firmly wedged in place by the crushed roof of the vehicle. Photographs of the wreckage clearly show the kink and bend which I was able to administer while under a moment of stress.

This bus accident was more than just a casual wreck. No one was killed but Larry Sheets suffered a punctured kidney and other internal injuries, while Margaret Knapp broke her collar bone. Both were transported by ambulance to a Calgary hospital where they staged complete recoveries.

To the best of my knowledge this was the first ever school bus accident in Canada. As such it has always been a mystery that the authorities did little to alter the wrongs that were so dangerous and obvious. No doubt, the happy outcome did much to dampen the publicity but in today's super sensitive society, commingling passengers with loose spare tires, tool boxes, and ten ton hydraulic jacks would never be allowed. Moreover, exposing school kids to the risk of splintering slats from a wooden bench would most certainly be a litigation lawyer's dream.

Playing Superman came at a price, since later, and for a few days following, my muscles were so sore that I could hardly lift my arms. To be sure, no one escaped without a few lumps, bumps cuts and bruises, but my smarting arm tendons were without question the most serious of my discomforts.

Adding to my agony, the accident caused me to miss Don Dunfeys's Gillette Razor Blade broadcast of the Joe

Lewis - Billy Conn fight. This heavyweight championship bout was the first postwar fight and the first that I had an opportunity to hear on the radio. It was preceded by a tremendous amount of hoopla and nearly everyone had been looking forward to this seemingly important sporting event.

In truth it was not the accident itself that was in conflict with the championship fight. It was several days later when someone decided that those of us who were in the wreck should be treated to a night out. It may have been a good idea but it happened to coincide with the Gillette broadcast.

Actually, as it turned out, the fight wasn't that great as Joe Lewis made short work of Billy Conn. For that matter, the night out wasn't terribly noteworthy either as it was simply a rather formal dinner party at the Empress Hotel in Calgary. It may have been an excellent hotel but its dining room, The Tea Kettle Inn, was a little too elegant to properly entertain a bunch of kids who were trying to forget a rather nightmarish event. They were even out of vanilla ice cream, and how was I to know that the finger bowl, graced with floating lemon slices, was not filled with consommé.

After the rollover, everyone fully expected that a new bigger and better bus would at long last replace the old mangled and made over bread wagon. No such luck. After a few weeks of transportation offered by Olie Chartrand and a few other parents, we got the old wreck back again. The dents had been banged out and its few windows had been replaced. Riding in it remained an intimate affair, as sitting on laps was still a requirement. Also all of the loose tires, tool boxes etc. continued to rest on the floor, sharing the limited space with the kids sitting on replaced wooden slat benches.

We were all disappointed but in fairness to the situation, new vehicles were almost impossible to obtain and there is little doubt that residual war time shortages were partially responsible for retaining the old wreck.

For me, I always took a modicum of secret pleasure in the now barely visible kink and crease that was still evident on the bottom of the driver's side door. Care had been taken to remove most of the bumps and bends but that special one was not easily repaired and the vehicle left the body shop in less than perfect condition.

****

Ever since David was making deals with Jonathan it has been fashionable to keep young boys occupied with some time consuming activity. Apparently there is a theory that supports the notion that a boy, any boy, with time on his hands is a rudderless soul that will automatically stumble into some unworthy event or dire situation. The most common cure for this congenital and unfortunate deficiency is membership in some club or character building association. Knowing this, a frequent prescription is membership in the "Boy Scouts." After all, learning how to tie knots and light a fire with no more than two matches is a worthy ambition that is certain to keep any young mind fully occupied. By corollary, such a meaningful activity should also guarantee a behavior that is acceptable to society.

Perhaps that sounds a bit cynical, but like so many of the young and potentially troublesome and misdirected souls that had preceded me, I joined a scout troop in the fall of 1946. For me it was a fresh and exiting venture. As well, it was almost new to Standard since the scout movement had not been active in the community for many years.

Those of us who joined all bought a stiff brimmed hat and a shirt. While there was more to the uniform, it was agreed that the balance of the attire could come later when there was some achievement and maturity within the group.

There were four packs within the troop. Gene Wheeler was the leader of my pack, the Wolf Pack. In spite of my cynicism, I enjoyed scouting but unfortunately it was in conflict with hockey. For that reason, the troop only survived for a few months when the skating rink beckoned and took over. I did however master a few knots and learned the proper way to fly the Union Jack. Lighting a fire with only two matches was well beyond my abilities.

****

The crop was in the granaries and the pig barn was full of growing porkers. It had been a good harvest and hog prices were holding fairly well. For us, prosperity was an unattainable dream but the occasion allowed for some improvement in our circumstances. Topping our wish list was a new car, but they were hard to come by.

For some reason it took an inordinate amount of time to retool the factories back to their initial and intended purpose from their wartime munitions production lines. New cars and trucks were in very short supply. Moreover, most of the car makers were beset with labor strife which made deliveries even slower.

In the interests of fair play, anyone seeking to buy a new automobile was only permitted to place an order with one vendor. Dad chose his friend, Mons Hansen, the local dealer for Chrysler products. In doing so he held the number two position for a new Plymouth. Despite this excellent spot for a new car, it was in fact a poor choice since all of the Chrysler plants were locked in a major strike that seemed to last forever. There may have been a few 1946 models but none arrived in Standard. New Fords, Chevs, and Pontiacs were slowly making an appearance but new Chrysler products were basically unavailable.

During the winter and while waiting for the new car, plans were made for a summer trip to the United States. Following the delightful experience of the summer just past, we were all excited with the prospect of once again seeing Grandmother and the rest of Dad's family in Iowa and Minnesota. I was thrilled for the chance to see Cousin Fred again but this was further enhanced by what was to be my first ever look at the United States.

I had always been intrigued by this vibrant neighbor to the south which seemed to have a tremendous influence on my life. For starters, both Mother and Dad had countless stories of the years past when they had spend time in the States. Mother had been born there but understandably had only a fleeting memory of those first four years of her life. She did however recount and relive many happy times, when as a teenager, she attended a church school, Atterdag College in Solvang, California. These were fun times and Mother's sharing of these joyful moments had a profound effect on my sister and me.

It seemed that almost everything was marked with the words "Made in USA." And of course there was a proliferation of American books, magazines and Henry Dam's comics. Also, most of the truly entertaining radio programs and movies were set in places like Detroit, St. Louis, Chicago and Los Angeles. Other exciting American venues included events such as the World's Fair, World Series, Indianapolis 500, Kentucky Derby, Championship boxing and of course, the new United Nations, which after a brief stay in San Francisco, was now permanently located in New York City.

Even America's infamous enjoyed titillating reputations that extended well into Canada. These villains were always of interest and at the very least aroused my morbid curiosity. And is it any wonder with Bedstefar always reminding us and making the boast that his niece, Mother's cousin, was married to Jesse James, a grandson of the notorious bank robbing gangster of the same name. With all of this, it is small wonder that the forthcoming visit to the

United States invoked much excitement for the whole family, especially so for Irene and me.

Spring came and the snow was gone but we still didn't have a new car in the garage. Without one there could be no trip and we were all extremely worried. The travel plans made throughout the winter had filled us with hope and thoughts of adventure but with the passing of each disappointing week, we were all in a doleful mood.

Actually, the winter had been generally uneventful but I did continue to play hockey. Indeed, with all the practice days, there was a slight but noticeable improvement in my hockey skills. Unfortunately, I remained the same relative size and was still the smallest player on the team. Despite this, I had managed to score a few goals. I didn't need any encouragement but as an inducement, Dad offered to pay a reward of one dollar for each goal or assist. He was certainly in no danger of going broke over such an offer but with the help of a few dubious assists, I was able to squirrel away six dollars.

Strangely, Strathmore had no hockey team and Rockyford was seldom available so most of our games were still scheduled with Cluny. We did however play one game with a team from the Hillhurst district of Calgary. They were a well balanced group being of similar age and were as a consequence all much bigger than me.

Without a doubt, the most memorable and certainly the most comical game of the year was played with Meadowbrook Hall, a small but distinct farm community situated between Gleichen and Standard. A school was not involved and as I recall, the team was entirely made up of stay at home farm boys. It is likely that these masters of the plow and milk stool were simply seeking a release from the tedium of a quiet Sunday afternoon.

Their equipment was limited to their farm duds some of which were blue jeans with a few splatters of cow manure on the lower cuffs. Many of these plow boys carried and played with a chained wallet protruding from the hip pockets of their tight fitting jeans. Uniforms were non existent and their skating talents had largely been acquired on a lake or slough having no walls or defined boundaries. To a man, they were all much larger than our team but seemed not terribly concerned with winning, should that ever be a possibility. They were a good natured, pleasant group and our few games with them were for the most part a lot of fun.

Our first encounter with Meadowbrook took place early in the season long before the old board fence surrounding our rink was backed with a solid snow pack. During these early winter days, very little snow had been scraped off the ice and the normal pile of snow behind the fence was yet to come. In the absence of this backing, the old boards surrounding the rink had considerable flex. In normal circumstances this would have gone unnoticed but for a rough and tumble group, most of whom could hardly turn or stop, it served as a challenge and created a new sport. Discovering the flimsy condition of the rink boards, the Meadowbrook gang took every opportunity to crash the wall in the obvious hope that it could be demolished.

Our coach, Mr. Bragg, quickly caught on and being concerned with our individual survival, urged us to be particularly careful and not to get in the way of a runaway Abner who was about to test the soundness of our rink fence. His advice was well taken but unlike a normal game when hitting and checking along the boards is an accepted part of the action, there was no malice in these often deliberate clattering collisions. Unfortunately, that didn't minimize the risk of becoming the meat in the sandwich and during the first two periods several of our team members inadvertently got smeared. A few two minute boarding penalties were handed out, but to no avail; the havoc continued.

With my diminutive stature I was especially cautious. It was well into the third period and while carrying the puck along the boards, I noticed one of these speeding but uncontrolled figures closing in. I stopped or ducked just in time as my adversary hit the wall with a shattering thud. It was probably intended to protect the cigarettes in his shirt pocket but whatever the reason, he turned his back to the wall at exactly the wrong moment. While this saved his tobacco and should have made possible a soft landing, the board that absorbed most of the impact gave way just enough to allow one cheek of his tush filled jeans to find the open space between it and the adjacent plank. Closing with a snap, the two boards now held him in a most unpleasant grip. The more he tried to escape, the tighter the hold. No doubt about it, he was in agony but everyone from Meadowbrook thought it was funny. I thought it was hilarious and if the rules had permitted, I and the rest of our team should all have been penalized for laughing.

What a scene! Mr. Bragg quickly came to the rescue with a hockey stick with which he pried open the boards so that the farmer could be released from his self inflicted trap.

The outcome of the game is long forgotten and of no importance. However, I well remember that the poor fellow quickly adjourned to the skate shack where in private he could examine the damage.

****

The winter ended with hardly a whimper as the snow melt was so slow as to be almost imperceptible. With the white gone we were left to wonder what happened to the runoff and flooding that was expected with each spring. The culvert and roadway that had so often washed away had survived and for some unexplainable reason the roads hardly got muddy. In a strange sort of way, we had transitioned from snow to dust. That was the good news, but we still didn't have a new car in the garage and that was the bad news.

By now the shortage of new automobiles was growing into a political fire storm and with this backdrop, the United States Congress reluctantly enacted the Taft-Hartley Labor Act. This quickly brought an end to all of the remaining labor disputes and production resumed in all of the Chrysler plants including Canada's Windsor, Ontario facility, which for lack of parts had been shut down.

Finally in late April, a black 1947 Plymouth arrived at Mons Hansen's agency. This new vehicle filled the first order and vaulted Dad into the number one spot, the next in line for a new set of wheels. We all harbored some lingering doubts about our chances for a trip to the States but now at least there was some reason for hope.

Both Irene and I had attended Pastor Jorgensen's confirmation classes throughout the winter. For Irene, it was her second year and she was scheduled to be confirmed in mid May. This was to be a big celebration, and as was the custom, the whole Rasmussen gang would attend. Some of the earlier confirmations of our Holm cousins had been outrageously festive and were in fact family reunions. Gasoline rationing had been done away with, leaving no one stranded for lack of fuel. Following the well established precedent set by older cousins, Irene's ceremony was to be followed by a mammoth dinner party. It was to be a marvelous event and we were all looking forward to it.

I think it was the week just before this gala affair when Dad was notified that a second Plymouth had at long last arrived in Standard. Its color was a mousy gray but for $1760.00 it was to be ours. I was ecstatic and doubt that I will ever forget the unmistakable new car smell of that Plymouth. Of more importance, we could now firm up our plans for an extended vacation and visit with Dad's family in Iowa and Minnesota.

Irene's Confirmation came off without a hitch and the Rasmussen love fest that followed measured up to everyone's expectations. Irene even had her picture taken with the new Plymouth in the background. Unfortunately, by the time all of my cigar smoking uncles had taken a turn sitting behind the wheel, the new car smell was nearly gone.

The end of the school year was approaching and Mrs. Young, my grade seven teacher, put her pointer away. In doing so she also contrived the most diabolical final exams that any of us had ever experienced. Throughout the year she had spent most of each day stalking the aisles between the desks like a drill sergeant. If, in her judgment, a student was seen not to be working, she would unleash her pointer with a sharp crack on the top of the wayward student's head. The only peace that we had from this onslaught occurred whenever she made one of her not so infrequent trips to the adjacent but partially hidden cloakroom for a cigarette. These brief nicotine fits were always announced by a loud scratch and snap, the unmistakable sound of lighting a large wooden match stick. Also, when her lungs were temporarily satisfied, the smoke smell filtered back with her as she reentered the classroom, leaving little doubt of her supposedly clandestine activities. We of course pretended not to notice these temporary sojourns for a smoke but she knew that we were not easily fooled.

To this day, I am convinced that her horrific six to seven hour final exams for each subject were a payback for our chortling and feigned ignorance of her tobacco addiction.

School was out and despite the lengthy exams, I had passed into grade eight. Also the long wait for our vacation was nearly over as our plans were quickly transforming into reality. Filling an absolutely essential priority, Dad found a man to care for the farm while we were away. The search had been difficult but at the very last moment, Hulbert agreed to take on the responsibility.

Hulbert was of Danish origin but the only Danish that he spoke were his eloquent cuss words. These obscene adjectives spiced up almost every sentence and were clearly verbalized with tremendous pride. While in Mother's presence he managed to keep his language within the range of decency, but it was easy to tell that these self imposed limits on his vocabulary made him uneasy. In this role he was also an incredible bore.

His most distinguishing feature was the shine on the tight skin of his well tanned face. He only shaved once a week but when he did, the razor went well up on each temple, exposing even more glistening skin and giving him an overall ghoulish appearance.

While Dad was explaining his duties, Hulbert was either rolling a cigarette or jingling a few coins in his pocket, giving the impression that he didn't care or feel the need to know. Undeniably, he was difficult to communicate with and I am sure there were times when Dad wondered how well things would be cared for. In truth, hiring a man for a short period of time was almost impossible so Dad's choices were limited to a very few. For sure, a top hand was out of the question.

Leaving Tippy behind was my major concern but Hulbert assured us that he liked dogs and that Tippy would be fed along with the other animals. This dubious assertion should have been comforting but the whole family remained anxious about it until we returned home nearly a month later. There is every reason to believe that Dad worried a whole lot more about Hulbert's overall competence.

Notwithstanding our misgivings, the gasoline tank read full and we were finally ready to embark on our safari to the States. The trunk was completely stuffed with boxes, bags and our only suitcase. Extra clothing was packed in boxes.

The voids in the trunk were stuffed with an array of quart sealers, each of which was filled with garden preserves that Mother had saved from the the year just passed. We certainly didn't have the wherewithal to visit many restaurants so it was planned that we would only stay in motels that had cooking facilities. Preparing our own meals was a nuisance but it was much cheaper and sure beat going hungry.

****

The exact date of our departure is unimportant but I well remember that it was extremely early in the morning. Even the best highways had posted speed limits of fifty five miles per hour so early starts were required if a reasonable daily distance was to be achieved. To make matters worse, Mother and Dad always stopped early in the afternoon to ensure that we could find a motel at an acceptable price.

A few miles could be saved by going directly south through Gleichen and Arrowwood. Unfortunately this road took us over the dusty Blackfoot Indian Reservation, and very near the site of our Sunday School picnics, the scene of my earlier spy fright with Henry and Kenneth. Sadly, by the time we reached the bridge, our car's new upholstery was laden with a layer of the light road dust that had been kicked up on the rutty trail. I think some of it stayed in the fabric forever, which along with my uncle's cigar smoke, made short work of the new car smell.

Irene and I promised ourselves that we wouldn't miss a thing but with such an early start these ambitious plans were soon forgotten and sleep took over. We both awoke in time for the border crossing into Sweetgrass, Montana. Everything went well but it did seem a bit strange to know that we were in a foreign country. Actually, the general topography of Montana and the Dakotas is similar to the plains of southern Alberta and I was a bit disappointed with the sameness of the land. There were however other differences which at the very least illustrate some of the subtle variations in our two societies.

During our initial gasoline stop in Shelby, I saw bubble gum for the first time ever. Added to this, the kid blowing the bubbles was riding a balloon tired bicycle. These had been pictured in magazines but to the best of my knowledge, none were available in Alberta. Dad quickly realized a difference when, after spending a travelers check for gasoline, he received all of his change in silver dollars. No doubt about it, Montana was one of the silver states.

As we traveled along it is likely that the most conspicuous dissimilarity with Alberta was the abundance of signs that cluttered the roadway. These flashy, almost gaudy billboards advertised everything from a cold beer to a drug store in Wall, South Dakota. The signs advertising Burma Shaving Cream were a unique medium that offered a welcome relief from the monotony of the road. These small signs were positioned along the highway in a sequence covering several miles. Each set of five or six small roadside markers contained a verse or brief story but one needed to travel about two miles to get the full message. One such series that comes to mind read "Car in ditch - Man in tree - Moon was full - So was he - Burma Shave."

Our path took us through Montana to Kenmare, North Dakota which was Dad's first home in America. We were never absolutely certain that we found the house in which he first lived after arriving from Denmark, but we know that we found the farm where he worked as a teen aged immigrant.

Overall the visit to some of Dad's old haunts was interesting and this included Minneapolis where he worked before migrating north to Canada. While in the Twin Cities area we were the guests of Uncle Chris and Aunt Alice who kept us busy visiting parks, museums and various other points of interest. Also, we spent a fair bit of time with Grandmother who had just moved into a senior citizen's home.

Chris, who was in the construction business, took us to one of his sites where his company was building a large concrete grain silo. I had never before seen so much wet concrete in one place. It was certainly very impressive. For all of that, nothing could match the shipyard on the Minnesota River, where during the war, he supervised the construction of a small fleet of T-2 Tankers. These 16,000 ton oil haulers were an essential part of the war effort, providing fuel to Great Britain and the Allies during much of the war. While several thousand were built, it was strange to think that some of these ocean going ships had been built on land that had previously been a corn field, hundreds of miles inland.

There were of course many interesting things in Minneapolis and St. Paul but one special and memorable event was our first ever viewing of television. Chris and Alice had one of these modern marvels in their living room. One evening everyone was there, including Cousin Garth who was in the process of finding his way back to civilian life after having served several years in the Pacific settling a dispute with the Japanese. We all sat down to enjoy Lipton Tea Company's "Arthur Godfrey Show." It was fun but Alice quickly turned to a different channel when a scantily clad chorus line did a dance number. Shucks, I was just starting to enjoy it. With such an untimely interruption, both Garth and I would have preferred a good Hopalong Cassidy shoot' em up western.

Corn, corn, and more corn, Iowa is most definitely farm country and from all appearances, Spencer was right in the heart of it. Clearly it was a healthy and mature agricultural economy. With few exceptions, the well treed farmsteads that dotted the county featured large barns, a reminder of a past era when horses were required to plant and harvest the crops. While they now enjoyed up to the minute equipment, I have always believed that Grant Wood's famous painting, "American Gothic", could easily have been set and posed for by an Iowa farmer and his wife.

During our Iowa visit, Cousin Fred and I didn't play catch but when we weren't being buffeted by a rain shower, we could often be found at Spencer's "Hart Baseball Stadium" watching the local heroes, (The Cardinals). It was hot and sticky but this was of little concern as all of the games were played under lights during the cooler part of each evening. It was really quite pleasant. Most likely a majority of Spencer's players were farm kids who had learned their craft by pitching cobs out of a corn bunk. They were however, very talented and the games were highly entertaining. I had never previously seen a night game and was surprised at how easy it was to watch a pitch or fly ball.

One night while taking in a game, the players suddenly ran off the field and the stands nearly emptied. It was still in the middle innings and while there was some thunder and lightening off in the distance, there was no rain nor was there an obvious reason to call the game or set up a delay. Fred and I were not only dismayed by this surprising behavior but were virtually left alone in the stands. We didn't have long to wonder at the reason when a lightning flash revealed a large tornado funnel hanging from a nearby cloud. It was scary but to the best of my knowledge this potentially deadly storm never did any serious damage. We did however join the rest of the crowd, most of whom were in the process of leaving the parking lot. We quickly headed for home but got caught in a terrific downpour. By the time we arrived at Uncle John's house we looked like a couple of refugees from Noah's Ark.

We divided our time between Minnesota and Iowa and while each day was filled with adventure and new experiences, the most memorable part of the visit was Dad's family. It was great to renew our acquaintances in Spencer but equally rewarding to develop new family ties with those who lived in Minneapolis. Our trip was on the lengthy side but the visits with relatives were in reality much too short.

Our stay in Iowa and Minnesota had been a delightful interlude but so was our trip home. This included some impressive drives through the South Dakota Badlands, the Black Hills and Yellowstone National Park. While these were awesome, none could rival the Little Big Horn Mountains immediately west of Sheridan, Wyoming. Not only were these mountains breathtaking, the trail on which we drove was beyond description.

Leaving Sheridan, the road across the mountains continued to shrink until it was but a single gravel path clinging to the nearly shear slopes of the mountains. Meeting an oncoming car would have been impossible and fortunately that didn't happen. When finally we had traversed this incredible road, a local resident told us of such a meeting. In this story, two cars met but there was no room to pass and neither of the meeting drivers had the courage to back up. To settle the argument, the owner of the oldest car, an apparent wreck, sold his vehicle to the owner of the newest car, whereupon it was simply pushed over the cliffs edge. The story teller went on to say that the vendor of the wreck was apparently quite satisfied with the transaction since he was later seen with a big smile on his face as he made his exit from a bank in Sheridan.

Just before leaving the United States we very deliberately made a slight diversion from sightseeing. Canada was still suffering from sugar rationing so before crossing the border, Mother, Dad, Irene, and I all trudged into a grocery store somewhere in Montana where we each purchased ten pounds of sugar. These four, ten pound bags were carefully stowed under the front seat of the car in the hope that the customs officials at the border would fail to notice our contraband. Our car wasn't searched but the concern associated with this smuggling operation could easily have been avoided if only we had known that all returning Canadians were entitled to carry ten pounds of sugar across the border. In retrospect, I am glad that we didn't know about this exemption since it wouldn't have been nearly as much fun.

It was good to return home and see Tippy again. He had been well cared for but was so happy to see us that he almost performed cartwheels. We had never before seen him so enthusiastic.

Apart from the mess in the house and the countless cigarette butts that littered the floor, Hulbert had done a reasonable job of caring for things. The bad news was our diminished immunity to the cleansing effects of our well water. We all suffered and it took several days before we got back to normal.

The trip to the United States was a happy occasion and I will forever cherish its memory. With some regret, the passage of time and my many subsequent visits have probably warped the attitudes and impressions that I carried home from that early exposure. To be sure, Canada and its neighbor to the south are not the same but square milk bottles, smaller gallons, a uniform currency color and fat bicycle tires are little more than superficial variations that are unique to a people of common roots, language, and religion. Following this first visit, I have always felt that these two societies have many more similarities than differences.

****

Having purchased the required text books at F.E. Osborne's exchange during our annual fall trip to Calgary, Irene and I were ready for school. Actually, I inherited most of the texts that Irene had used in grade eight while she traded my grade seven books for those that she needed for grade nine. It wasn't without some cost but by shopping early, we could usually acquire some used ones at a reasonable price. Also the book exchange was anxious to get my used texts so that they would be available for the big rush that could be expected right after classes started.

What a deal! Not only was I fully equipped for school but when Arthur Grant showed up, he was driving a school bus that actually looked like one. I could hardly believe my eyes. While it was a secondhand rig, it had been freshened up with a new coat of red paint. More importantly, all of the seats faced to the front and there were windows on both sides. There was space for everyone and it was no longer necessary to sit on someone's lap. With a nearly fresh set of books and a state of the art bus, what could possibly go wrong?

Boy! Was I in for a shock. My grade eight teacher turned out to be one of the strangest men I have ever known. It may be inappropriate to criticize but it is hard to understand how or why this man was hired to teach in a classroom. No doubt Mr. Morgan had the credentials, but as an unstable derelict with some serious mental deficiencies, he never earned the respect of his colleagues or his students. His teaching skills were negative and he seemed not to care if anyone learned anything except a few words of French, his native tongue.

He came to town an old "Indian Motorcycle" which carried him and his entire stash of earthly goods. During the five or so months that he was charged with teaching grades five through eight he never once changed his filthy clothes or homemade moccasins.

His thin but straggly gray hair fell from the outer edges of his balding head to his shoulders. Here, the tangled ends more or less disappeared under his open shirt and the incredibly dirty bandanna which encircled his grubby neck. He shaved his face just often enough to give dimension to a ragged mustache which was divided by yellow stains immediately below each nostril. These ever present land marks were particularly noticeable if he happened to have a cold. During these horrific times his dripping schnozzle was taken care of with a loud snort and a sideways swipe from a grubby sleeve. As the winter progressed the left sleeve of his already filthy sweater took on the appearance of a vambrace from a mediaeval coat of armor.

Mr. Morgan's special talent and obviously a first love, was music. He didn't seem especially talented but did play a flute well enough to provide a modicum of background for our frequent interludes of musical instruction. He stored his treasured but tarnished instrument in a tattered black case which in better times had been velvet lined. Unfortunately, his musical joy was now held captive in a putrid, broken down carton, akin to a blacksmith's tool box.

Our teacher truly loved his flute and when it was in his grasp, his eyes twinkled like that of a child viewing a Christmas tree for the first time. Whenever he played this musical relic he would shamelessly remove his gooey false teeth, popping both upper and lower plates into one of his filthy pockets. At these moments, his face would cave in giving him a shallow, gaunt appearance. In the absence of his choppers, conversation was punctuated with a spray of foul smelling saliva. No one wanted an intimate conversation.

If he played for any appreciable length of time, the open end of the old silver pipe continuously dripped moisture, leaving large wet spots on the oiled floor which he carelessly tracked through as he kept time by thumping the heel of his disgustingly grimy moccasins.

Our class had several students who were there because they were still too young to quit. The law demanded their presence but could not force them to study. It soon became apparent to these unwilling desk sitters that Mr. Morgan could be manipulated by flattering him with regard to his musical prowess. With hardly any coaxing, he would instruct everyone to put away their work while he played a few of his favorite melodies. These included some real uptown hits like "Swing Low, Sweet Chariot, Who is Sylvia, and Alouette."

During one of these work stoppages, Alvin Shear happened to be seated near the wrong end of the flute. He was not directly under the drips but was in fact slightly behind the maestro. As such, he was not in Mr. Morgan's vision.

Now Alvin was a resourceful fellow who enjoyed the stage if one was provided. Here at the front of the class but just slightly behind the performing Mr. Morgan, the temptation to cutup was overwhelming. Alvin started his solo mime with a simple squint into the open barrel of the flute. This innocent gesture was quickly followed by a gruesome face and a pretended retch and upchuck. The class was enjoying his antics, and being a ham, Alvin knew that he was on a roll. Depending on your perspective, it was bound to get better or worse. Sure enough, right at the height of a screeching crescendo, Alvin flicked a wad of chewed paper into the open end of the flute and to everyone's surprise, it stayed there. The music went on for a few more bars but after a few more flicks combined with a few more wads of paper the sound went south. At this, the whole class broke into unrestrained gales of laughter.

Mr. Morgan was totally unaware of Alvin's prank but thinking that we were making fun of his flat notes, he lost his cool. Becoming completely unhinged, he produced a small vial from his pocket which he declared to be acid. Raving in anger he then ran up and down the aisles fuming and sputtering. In the absence of his teeth, which were still in his pocket, his warpath orations were not that easy to understand but it was clear that he was threatening to throw the acid at anyone who even dared to smile. No one did but with these threats, the school board finally dealt with the man and the absolutely ridiculous situation that had prevailed since his arrival. He was not in class the following day and no one ever saw him again.

Alvin may not have realized it but he did us all a tremendous favor. He may also have done Mr. Morgan a kindness since the poor fellow should never have been in a classroom in the first place.

By any measure, Mr. Morgan was one of the most fascinating characters of my early life. In other circumstances, knowing him could have been a worthwhile experience but wasting a half year at school tarnished the entire episode beyond redemption. It wasn't that I was terribly motivated but I did have intentions of going on through high school. A setback in grade eight would at the very least, make grade nine and its worrisome Departmental Examinations a catastrophic screwup.

****

No doubt the grade nine board exams were really intended to standardize the Alberta school system but in so doing they also held the threat of streaming students away from any and all academic pursuits. They certainly had to be taken seriously as they were in fact a prerequisite to any thought of a university education. Preparing for them started in grade eight so being under the tutelage of a vagabond minstrel was not a good omen.

Good teachers were hard to find and getting one in mid term must have given members of the school board some sleepless nights. For sure, there were a few more misfires but in the end we got Miss Patchet. One would have to think that her previous position had been in Heaven, since almost everyone thought she was an angel. Truly she was a quintessential school mistress who seemed not to mind the challenge of a room filled with kids who were totally out of sync with the curriculum.

Not only was she a no nonsense lady, she was mighty attractive and most of the rogue scholars who would rather not have been there were quickly tamed and started to enjoy their surroundings. Oh yes, Miss Patchet had a temper but even this was put to good use as we scrambled our way back to reality and some serious studies. After all, there was always the hope that the year could be salvaged.

****

Indeed, it was a never to be forgotten school year, but for all of its tumultuous twists and turns it was nothing compared to the weather of late winter and spring. Actually, the early winter had been quite ordinary and could easily qualify as pleasantly mild. October through January came and went and as the daylight hours increased, the higher sun started to melt the dirty snow along the roadways. These soiled snow ridges were now laced with little sun melted snow crystals, hinting that winter was on its last legs.

But not so fast, it was a Saturday in mid February when winter turned its back on the calendar with a vengeance and we experienced the worst snow storm of the century. It started before morning with both wind and snow. There is no telling how much it snowed but by late afternoon Dad and I ventured out into its blinding fury. By then, the pig barn was nearly buried, and to avoid a disastrous collapse of the building we quickly removed the weight of over three feet of snow from its roof. Reaching this snow pile was easy as the drifts were lying firm right up to the barn's eaves. To gain entrance into the barn we were obliged to dig down to the hay loft entrance which was normally some eight or ten feet above ground.

The wind and snow reduced our vision to only a few feet so when the storm abated we were somewhat surprised to discover a humungous drift right in the middle of the yard. When finally the wind let up, this drift measuring to a height of approximately fourteen feet, was set in a sea of white which varied in depth but averaged at least four feet over the length of the driveway.

With a nearly super human effort from the whole family, this pathway to the outside world was cleared out by late Monday. Unfortunately, the road to town took longer and before we were able to use the car, our mega storm was bested by an even larger one which once again drifted in the driveway. With the path from our yard flanked by piles of snow from the earlier dig out, the snow covering it was now over six feet deep. These anomalous winter blizzards continued every few days until late April or early May. By then we were not only digging out the driveway we were uncovering the telephone line which, during a tranquil summer day, was suspended some twelve feet above the now totally buried caragana hedge which grew beneath it.

Standard was by no means the only area beset with wind and snow. Virtually all of southern Alberta was suffering the wrath of this awe-inspiring weather. Modes of transportation were essentially limited to small ski planes, snowmobiles, horses and large tractors affixed with snow plows. Size was not necessarily an asset as even large steam locomotives were all but stymied by the ever increasing mounds of snow. The train serving Standard had a huge plow mounted on its front but even this offered no guarantee that it could get through.

I recall watching it for nearly an hour as it repeatedly rammed into a particularly large snow bank. Each smashing attack resulted in little more than thirty to forty feet of track being cleared. From a distance all that was visible above the towering snow banks was a burst of smoke each time the laboring engine thrust at the snow that blocked its path.

With mobility confined as it was, it's no surprise that many communities ran out of food and cattle feed. It is hard to believe now but on one occasion supplies were brought to town by way of a Caterpillar tractor and a small army of miners who trudged along to dig it through the numerous snow banks that covered the road. It's possible that these stalwart volunteers were largely motivated by the need for a fresh supply of beer but that didn't minimize the value of their contribution to the community.

Irene and I stayed in town for well over a month during this incredible winter. We were hosted by Mr. and Mrs. Bragg who like so many of the townspeople opened their homes to the many country kids that would otherwise be stranded at home and away from school. The Braggs were very hospitable but despite their many kindnesses, I often became terribly homesick. This was especially true on weekends when the roads were totally impassable and even Ray Green's horse and sled outfit had no way of taking us lonesome kids home.

It was probably late April when finally the wind and snow relented and the roads were cleared. The calendar claimed it to be springtime and while the sun was bright and high, the land was still completely shrouded in snow. Being outside without dark glasses was sure to result in a terrible case of snow blindness. Like so many others, I fell prey to the blinding light and for several days my eyes would hardly open. When they did, I felt as though I was packing a handful of sand behind each eyeball. If that wasn't enough, the sunburn which I incurred was equally severe. With the reflection and the refraction of light virtually blasting off the reflective snow from every angle, my face became a huge blister. I was a mess.

It was a late spring, but normalcy finally descended on southern Alberta. It had been brutal but in the end we all recovered from what must remain to this day as the winter to end all winters.

****

I was confirmed on Pentecost which fell on May 16th. It was a beautiful warm Sunday and the last vestiges of our mammoth snow drifts disappeared into the mud sometime during that afternoon. My Confirmation was a momentous event but seeing the last of our winter snow almost overshadowed the entire affair.

In preparation for the occasion, Mother and Dad bought me a brand new double breasted, MacLeod Brothers suit. It was brown in color and with a solid yellow tie, I thought it was absolutely smashing. With this new "uptown getup," I felt very grownup and hoped that nothing would happen to spoil or alter this adult feeling of well-being. I was after all just a few weeks short of being fourteen.

Now to be honest, my new duds were slightly on the big side since it was assumed that I would still add a few inches to my stature and increase my weight by a few pounds. Notwithstanding my suit and its size, Confirmation changed my appearance forever. It wasn't my idea but with the many years that have followed, I must admit that it has turned out to be a efficacious turning point to my bashful appearance and demeanor. At the time, having a finger wave in my forelock was the farthest thing from my mind but for such a special occasion, Mother persuaded me to give it a try.

Actually my hair takes a shape rather easily but on that particular Sunday morning it was as straight as a rifle shot. That didn't stop Mother who simply wet it down and positioned a wave with the help of a strategically located bobby pin. Sure enough just before church when the bobby pin was removed, my hair featured a neat wave right above my brow. Unknown to me, the bobby pin had left a residue of rust and throughout the day, I sported an obvious rust line right across my almost white thatch.

Pastor Jorgensen had eight beaming Confirmands in the class of 1948. We were all eager to formalize completion of our classes and like everyone else, it seemed reasonable to assume that with Confirmation, I would suddenly become an adult. Sadly, I could still not be trusted to drive a car but would become an adult member of the church and a bona-fide member of Luther League. Later in the summer this affiliation allowed for my reintroduction to hair snakes at what seemed to be the much overrated Lutheran "Sylvan Lake Bible Camp". Even riding to and from the camp in Howard Rasmussen's jazzy Studebaker could not make up for my disappointment with this much touted Bible retreat.

As in Irene's Confirmation one year earlier, my Protestant Bar Mitzvah was a festive event with almost the entire Rasmussen gang in attendance. Gifts were customary and gifts were received. These included a baseball bat, a few books, some fish hooks, money and if you can believe it, a Ronson cigarette lighter. Mother and Dad gave me a much appreciated wrist watch which added to my grown up feelings.

****

No doubt about it, my confirmation was both a milestone and an important inflection point in my life. It was however nothing compared to my fourteenth birthday which came a few weeks later. With this behind me I could for the first time legally obtain a much wanted bird hunting license and could look forward to the forthcoming duck and upland game season. I didn't have a shotgun but had the hope of borrowing Bedstefar's double barreled, twelve gauge.

Actually, I had been shooting gophers with Dad's twenty- two for several years and had gone as a dog with Uncle Martin whenever he showed up for some bird shooting. I was far from a skilled hunter but had been exposed to the sport enough to know that I would love to hunt with a shotgun.

At last, everything was in readiness. I had paid three dollars for my bird license the very first day they became available at Dora Paregaard's Standard Post Office. Equally important, I had managed to save most of my Confirmation money and had two boxes of number four, Canuck shotgun shells. It would have been preferable to have the more potent high base Imperials but they were four twenty five at Chas Madsen's General Merchandise while Canucks were cheaper at only three dollars per box. Bedstefar's double barrel was in my custody and to mitigate some of the recoil, the butt plate had been removed and replaced by a bunched up woolen sock.

The warmth of August was already a tired memory but the ugly days of rain and light snow that fell over the Labor Day weekend had been replaced by a most welcome burst of what almost seemed to be Indian summer. Discouragement and impatience were giving way to a modest amount of farmer's optimism and with a few more drying days, a hurried harvest could once again be in full swing. To be sure, there was still a threatening bank of gray off on the northern horizon but this appeared to be retracting with each sunny hour. Meanwhile the golden stalks of grain that stood in the sodden fields were put on hold, in wait of more clement weather and drying breezes.

The shoddy weather had interrupted the harvest but in so doing it had given me a break from what promised to be a very busy time. The rights implicit with my new hunting permit were mine to exploit against pheasants, partridges and the wily flight of Mallards, Pintails and whatever. After school I immediately jumped into my twelve inch rubber gum boots, grabbed Bedstefar's twelve gauge Hopkins and Allan and headed out for my first ever solo duck shoot. What a terrific feeling!

With the huge winter snowfall and late spring there were lots of ducks and having the notion that filling a limit of ten birds would be easy, I had left one of my two boxes of shells back home. Now under a small willow bush at the east end of Alfred Petersen's slough, I had only to wait for the return of my prey, all of which had vacated their lazy afternoon water rest when I first made my appearance.

Sure enough, it wasn't long before a small flock appeared to be heading directly my way. But wait a minute, it soon became obvious that they were getting smaller and had without my notice flown directly over my head.

Settling down to wait for another sortie, I convinced myself that a vigil could be maintained in all directions, thus ensuring that no bird would go unnoticed - at least that was my hope. Scanning the open skies, it wasn't long before another small flock appeared in the distant southeast. They looked somewhat encouraging and to make sure that there wouldn't be another sneak flyby, I faithfully kept my eyes on them.

Suddenly, there was the tearing of air over my left shoulder as two speeding teal came banking in over the water's edge. They came out of nowhere and seemed determined to set down on the glassy surface of the slough. "Bang! Bang!" roared the gun as I vainly spun around to face this unexpected challenge. Despite a valiant effort, both barrels were a clean miss as my unbalanced swing never came close to catching up with those fleet winged beauties.

With all of this commotion there was now little chance that my much watched flock in the southeast would consider even a look in my direction. As I dropped two fresh shells into the smoking barrels, there was time to consider my situation and choice of cover under the nearly naked willow tree. With all of the rain and snow of the last few days, the long coarse grass that encircled the ten to twelve acre water hole was much too wet to kneel or sit on. This autumn brown tangle looked dry but the warm sun had yet to penetrate to its soggy roots and judging from the wet shine on my rubber boots, there was no comfortable way that I could lower my profile. Considering the limited alternatives it seemed wiser to remain standing with at least partial concealment under the short willows. Unfortunately, this put the late afternoon sun squarely in my eyes as I looked out over the motionless water. Even worse, in the bright sunlight, my light blue school jacket probably resembled a lighthouse to any high flying but wary duck.

Apart from these disadvantages, it was an incredibly marvelous afternoon and I was enjoying it. The early frost of late August and the more recent cold and wet snap had all but eliminated the mosquitoes. Also, the noisy crickets and grasshoppers were long gone. It was so quiet that I could easily hear the complacent mud hens clucking and gurgling at the far end of the pond. Occasionally Ray Green's cow could be heard bawling her complaints as she waited to be milked. Were it not for the sound of a tractor or truck coming from some remote farm yard, there were moments when I could easily imagine that I was the only person enjoying the beautiful sunlit world.

The windless clear afternoon was not at all ideal for duck hunting but intermittent distant reports from a shotgun blast hinted that other hunters were enjoying some activity. Having previously spent many happy hours on a duck pond with Uncle Martin, I knew that these sporadic but far away shots would keep the birds on the move, making my water hole a possible point of interest. Equally important, it was opening day and there was every reason to believe that the local birds were not yet gun shy.

All of these suppositions were correct and indeed there was a steady flow of birds seeking a night's refuge on Alfred's slough. Some came in flocks of twenty or thirty while others came as pairs and even singles. Almost all were miles high as they crossed over the outer edges of their intended resting place. There were however an adequate number of birds to shoot at and if one had been counting, it could easily be assumed that there would be a pile of ducks at my side.

No such luck, it was becoming clear that even a slight motion under the exposed willow tree caused a promising duck to veer from its flight path, causing me to miss what should have been an easy shot. If I waited until a new direction had been established, the range would invariably be well beyond that of my low base Canuck shells. By the time the sun was setting into a beautiful red haze on the horizon, two thirds of my ammunition had been blasted away and I had yet to loosen so much as a tail feather.

In the end, twilight took over and lifting the gun to shoot became slightly less discernible to the now hordes of ducks that were intent on spending the night on Alfred's slough. With this new freedom of motion, I finally managed to tag a lone bird that tumbled into the water with a satisfying splash. I was delighted but as it was fifteen to twenty yards from the shore line, there was little hope of retrieving it with my limited depth gum boots. There was no breeze to drift my prize to shore but nothing would prevent me from gathering in this lone trophy. Removing my boots and socks, I managed to wade out into the chilled water which finally reached well above my rolled up trousers. It was impossible to know how much was water and how much was mud but I soon found out that there was a good deal of both.

Thinking that there may be other opportunities to shoot a careless duck, I took the shotgun with me as I ventured into the gooey muck and chill of the water. That proved to be a reasonable idea as I had barely reached my luckless prey when a clear shot at a brace of gliding Pintails presented itself.

Their wings were set and in the dusk of the evening it was clear that my presence had at least momentarily gone unnoticed. This changed quickly when I lifted the old twelve gauge to answer the challenge. At this, both birds flared up and over my head forcing me to lean back in an overextended position. My first shot was a clean miss so I promptly went to the second trigger only to find that my left foot was temporarily stuck in the mud and would not move quickly enough to coordinate with my trigger finger. That was bad news since the recoil of the second blast was just enough to rock me back from an already precarious situation.

Now I wasn't really off balance that much but despite my frantic and futile efforts to dislodge and reposition my left foot, there was a distinct feeling that gravity had the upper hand. It seemed to take forever but the inevitable outcome was obvious long before I found myself flat on my back and totally submerged in the cold muck and mire. Plunging my free hand into the boggy morass, I soon resurfaced, a total mess but otherwise unhurt.

There was a good deal of coughing, sputtering and spitting as under the weight of my water drenched clothes, I waddled back to shore. Lamentably, the damage was done and Bedstefar's shotgun was certainly entitled to a thorough cleaning before it could be fired again. While I still had five or six shells and was nine ducks short of my limit, hunting was over for the day.

It was well after dark when I finally arrived home. Being late had fostered some worry and the whole family was upset with me. Also I was cold, wet, dirty, smelly and in need of a bath. I had missed supper and still had some chores to do. Mrs. Sorenson, my grade nine teacher had assigned homework that would require at least one hour to complete.

After blasting away nearly a full box of shells, my lone success turned out to be a scrawny Shoveler (Spoon Bill), which needed cleaning before bedtime. More urgently, I needed to strip down, open, dry and clean the inner workings of my borrowed shotgun. The middle finger on my right hand was bleeding and half broken from the recoil received from the trigger guard on Bedstefar's fowling piece. My new light blue school jacket was beyond salvage and there was water lodged under the crystal of my nearly new Confirmation wrist watch.

With all of these complications and discomforts, I had just experienced one of the happiest and most memorable days of my life. Even a partially insane fellow hunter may find it difficult to understand, but my afternoon on the slough had been an absolute delight.

There have been other, indeed many more pleasant and successful forays onto a duck pond but this first solo affair was truly special and I wouldn't trade its enduring memory for anything.

Over the many years that have followed, I have enjoyed countless hunts with varying degrees of success. Regardless of the results, I never failed to delight in the quiet peace of a sunset over a wetland filled with fidgeting waterfowl or the frosty chill of a dawn as the clamorous birds started their day. I have been wet, cold, hungry and hurting but despite these discomforts and hardships, I still place duck hunting at the top of my sports interests. With time and practice I developed some improvement with a shotgun and in due course found ways to better camouflage my presence. Also, I never again purchased low base ammunition for ducks.

Hunting spawned a keen interest in ducks and the habits of these wary migrants. For a number of years I could predict with some accuracy the arrival dates of the migrating Scaup and the annual disappearance of the Widgeon. I have tried to emulate their calls and have carved their likeness in wood. For all of this, I never became a crack shot and have never considered myself to be a master of the sport. In truth, I have suffered many more defeats than victories.

While Mother and Dad never shared my ardent love and interest in the shooting sports, they seldom interfered or deliberately impeded my activity. They did however insist that I pluck and clean every bird that I brought home. This not so pleasant part of the hunt often motivated me to pack up, empty my gun and leave my blind well before a legal limit was in my game bag. Following such a decision, the birds always seemed much braver and even brazen as they flew ever closer.

Perhaps more meaningful were the many duck nests that were moved out of harms way whenever I helped Dad till the spring stubble. This act of mercy and conservation always provided a good feeling when Mrs. Duck was once again sitting on her eggs as the tractor and cultivator passed by on the next round. Unfortunately, the exact opposite was true if I failed to notice a nest and carelessly allowed my spring plowing to destroy it and a clutch of eggs.

I don't specifically recall it happening with ducks, but there were several occasions when Mother invited Sunday company for a meal of pheasant and partridge. For these special events I was encouraged to head for the fields and bring home enough wild fowl to feed a modest throng of guests. I never failed to produce but the pressure to satisfy a specific need removed some of the pleasures of the hunt.

****

Duck season was over and with the diminished warmth of the sun, winter was upon us. Looking back, it had been a momentous summer since on July 22, Newfoundland had become Canada's tenth province. The event was hardly noticed by a klutz like me but Canadians as a whole rejoiced and celebrated this important addition to Confederation. Now in the cold light of winter it was clear that assimilation would take a good deal of time and some misgivings were starting to creep in.

The event itself was largely a Newfoundland matter where not everyone was happy with the idea of becoming a Canadian. While Newfoundland dates back to 1583 as a British colony, for the fifteen years immediately preceding provincial status, it had existed as a British colony in a state of suspended democracy. This strange circumstance came about when in 1933 the island colony declared bankruptcy and voted self government out of existence. Starting with this declaration, its people were governed entirely by a British Commissioner having the absolute power of a benevolent dictator. With this background, it is not surprising that the vote to join Canada was less than enthusiastic. There were only seventy three thousand who voted for Confederation while seventy one thousand asked for a return to self government. Had the choice of keeping a dictatorial British Commissioner been offered on the ballot, it would probably have won the day.

On a lighter side, this extension to Canada's borders had to be bad news for the Northwest Territories since the only blank shield left in the Ottawa parliament building rotunda would now he carved into a Newfoundland Coat of Arms. This, one of ten limestone shields, had been intended for that portion of Northern Canada which was left out in 1905, when Alberta and Saskatchewan became provinces. Apparently the forward planning by Canada's architects had not contemplated Newfoundland as a province.

****

It was finally going to happen, poles had been set and the wire had been strung. Yes, it was true. Our farm was about to have electricity. This wasn't part of the rural electrification program that swept through the province later in the fifties and sixties, rather it was brought on by the delightful and persuasive intimidation from one of our neighbors.

The whole idea was Ray Green's who was particularly anxious to electrify his farm. While there were several possibilities, the easiest and most promising was electrification by way of Calgary Power, the major power company in Alberta and the only one in our area.

Calgary Power was quite happy to supply the electricity but was unprepared to endure the capitol costs of extending any lines from their already mature power grid. In Ray's case this meant that he would be responsible for the feeder line that was required to reach the twenty two thousand volt system, one and one half miles to the north of his farm. From our perspective, any line to the Green farm would be obliged to go directly past our place. Ray was angling for a way to reduce his cost and this could best be done if Dad and Alfred Petersen could be convinced to join in the project. Understandably any additional participation would result in a sharing of the costs. Carrying the line farther south was never considered as Leo Larsen's farm, which was immediately south of Ray's place, was equipped with a Kohler plant. This self contained electric generator was powered by a gasoline engine and was quite capable of generating adequate power for a typical farmstead.

Persuading Mother and Dad to join was probably an easy task since the merits of electricity were never in doubt. We would be able to pitch out the old kerosene lamps and rid ourselves of the terrible fire risk that went with their use. Throughout my childhood there was never a stronger and more forceful admonition than that which Irene and I constantly received about the careful use of kerosene lamps. Despite the obvious danger, these light sources were of necessity always on the move, being shunted from room to room. Falling and breaking the glass globe that held the fuel would at the very least set the house on fire.

We never knew the reason, but Mother was deathly afraid of Coleman gas lights and lanterns. Dad knew that their steel fuel tanks were much safer than the fragile glass globes of a kerosene lamp, but in deference to her fear, our home never enjoyed the much brighter and safer light of a Coleman.

Anyway, it was finally agreed that all three farmsteads would become electrified. Tommy Enevoldsen, one half mile north and virtually adjacent to the power grid declined involvement. Moreover, at the very outset, he was quite unhappy with our power line which had little choice but to run by his farm.

Since the early thirties, Tommy had owned at least one airplane and maintained a fine multidirectional grass landing strip right in the middle of his field. The power line going south along the roadway passed directly through the glide path to the northeast portion of this landing area and was certainly a considerable nuisance. For a time Tommy considered going under the wire as he landed but I doubt that he ever did so. In time he became accustomed to the hurdle and carefully learned to traverse it each time he brought one of his several planes back to earth.

It was just before Christmas when our house was first illuminated with light bulbs. As yet there were no light fixtures but Walter Hansen, the local electrician, had placed temporary bakelite receptacles in every room and while these were certainly not fancy, there was light.

That Christmas was something special since for the first time ever, our Christmas tree was decorated with a string of twelve electric light bulbs. This was great when all were working but the string was wired in series and a loose or faulty bulb turned off the entire set. It seemed that Irene spent the entire holiday season looking for culprit bulbs.

To help celebrate our new found light, Mother and Dad bought a record player and the only three 77.5 RPM record albums in town. We played "The Ink Spots, Andrew Sisters, and "The Browns" throughout the holiday season. To this day, Christmas always comes to mind whenever I hear the song about "Little Jimmy Brown."

It was several months before the yard, barns, and garage were wired for electricity but once again Walter Hansen did an excellent job. All went well, although he did have a worrisome afternoon when the job required a wire to pass directly over a pen which held a huge Yorkshire boar. This porcine brute of nearly a quarter ton had a very unfriendly disposition and understandably, Walter was less than happy with the need to be in his pen. To help, I was assigned the task of keeping this diabolical porker at bay. A pitch fork made the job easy but I did notice that Walter looked over his shoulder more than usual and he definitely had a propensity to drop things when the grunting and snarling tusker was a bit too close.

The real plus with this outdoor addition were three yard lights which made late chores a breeze. Equally important, an electric motor on the pump was much easier to start than the old John Deere one cylinder gasoline engine.

****

Grade nine had started in September but it wasn't until it became too cold for recess baseball that I became fully cognizant of my fortunate situation. Hardly anyone had taken notice, but at long last we had arrived. It was hard to believe but my classmates and I could now sit on the regal window sill that dominated and held sway over the lower classrooms and their diminutive inmates. My class had finally reached the upper level where we shared a room with grade ten. Reaching these giddy heights had seemed almost insurmountable when I first came to the Standard School from Craigantler. Now I had made it, and this prestigious window sill was at long last, mine to sit on and enjoy.

Grade nine, our last year before high school, was particularly important since it would set the curriculum for grades ten through twelve and determined whether we could or could not matriculate. We were lucky to have Mrs. Sorenson as our teacher. She helped us all make up for the many shortfalls and mix-ups that were left over from the previous year.

I remember working and studying hard but it is no lie to say that my most vivid memory of grade nine revolves around pimples. It was an epidemic. Pimples, pimples, pimples, they were everywhere. These ubiquitous blemishes were taking over. Some were red, some were inflamed, some were bumps, while still other were dints. Although some members of my class had only a few, there was no complete immunity and there was certainly no justice. The kids who were pristinely clean and virtually consumed with their personal hygiene seemed to be the worse for it. Those who washed their faces every Tuesday, if it was convenient, seemed least likely to have the affliction.

I had only a minor problem and could justifiably afford to be selfishly unconcerned. Despite this good fortune, I could not avoid hearing the serious recess talk which often centered on someone's facial zit. Invariably, this stimulated and aroused discussion on someone's recent success with a new treatment. There were lotions, salves, powders, soaps, pills, sun lamps, and diets, all of which offered new hope for the treatment of acne. Throughout the year, recipes for clean skin were traded around like a January cold in a Saskatchewan kindergarten. Nothing seemed to work and in the end almost everyone realized that the misery of the scourge was simply a part of growing up. Living with teenage vanity was not easy, but staying away from O'Henry chocolate bars probably helped. For the girls, the first use of lipstick was often thought to be the villain and the use of makeup was sure to create some really awkward choices.

****

It wasn't a shooting war but once again I had an uneasy feeling about the future. Newscasts were filled with concerns about a nuclear holocaust, often implying that our generation would be the last members of civilization. No doubt the reports were exaggerated but it was certain that a conflict of some order was brewing. Unlike the war just won, which was largely confined to Europe and the Pacific, this debacle, should it erupt into a serious conflict, promised to make Canada the meat in the sandwich. Nobody was entirely exempt but there is little doubt that we in Canada would be guaranteed a front seat exposure to any hostilities.

Having in mind that the Krauts were the antagonists in both W.W.I and W.W.II, the western leaders and the Soviets had carefully crafted a division of Germany. The intent of this measure was to safeguard the peace by fracturing the country and thereby diminishing its potential for a new military buildup. This division, agreed to at the Yalta Conference some three months before the final European armistice, effectively split the Rhineland into two sections - east and west. The partitioning also paid special attention to the city of Berlin, which while located in the eastern sector, was also divided into a Soviet and Western Alliance portion. To facilitate access to West Berlin, a special railway and motor transport corridor was provided which of necessity ran through a part of the Soviet zone.

Doubtless, this division constructively diminished Germany's ability to rearm and wage war. Unfortunately it also provided the Soviet Union with the opportunity for mischief and debauchery.

The war in Europe had been over since 1945 but this renegade member of the World War II alliance was becoming more and more belligerent with each passing day. Its uncompromising threats and quarrelsome behavior seemed to grow in intensity each time a Soviet official stood before an audience. This intimidating rhetoric was finally transformed into action when they blockaded all movement through the Berlin corridor, thus preventing all contact by land from the western sector to this isolated city. This blockade was finally lifted on May 12, 1949 when at last, the Soviet's realized that Western resolve would not allow any part of Berlin or West Germany to fall into their gluttonous hands. Despite the expense and inconvenience, the United States and the other members of the alliance had for 328 days airlifted everything needed to sustain this isolated and otherwise helpless city.

It wasn't totally obvious at the time but there is some suggestion that the formation of NATO had much to do with Stalin's realization that the Berlin Blockade was little more than a fool's errand. The North Atlantic Treaty Organization, embracing twelve nations, had been formalized on April 4, 1949, just one month before the Soviets allowed the Berlin corridor to reopen for ground transportation.

We were all happy when the blockade came to an end, but our euphoria was short lived, as on September 12, new and even more ominous treachery loomed in the mud of human destiny. Using stolen technology, the Soviets successfully tested an atomic bomb for the first time.

We did not know the motives or intentions of Joseph Stalin, the Soviet leader, but there is little doubt that his bombastic threats and intimidation's had to be taken seriously. At the very least, there was a constant cloud of uncertainty hanging over the tenuous peace. This was especially so for

Canadians since any real conflict would place us right between and in the path of the two major combatants.

Clearly we were embroiled in a very risky cold war and while there had been no loss of life, it was adversely effecting the national demeanor. Newspaper headlines and radio broadcasts invariably made reference to the Soviet Union's continuing threats and intimidation's.

Meanwhile, I was living through and surviving the awkwardness of feeling grownup but still to young for a driver's license and still not old enough for a summer job. For all of this, I had enjoyed a most memorable summer. Quite frankly, neither my wish to be older nor Stalin's menacing behavior and his nuclear status could dampen my enthusiasm for high school and the year ahead. Moreover, the months just past had been punctuated with a whole litany of pleasantries.

For starters, Irene had found summer work at Kinbasket Lake in the mountains of British Columbia. Here at this tourist camp, located on the Big Bend Highway, she would be employed as a waitress for the months of July and August.

Mother and Dad were delighted with Irene's resourcefulness in finding such a fine summer job. While other kids from Standard had previously enjoyed vacation employment at Kinbasket, it was a relatively isolated spot and little was known about it. Therefore, it is not surprising that we were anxious to see it and besides, it wasn't long after Irene's departure that we began to miss her. Finding a remedy for these problems was easy and plans were quickly made for a few leisure days at the mountain resort of Kinbasket Lake. Not only did we see Irene, Dad and I went fishing and wonder of wonders, we even caught a few.

****

317

We had barely arrived home when I undertook a second vacation at the Sylvan Lake Bible Camp. Unlike the previous year which was fraught with boredom, I met a whole bunch of super kids, some of whom exhibited some admirable qualities and maturity. To this day I credit those few days as a turning point that helped shape many of my plans for the future. As an example, it was at this camp that I firmed up my resolve to leave the farm. I had known for some time that the possibility of becoming a farmer never really existed, but despite this knowledge, I had never made serious plans for an alternative life style. Dad had burned the farm's mortgage in early spring but having three hundred and twenty acres in the family didn't provide much of a basis for a father and son operation. Moreover, buying my own land and equipment was out of the question as the interest that had accrued to my Royal Bank savings account was grossly inadequate. Finally and more importantly, if there was ever any doubt about finishing high school, those thoughts vanished during those few but constructive days at Sylvan Lake.

Arriving home I found that my grade nine results had arrived from The Department of Education in Edmonton. I had passed with a solid grade which allowed me to extend my education and pursue a senior matriculation program. While I had no specific plans, I was delighted since it was now possible to at least harbor the idea of attending university.

****

The summer of 1949 was a blast but as the days grew shorter and the leaves lost their luster, Irene returned home from her summer employment. As usual, we made our annual preschool trek to Calgary for clothes and books. This year we were a bit late and F.E. Osborne's book exchange on 8th Avenue was a virtual mad house. While most of the used texts in good condition were gone, we did manage to elbow our way through the crowd and save a buck or two by picking up a few that were used but still contained most of the requisite pages. In the end, I brought home a mix of new and used books which may or may not have helped with my education.

The content has long since been forgotten but I still have a clear memory of the French text. This well used reference came complete with the picture and address of the previous owner. Charlotte was her name and she lived in Nanton, Alberta.

It was no big deal but it was obvious that Charlotte's picture and carefully scripted address was a clear invitation for some serious correspondence.

I don't recall if I ever really intended to write Charlotte a letter but it wasn't long before the whole class knew of the address and picture in my book. Unknown to me, almost every guy in the high school copied her address and beating me to the punch dropped her a line, and what a line it must have been. Long before I came to grips with my own procrastination's, they had all received her less than friendly reply. Adding to the insult, all of the letters were identical, having been duplicated on a hectograph. We all made good sport of it and for the balance of the year, the daily greeting among my colleagues was, "Have you heard from Charlotte?"

Returning to the hectograph, this marvel of years past, was one of the few tools that teachers had at their disposal for producing multiple copies of printed matter. In the absence of more sophisticated copying machines, the hectograph was frequently used and was available in every classroom during my early school years. The copying process was messy but simple.

First of all, using a special indelible pen, the teacher wrote out the material on a normal sheet of paper. This first copy was then carefully positioned face down on a glycerin coated sheet of gelatin. In so doing, the written message was transferred to the glycerin. From this, additional copies could be lifted by positioning other blank sheets of paper over the gelatin surface. Each copy was progressively fainter than the one that preceded it but with care eight to ten readable copies were possible. Some of Charlotte's letters were nearly illegible.

Everything else aside, grade ten was unusually agreeable and moved along without serious incident. For the first time, I had two teachers, Mr. Bragg and Mr. Jardine. Actually, there were three counting Mr. Hebert, my once a week shop teacher.

To accommodate a growing number of younger students, an old unused school house had been moved into the school yard. This additional classroom allowed for a reshuffling of the classes, leaving all of the grade nines back with the grade eight's. It also left grades ten through twelve in Mr. Bragg's home room. For the most part the kids who wished to be elsewhere and were not interested in further studies had left for the big commercial world, thus leaving our classes generally productive with fewer interruptions and less foolishness. Those of us that remained were small in number which probably accounted for the tremendous camaraderie which we all enjoyed. Except for those who lived in town and went home for lunch, every noon hour became a most pleasurable social event. Adding to this, we almost always topped it off with a downtown trip to Betty and William's Restaurant for a Pepsi, or for those few who had the money, a butterscotch sundae.

If the weather was inclement and the downtown trek was out of the question, Stanley Mellsen and Dennis Myrthu, both grade twelve students, could usually be found in the chemistry lab attempting to produce nitroglycerin. On cold days this escapade had the potential for warming things up. This was especially so when a teacher happened to make an unexpected appearance and the whole mess would quickly be tossed out of the second story window.

****

School had suddenly become a lot of fun and except for French, I was enjoying all of my classes. Mr. Bragg had a way of making most of our studies interesting and on occasion, a real kick. Probably English was his favorite subject and it showed.

Without a doubt, one of his most famous lessons was taught when he requested a writing assignment which was intended to duplicate a report suitable for a newspaper. I chose to pen an article for the sports section in which the home team won. As you might expect, there was a fascinating array of subjects with each student selecting one with which he or she had some level of comfort. Time has faded the event but I think it was Miriam Nielsen who chose to write a social page story about a lavish wedding. While none of our compositions were factual they were expected to represent a realistic situation. Had it been authentic, Miriam's story would most certainly have described a glorious affair. At the very least, it would have been nice and indeed that adjective was used incessantly throughout the article.

Clearly Mr. Bragg thought that the word "nice" had been overworked and to make the point, he asked Miriam to read her assignment to the entire class. That would probably have been easy except for his insistence that she insert the world "damn" before each offensive but descriptive "nice". After the first few sentences Miriam and the whole class were laughing hysterically and reading further was out of the question. Had she done so, her story would have gone something like this.

"In a double-ring ceremony on a damn nice sunny day, Jean Nielsen and Harry Brown exchanged wedding vows.

Jean, the daughter of Pete and Mary Nielsen, was given in marriage by her father at Nazareth Lutheran Church. She had chosen a damn nice traditional satin gown with a dropped waistline, full skirt and a damn nice cathedral length train. The net bodice featured damn nice pearl chevrons front and back and full length lily point sleeves with damn nice pearl on lace appliqués and matching lace inserts.

Her damn nice chapel length organza veil was gathered at the back and secured by a damn nice headband of braided pearl strands, matching her damn nice pearl earrings, a gift from the groom. She carried a damn nice cascade bouquet of white silk lilies, gladioli and miniature orchids.

Jean's attendants each wore a damn nice floor length dress of powder blue satin. The gowns were highlighted with damn nice bouquets of multicolored spring flowers.

The groom, son of Don and Nancy Brown of Calgary, wore a damn nice black three piece tuxedo with tails, a damn nice bow tie and a boutonnière of damn nice miniature orchids."

The article went on, but with apologies to Miriam, the foregoing excerpt speaks for itself. When the report was read, it portrayed good solid humor but no one missed the point and it is unlikely that any of our class will ever again use repetitious adjectives.

****

With the arrival of spring came my sixteenth birthday and a most important milestone, a driver's license. It is amazing what a two by three inch piece of paper can do for one's persona. Curiously, being able to drive was not a prerequisite as in those days no one was required to prove a competence behind the wheel. Three dollars and proof of age earned anyone the right to drive an automobile or a truck having a gross weight of not more than twelve thousand pounds.

Equally important, at this advanced age I was now qualified to accept employment and had every hope of finding work during the forthcoming summer months. Apart from the prospect of a job, I was ecstatic and fully intended to add to the small fortune that had been amassed during the winter and early spring. It was about to end but Dad had paid out quite a few dollars for the goals that I had managed to score during the hockey season. Added to this, I was about to cash in on my best ever fur catch.

My trap line for the winter just past had been particularly profitable as it had included two beaver, approximately two dozen muskrat, several rabbits and one weasel. Actually, the beavers had been residents of a local irrigation ditch. While otherwise a protected animal, I had obtained a special nuisance permit from the R.C.M.P. office in Strathmore and had permission to trap them. Left in the ditch, these busy little fur bearers could quickly destroy an irrigation system. Skinning, scraping, and stretching my beaver pelts had been a lot of work but I was glad to have them. They alone represented a good part of the sixty some dollars that Simpson and Lea, fur buyers, paid for my extracurricular winter's work.

To effect the sale of my furs, Dad delivered me to the nine mile corner, where for the princely sum of one dollar and thirty cents, Greyhound carried me and my shopping bag filled with furs right into the heart of Calgary.

The leather part of my pelts were as dry as parchment but in the heat of the bus, it soon became clear to everyone that something was amiss. By the time we reached the city the entire bus smelled like an eighteenth century Indian encampment and I was embarrassed. I was however nicely dressed and remained very circumspect throughout the trip. As far as is known, no one knew that my bulging shopping bag was the source of this unique and overpowering fragrance.

****

Grade ten turned out to be a fantastic year. To be sure, it was not all shenanigans but the camaraderie with my fellow students and the quality of the teachers made everyday a worthwhile experience. During almost any recess, which happened to be combined with decent weather, most of the older boys, yours truly included, could be found catching fly balls hit by Raymond Klemmensen. Raymond didn't really play baseball but there were few who could hit fly balls better. I was always on the catching end and it was a lot of fun.

Throughout the entire winter and spring, the noon hour refreshments at Betty and Williams continued to be the cornerstone of our classes social activities. Our stroll to the downtown wooden sidewalks of Broadway also included a peek at the local movie billboard. This newspaper sized Hollywood humbug announced the next feature to be shown at the old, soon to be demolished S & S Hall and was as a consequence changed weekly. For maximum exposure, the advertisement was positioned within a wooden frame that was spiked to a short weather beaten fence that spanned the gap between Walter's electric shop and the post office. The paper flyer was firmly held in place by a chicken wire screen that covered the whole set.

In most cases the gaudy message was of little help in predicting the quality of the next scheduled flick. Indeed, it seemed that the kaleidoscopic colors and exciting art work shown on the posters were more often than not inversely proportional to the actual character and nature of the forthcoming show.

I never paid much attention to this false advertising since the picture show was little more than an excuse to formalize a Saturday night rendezvous with some of my friends. During the winter Raymond Klemmensen did the driving but following my birthday and drivers license, I was able to drive myself. Having the trust of my parents for use of the family automobile was something very special.

Realistically, a sorry show viewed from the hard and sliver filled benches of the hall needed more than a little help to make a worthwhile night out on the town.

Looking back I can't recall any of the movies that were shown and in fact, time has also challenged my memory of the activities that followed. The little that comes to mind always involved the ambiance of Betty and William's Cafe where much of the post movie visiting and chin wagging took place. Here in one of the painted plywood booths there was room for at least six kids. If there happened to be a gang of eight that could work equally well with a little crowding. In any event no one was expected to spend more than a dime for a Pepsi and few did more. Equally important, it only cost a nickel to crank up the glitzy juke box that stood near the cash register and which was loaded with all of the latest hits. Our visits could not possibly have been cost effective but for some reason both Betty and William seemed to enjoy our sometime lengthy visits.

When finally we had overworked the generous hospitality of our hosts, we could always find more to talk about out on the street or in Raymond's car. Life was good.

While the curriculum, as set by the Department of Education, was not strictly adhered to, everyone benefited from the less rigid class sessions during which time many of the more fundamental and useful social needs were emphasized. Perhaps it was for this reason that Mr. Bragg had only a modest objection when Mother and Dad chose to revisit the United States nearly a week before the term was scheduled to expire. Both Irene and I had the good fortune of missing final exams but were advanced to the next grade on the basis of our year's work and the marks that we achieved during the many exams that were held at various intervals throughout the term.

****

I think it was June 23, 1950, when we left home for our second vacation to Iowa and Minnesota. There we could visit Grandmother, uncles, aunts, cousins, and one of Mother's friends from her teenage years at Atterdag College in Solvang, California.

Speed was of the essence so there was little chance that any of us would mistake this hurried junket with a sightseeing venture. Upon entry to the United States we barreled along Highway 2, reaching Reserve, Montana, early the second day. Here we met Cousin Ronald Jensen, and his young bride, Arlene. Ronald, a Lutheran pastor, had just recently moved to this remote community where he served several country congregations. We became aware of his hectic schedule the following day which was a Sunday. After conducting service and preaching a sermon in several churches, Ron rushed home to pick up his baseball equipment, whereupon he ventured forth to pitch the locals to victory. I was much impressed.

By the fourth or fifth day we were through North Dakota and scheduled to arrive in Minneapolis in late afternoon. We were still a few hundred miles from our primary destination when we learned that President Truman had ordered air and naval units into South Korea to fend off the aggressive excursions of China and North Korea. These military ventures carried the offensive actions of North Korea south of the thirty-eighth parallel, the dividing line agreed to after the Japanese surrender in 1945.

Dad had been tuned into the world scene and was not terribly surprised. For me the news, supplied by the gas station attendant, was a particular shock. It seemed that the war to end all wars had just recently been won. Now the world was once again embroiled in a bloody conflict. I was terribly disappointed.

The visit to Minneapolis allowed me to become better acquainted with Cousin Garth whom I knew to be interested in hunting and the shooting sports. I was of course keen to see all of my relatives but in addition hoped that I would have the opportunity to purchase a shotgun. To this end, Garth was a terrific help. It was the first or second night in Minneapolis when he took me to his shooting club. Here under lights, there was opportunity to shoot dozens of new and used shotguns, all of which were for sale. It was a difficult decision but in the end, a new Model 12 Winchester was selected. I had been prepared to spend a good part of my savings but with Garth's help and his club connections, an excellent fowling piece was purchased at a very reasonable price.

During the next few days Garth showed me how to call crows which led to some excellent shooting near the metropolis of the Twin Cities. I didn't shoot nearly as many as Garth, but I did score a few hits which gave me a good deal of confidence with my new twelve gauge smooth bore. Added to this, Garth gave me one of his old tan hunting jackets. It would certainly offer better camouflage than a brightly colored school jacket.

Since Cousin Fred was attending university in Denmark for the summer, I would have preferred to stay in Minneapolis where I could continue to pop a few crows with my new thunder stick. This was not to be and while most of our Iowa time was spent in Spencer with Uncle John and Aunt Ragnhild, Mother was determined to visit an old college friend who lived in a southern sector of the state. A common acquaintance had told her that this classmate from years past was living with her family of four children in the Audabon Hills near the small town of Elk Horn.

Our trip to Elk Horn represented a relatively modest drive of about one hundred miles. It was however anything but pleasant since it was several degrees above the century mark and the humidity was so heavy that one could almost see it. Our car was not air-conditioned and shooting crows under a Minnesota shade tree seemed infinitely more gratifying.

It was a sticky, tiresome ride but in late afternoon we finally located Mother's college friend. In spite of the uncomfortable heat and humidity, we were all pleased that she would be able to visit this dear friend from her teenage years.

The whole county of Audubon is laced with hills and the farm buildings of Mother's friend were located on particularly uneven ground. Each major building sat on its own isolated berm or hill. The weed infested valleys between were cluttered with rusting farm implements ranging from abandoned horse mowers to old steel lugged tractors. The whole scene was classic hillbilly and should have been in the funny papers.

Our arrival quickly brought Mother's college pal to the front door. Before she rushed out to embrace Mother, she removed her soiled apron with which she shooed away a flock of chickens that had been resting in the shade of the front porch. While the sagging verandah had broken away from the house, it provided shade both above and below. The commotion of our arrival in combination with the noisy welcome caused a copper colored sow to retreat further into a gaping entry that had been burrowed under the porch. The half dozen piglets that had been nursing complained but soon settled down amid the spent corn cobs and dusty shade of this domestic lair.

Upon entry into the front parlor, we met the rest of the family. The four barefoot children ranging in age from about sixteen to less than school age were trying desperately to deal with the heat of the day by lounging on the cool linoleum floor. With shades fully drawn, the room was dark except for the glowing dial of a small radio in one corner. We hardly noticed the man of the house who sat with his ear fixed to its speaker. He seemed not to notice our arrival and it soon became clear that he was tuned into a local news broadcast that was probably covering the police action in Korea. While not a mute, he was a man of few words and even without the distraction of a Des Moines newscast, said very little. It was Mother's friend who did all of the talking and it was clear that she was in charge.

Dinner was served in a large formal dining room and while there was a place for everyone, the children chose not to sit. Instead their food was plucked from the table in handfuls whereupon they retreated to a corner or side sofa for ingestion of each morsel. In any event, the vittels were wholesome and there was certainly nothing lacking in the hospitality.

Apparently it had been discussed earlier as Mother didn't protest when we were invited to stay for the night. At first, sleeping arrangements were a bit bizarre but when final positions were set, Dad and I found ourselves sleeping under the tin roof of a storage shed. It had been a hot day but that was nothing compared to the temperature and stagnant air of this small shelter. With no windows, there was absolutely no air movement and the sun's rays of the day had left the tin roof as hot as a blacksmith's forge. Neither Dad nor I slept and if he hadn't been so angry with the whole affair, it would have been a good time for some solid conversation. As it was, I couldn't get him to stop talking about the heat and the miserable visit.

We left immediately after breakfast. Everyone in the family was glad to see the Iowa hills and ramshackled farmstead fade from view. Dad very wisely kept his thoughts to himself and Mother said very little about the visit. Indeed, she hardly ever spoke of her friend again.

****

Leaving Elk Horn, we drove directly home stopping only for gas, food and sleep. Oh yes, we did take a few photo opportunities at the Corn palace in Mitchell, South Dakota, the Wall Drug Store, and the advertised geographical center of the USA. In having this balancing fulcrum in South Dakota, it would seem that some clever engineer embraced Alaska and Hawaii in his rather imaginative calculations.

COMING OF AGE

Returning home from our junket to the United States was especially important for Irene since she immediately left for a second summer at Kinbasket Lake. I had applied for employment too, but had been informed in early June that the Tourist Villa's staffing requirements had been satisfied. The letter had the usual placation, "we'll keep you in mind if our needs change." Knowing that these words were common to all rejections, I paid them little heed.

It was nearly a week later when Dad and I were preparing to irrigate the alfalfa field that I received an urgent telegram from Kinbasket which read, "Get here, the tourists are coming in great numbers and we need you." I was delighted and left the next day for Kinbasket Lake via a Greyhound bus. Dad didn't really need my help.

Kinbasket Tourist Villas was on the Big Bend Highway some seventy two miles north of Golden, British Columbia. This dusty, pot hole infested trail, open only during the summer months followed the large northerly bend of the Columbia River and traversed some 193 miles from Golden to Revelstoke. The more recently completed and more direct Rogers Pass Highway shortened this distance to slightly less than one hundred miles.

The lake from which the tourist camp took its name was approximately twelve miles long and two miles wide. It had been named in 1866 by Walter Moberly who in surveying the Selkirks received considerable assistance from the great Indian Chief, Paul Ignatius Kinbasket. In many respects this body of water was little more than a widening of the mighty Columbia River which flowed into the lake at its southern limits and rushed out at its northern shore en route to the Pacific. On a calm day the enormity of the stream left a distinctly visible current on the water's surface.

Sitting like a pearl on a string, the lake and the Columbia flowed between the rugged Rocky Mountains to the east and the craggy Selkirks to the west. These magnificent towering features were softened by mature stands of cedar and balsam fir which stood tall and thick on the lake's shores. It was truly a beautiful spot in which to spend the summer.

The tourist camp was located on both sides of the highway. On the west, adjacent to a small gravel bottomed pond, stood the coffee shop. This gaudily painted centerpiece of the camp, also serving as the motel office, was built much like a barn with the interior showing water stained two by four studs and rafters. On a warm sunny day it was unpleasantly hot and during a rainy period, the cold crept in along with a few drips from the underside of its vaulted roof.

The public area of this barn like building featured a comfortable lounge with several sofas and an old upright piano. It was intended to provide a quiet atmosphere for road weary travelers and many took advantage of its rustic ambiance.

Behind the foyer, the guest tables stood in well organized rows. These were painted relics, all draped in oil cloth with adjacent wooden chairs, none of which seemed to match. More importantly, the simple sandwich lunches, prepared in a modest kitchen at the rear, were wholesome and well liked by most of the patrons. As a Greyhound Bus stop, short orders were the specialty and to accommodate the sudden rush of business, the girls who served and waited on the tables were expected to hustle.

The remaining part of the west campus was represented by a dozen small cabins of various size and shape. These rustic cottages enjoyed wood stoves for heating and cooking but no bathroom amenities. Showers were only available at a common bath house next to an outdoor privy. Despite the mosquito infestation, these crude facilities were filled with tourists virtually every night.

The east side of the highway featured a service station, a staff house, and a campground for those who wished to pitch a tent or had the courage and resolve to pull a trailer over the winding dusty highway. This primitive parking and camping facility, adjacent to the staff house, was bounded on its northern boundary by the Sullivan River, a rather large glacier fed stream which dumped its silt filled ice melt into Kinbasket Lake at that point.

The service station, my place of employment, like the buildings opposite, was anything but fancy. The crude filling station office was attached to a dirt floored, three bay garage which stood behind two old fashioned gravity gas pumps. Here the visible glass columns each held ten gallons of Ethyl gasoline which was sold for fifty cents per gallon. In its day that was expensive and very few tourists accepted a tank of fuel without making some comment about the price, which in a less remote area would be in the order of thirty five cents per gallon.

Selling gasoline provided me with my first ever exposure to credit cards. This marketing tool was in its infancy but there is little doubt that it enhanced oil company profits by encouraging travel. While the "buy now - pay later" syndrome was alive and well, it was employed with considerable caution and as such gave rise to no end of problems for those of us working the pumps.

In those early days, Esso offered several credit card arrangements which presumably reflected the credit worthiness of each individual customer. For example, a white card, available to those with top credit credentials, was valid for one year and more or less offered unlimited usage. In contrast, a tan colored card was valid for three months and carried some restrictions which precluded its use for expensive motor repairs. In normal circumstances these cards offered few if any problems to the gasoline vendor. The darker, almost brown card, was fraught with problems as it was usually issued to a poor credit risk for a very limited period. A vacationing carrier was often miles from home when his card expired. In addition, these limited purpose cards had upper limits which denied their use for the purchase of a tire or any costly automobile repair.

Hardly a day would pass when we were not obliged to refuse a traveling motorist of a much needed item such as a tire or battery since he was deemed to have insufficient credit. Also we received weekly lists of card numbers that were no longer valid and which we were expected to lift from the carrier when presented for use. At times this could be a bit awkward.

The Chapmans, owners of the tourist camp, were truly excellent people to work for. John supervised the service station and performed all of the difficult mechanical jobs while his wife, Gladys, managed the coffee shop and cabins. Both insisted on a high standard of service for their customers.

At the Esso gas pumps, a single car driving up would cause a sudden explosion of activity with me at the gas tank, Bill Craig cleaning the windshields and Gerald Knowlton asking the startled tourist to pop the hood so that he could check the oil, fan belt etc. It was truly an unusual act and no car drove off the pumps without the suggestion of an oil change and a new fan belt. During the two summer months when "Kinbasket Service" was fully staffed, it was the largest Atlas tire and accessory outlet in the province. Tires were a big item since the potholes and graveled bed of the highway could be sure to do their part.

Gerald Knowlton was an exceptional salesman and selling these extra items made the service station a major profit center for the entire facility. While my salesmanship was a poor second to Gerald's, I did on one occasion sell seven fan belts and two oil changes before breakfast.

During the busy intervals there wasn't any regular time off for we three who worked the gas pumps and garage. Each day started about 6 AM and usually ended after dark. Apart from pumping gasoline, there was also the business of changing oil and fixing tires. The work wasn't exciting, as messing with gasoline, oil, tires, and fan belts more or less provides a complete job description. There were however exceptions such as spraying DDT into the mosquito infested brush that surrounded the guest cottages. This was done on an almost daily basis and for some reason this task fell to me. DDT, the now outlawed insecticide, was used throughout the summer and although I handled gallons of the stuff, there were no obvious ill effects from its toxicity or the incredible number of bites that I earned for invading the mosquito's favorite domain.

As you might expect, with such a busy schedule, there were few opportunities to hike, fish and explore the area. One notable exception comes to mind. On this occasion, during a slack period, I decided to take a walk over the nearly quarter mile wooden bridge that spanned the muddy estuary of the Sullivan River. I was approximately half way when coming my way was a car chasing a black bear directly toward me. The car was sounding its horn and with only one direction available, the bear was in full flight. Blocking a frightened bear's exit from trouble was not my idea of fun and it was clear that quick action was required. As the bear and car sped by, I found myself hanging onto the outside of the guard rail hoping that I wouldn't fall into the river below or that the panicked black brute would feel threatened by my presence. Somehow I managed to stay clear of the silt filled glacier water that was streaming below and surmise that the speeding bruin was not intimidated, nor did it notice the white knuckles that were clutching the top rail of the bridge as it zipped by.

Kinbasket was great but by the end of August Irene and I were happy to return home. Sleeping-in for a change was a real treat but having nearly two hundred dollars to deposit in the bank was even better. Tippy was particularly happy to see us. Also our being away was a new experience and it is certain that Mother and Dad had missed us as well. The bad news was the well water, which after a two months absence, showed its temper once again.

****

Although Dana School in Standard offered all grades through high school, the modest teaching staff was unable to handle the entire grade twelve curriculum during one year. The requisite courses for a high school diploma were offered but a matriculation standing could only be achieved if the student was prepared to spend two years in grade twelve. Actually, this idea had some merit due to the complexity of the grade and the difficulty of the departmental exams.

Irene was eager to throw off the shackles of school so she decided to enter Mount Royal College in Calgary. Here, she could focus on all of the courses, wind up her final year and obtain her senior matriculation. With her leaving I was once again without her companionship.

For me, grade eleven was little more than a continuation of grade ten. My teachers were the same and there was still a strong camaraderie and good spirit among all of the students. Indeed, it was even better as the grade ten group entering our room was much larger than the four who graduated back in June.

The real change in my life was my continuing ability to drive to various events. This meant that I could enjoy a whole host of social activities without troubling Dad or someone else for a ride. Even coming and going to school had improved since my friend, Kenneth Larsen, had acquired his own automobile which he drove to class almost every day. He was always very generous with his Ford coupe and a ride was available on an almost daily basis.

During the same year Svend Nielsen started to arrive at school via a new but very small Morris Minor. This tiny British built automobile sported four seats and could under considerable duress be expected to haul four small people. This was often put to the test when at lunch hour many of us made our daily excursion to Betty and William's Cafe for a Pepsi or milk shake. I don't recall the count but Alex Christensen, the local butcher, swears that he once counted eleven kids unload from that mini automobile. It was of course a challenge and if memory serves, we once managed to pack in thirteen kids. Unfortunately, there was no room for the driver

With such a load, and in deference to the springs and tires, the short trip to the cafe was driven slowly and with extreme care. This caution was not at all obvious if Svend's little car was in need of repairs and as a substitute he drove his father's new Packard. When this rare event occurred, one could almost see Eldon Rasmussen salivate. Eldon loved cars and he loved speed. More importantly, he could at times cajole Svend into letting him drive this beautiful luxury automobile. That always produced a short spin into the country and if anyone happened to be along, they were sure to get a fast ride.

Eldon was a superb driver and he handled speed with incredible aplomb. No one was surprised when a few years later, Eldon could be seen as one of the drivers in the annual Indianapolis 500.

****

For some reason, the village of Standard didn't bother to operate the skating rink during the winter of 1950-51. While there was a fair bit of complaining, I didn't fuss about it much. It was almost a treat not having to attend all of the hockey practices. Besides having access to the family car opened the possibility of playing for the Gleichen Gunners. They had a great hockey program and Buster Stott, their coach, didn't much care if you were from Gleichen or the planet Mars. Rex Green, Norm Devitt and I ventured south to Gunner town for a few games but it soon became obvious that without easy access to practice ice, we were out of our league.

It seems funny now but in the absence of hockey, I decided, as a substitute, to join the church choir. Nazareth Lutheran Church always had a terrific choir and some truly superb singing voices in every section. I was not foolish enough to think that my voice would add to the pool of talent but as a bass, I knew that there was a spot in the back row where I could hardly be seen and hopefully not heard. As expected, I ended up in the back row and as a bonus, lucky enough to be seated next to Alfred Jensen (no relation) who helped keep me in line and occasionally on key. Unfortunately, Alfie could only do so much.

Stanley Rasmussen, an exquisite baritone, was also an excellent and very talented director. With his help and fastidious dedication, I soon blended in or more accurately, next to Alfie's strong voice, became generally unnoticed with little damage potential.

After a few Thursday night practice sessions, the choir was all set to sing a special anthem for Sunday service. Everything was going along just fine when suddenly my voice cracked. The offending verse escapes memory but for sure and certain, neither Stanley nor Martin Luther, the composer, intended to have a burst of falsetto appear right in the middle of "A Mighty Fortress Is Our God," but there it was and there I stood, red faced in the back row.

Poor Alfie pretended not to notice but the smile on his face belied the truth. Also there were a few backward glances from the altos and sopranos. That was all that I needed. The next Sunday found me safely back in the pews where little damage could be inflicted on the service. Once again Nazareth Lutheran Church could continue in the tradition of having a fine choir.

****

Sitting back in the nave and studiously avoiding the hymns gave me the opportunity to think about and ponder my future. Time was moving quickly and my seventeenth birthday was approaching. Since starvation was not a viable choice, a career in music was never considered. Thankfully there were other possibilities.

It is probable that every Canadian boy has from time to time fantasized about becoming a Mountie. Certainly I did and while my interest had diminished, there was in my possession a whole file of information regarding a career in The Royal Canadian Mounted Police. Having fully recovered from the cop fright that I endured as a five year old, there were rare moments when the thought of becoming a policeman made sense. In fact my attraction to this occupation had first been kindled when Irene and I played an important role in the capture of two car thieves.

This noteworthy event had occurred a few years earlier in September, 1947. As it happened, Mother and Dad were briefly away and Irene and I had just arrived home from school. It was raining like a ruptured water main and our road was almost impassable. Despite these horrid conditions, a relatively new car managed to make its way into our yard with two male occupants. It was clear that the vehicle had been driving on side roads as even the inside of the front door panel was plastered with mud. While both came to the door, the driver, the apparent spokesperson, advised that they had been stuck and were nearly out of gas. He asked if we could supply some so that they could make their way back to the highway. He went on to say that he didn't have any small bills or change on his person so would be unable to pay for the fuel until the following week.

As the story sounded plausible, I ventured out into the rain and poured about three gallons into the car's gasoline tank. The stranger wanted more but I held to the three gallons knowing that it was less than five miles to the less muddy highway and Arthur's filling station. The driver accepted this without complaint and confirmed that they planned to go directly to the service station for a real fill up.

For some reason it seemed that the pair were less than truthful so I took the trouble to record the car's license number on the gas drum. Curiously Irene, who was watching the entire affair from the kitchen window, was also skeptical of their behavior and she recorded their tag number. We became even more dubious of their actions when my travel instructions were totally ignored and they headed south instead of north toward the highway and service station.

It wasn't long before Mother and Dad came home and we persuaded Dad to phone the RCMP office in Strathmore. Sure enough, it was a hot car and the police were looking for it. As a result of our suspicions and Dad's call to the police, the car was recovered and both thieves were apprehended a few hours later.

A few weeks later Irene and I received a special letter of commendation from the Alberta superintendent of the RCMP. More importantly the crooks earned a year's room and board at government expense.

The incident of the car thieves briefly spurred my interest in a police career but learning that mounties were still expected to ride horses put the kibosh on the whole idea. There was still a strong memory of working the potato patch with Diamond.

****

In my search for a livelihood, there was a very brief period when becoming a minister was considered. In point of fact several of my Jensen cousins were on that path and of course Uncle John M. Jensen was a well known pastor in the Lutheran church.

For various reasons, becoming a man of the cloth had some appeal. Being inherently lazy, it also occurred to me that the job required only one fully developed sermon per week. Moreover, if Standard was any example, a congregational change could be expected every five to six years. As a very worst case and allowing for vacations, that meant that a pastor could realistically get by with a life time production and repertoire of no more than three hundred sermons. With the probability of a new parish every five years, the entire series could be repeated and no one would be the wiser. Besides, I had already read the text book and that wasn't likely to change.

During these deliberations I became particularly sensitive to the role of our new pastor, Lief Kirkegaard. He was my only real contact with a member of the clergy and except for the week that had been spent at Sylvan Lake Bible Camp a year earlier, there was little opportunity to observe the role of a Lutheran preacher. Watching Kirkegaard was not terribly revealing but his style did allow me to focus on a few of the not so nice elements of the job.

He had arrived in September and brought with him the epitome of "preacher's kids." Not one, but three. Yes count them, Carl, Paul and Celestia. No doubt they have grown up to become fine citizens but as youngsters they had all of the attributes that gave PK's their unsavory reputation.

Being tolerant of his children's behavior spilled over to the church services and it wasn't long after his arrival that the entire Sunday morning service became something of a zoo. In this atmosphere, developing an attitude and insight into the business of becoming a man of the cloth was all but impossible. The distractions were enormous and all thoughts of following Uncle John's vocation were certainly put to the test.

In Kirkegaard's Sunday morning service, parents often allowed their small children to play under the pews. In theory this could be expected to keep them occupied and quiet but regrettably this was not to be. For starters, there was always more than one child banging around the senior parishioners feet. To make matters worse, some of them had toys that produced a good deal of confusion and some very unfamiliar and irreverent sounds. Finally and more importantly, there wasn't much head room on the underside of the church furniture. Standing up in this perilous situation was fraught with risk and guaranteed to produce a loud "bonk." Predictably this seemingly innocent sound would bring on a explosive outburst of excruciating anguish that every mother should recognize.

On one occasion the eruption was so thunderous that I thought the windows would shatter. Through it all, Reverend Kirkegaard hardly grimaced and it became obvious that I could never emulate such an unabashed response to this absolutely deafening paroxysm. With this as a background, it became easy to forever give up the idea of becoming a preacher.

****

With spring came baseball and as usual Standard had a truly noteworthy team. This year was even better as it had been organized by Stan Larsen, a relatively new resident, who had a true passion for the game. The old fashioned idea of playing Strathmore, Rockyford, Chancellor or Rosebud was now deemed to be archaic since Stan had ensconced the team into the Chinook League. This federation included teams from larger centers including Calgary and Drumheller. To be competitive the towns that were previously foes were now an important source of talent for the super team that Stan was so eager to manage and put on the road. To be sure, there were many top quality players in our own community but the schedule and competition demanded more than Standard could provide.

I played center field for the high school team and for a brief period wore a Standard uniform but that was as far as it went. Actually, another summer at Kinbasket was being planned so early in June I turned in my team equipment.

Before leaving for the summer, there was opportunity to be a spectator at some of the Chinook League games. They were excellent and the locals were incredibly loyal and supportive. More often than not, the entire baseball field was surrounded with automobiles. While the stands behind home plate were always filled, it was the cars that evidenced the truly outstanding sponsorship of the team. A hit by the home team brought on an almost deafening applause with several hundred car horns all blasting at once.

****

Except for the inordinate number of tire repairs required by Greyhound and listening to the yarns of the exploration workers across the lake, my summer at Kinbasket was basically a repetition of the previous year.

During August, Canada had a national rail strike which put considerable pressure on the bus systems. To meet the challenge, Greyhound pressed most of their old equipment into service. Their tires were in terrible shape and hardly a day went by when I wasn't required to break down and repair several of these heavy truck tires.

As for the exploration, Consolidated Mining and Smelting Company owned a lease across the lake and were busy studying a lead zinc deposit. I became acquainted with the project engineer and the foreman of T. Connors Diamond Drillers, the company responsible for working the find. These were interesting people and I was inspired to consider many new ideas and possibilities for a career selection. While mining didn't particularly appeal to me, being an engineer in the earth sciences appeared to have some potential.

Apparently the mountain on the opposite shore was virtually a solid lump of lead- silver but that didn't stop the bears from raiding the kitchen and wrecking the driller's camp. The workers had to eat but in an effort to avoid more carnage and bear trouble, the foreman moved most of their food supplies next to Sid Webber's trappers cabin which was on our side of the river. This single room log cabin was approximately one mile south of the tourist villas and while the food was stored in an adjacent tent everyone thought that the new location and its proximity to the cabin would offer some protection.

It all sounded good but the strategy was short lived. Within a few days, the bears on our side discovered the food cache and of course they brought their appetites.

The drillers were not missing any meals but Bill Craig and I were given every encouragement to shoot the bear or bears if possible. It sounded like great sport but the only free time that we had was late at night when the tourists were off the road and we should be asleep. That didn't stop us and for several nights, we sat outside in the dark next to Sid's cabin waiting for a bear. We had John Chapman's old 95 Winchester with a flashlight taped to the underside of the barrel. We were all set for a bear but were totally unprepared for the hordes of mosquitoes that nearly ate us alive. On each occasion, we surrendered to these vulturous creatures just after midnight only to learn that the hungry bruins came to dinner some twenty minutes later.

We never did get a shot at a bear but Sid's wife did and to the best of my knowledge, her marksmanship solved the problem. The August hide was worthless, and as Mrs. Webber wanted to get rid of the carcass, Bill and I helped her push the dead brute into the river. All that we got out of the affair were the countless swollen welts, evidencing the feast that we had provided to our nocturnal insect visitors. We itched and scratched for days.

The only other excitement came about when Bill Craig found part of a human skeleton. There were few opportunities for recreational activities but Bill occasionally found the time to wet a line at the mouth of a small nearby creek that flowed into the lake. It was here that he spotted a human skull. If there were any fish in the creek, Bill left them there because at that moment, he made a hasty retreat back to the camp. Who knows why, but it was several days before he shared this ghoulish discovery with the rest of us. When he did, we quickly brought John into the picture. John insisted that Bill take him to the creek and show him the grisly mess. Sure enough, there it was, a complete skull, a few ribs and other sundry bones lodged in the swampy grass filled effluent of the creek.

John retrieved the skull and taking it back to the service station, placed it in a cardboard box. It remained there for a few days until the Esso gasoline truck made a delivery to our underground tanks. Without revealing the contents of the sealed box he asked Walt, the truck driver, to deliver it to the RCMP office in Golden. This office was run by Bill

345

Craig's father and it is not surprising that Walt asked no questions and was not at all suspicious of the item.

Now of course, we were not present when Constable Craig opened the box but learned later that Walt's obvious ignorance of the situation prompted a complete and detailed interrogation. It was John's idea of a joke but it is doubtful if Walt ever forgave those of us who were part of the conspiracy.

Meanwhile, it didn't take long before Constable Craig paid a visit to Kinbasket and the swampy area of the creek where he retrieved a few more bones and body parts. (Another good reason not to join the mounties).

In due course dental records helped to identify the remains and a proper burial was arranged. It was truly a sad affair and our silly antics were not at all appropriate. In the end however, we were pleased that we had found the remains of a missing person and that we had been able to help with the resolution of a tragic mystery.

Returning from Kinbasket produced the usual bout of tummy trouble but it was worth it. Besides it didn't seem too bad this time.

****

Harvest was always a priority and helping with this annual undertaking provided a temporary excuse from class. Contrary to the rules, which assumed that each missing student was required at home, I had in fact taken a job with our neighbor, Alfred Petersen. Alfred had twisted his back and was likely to be incapacitated for most of the harvest season. I didn't jump out of a telephone booth with an "S" on my shirt but did feel it worthwhile to help a neighbor in need.

Truth be known, grade twelve wasn't likely to be very taxing since I had opted to stay in Standard for the two year matriculation program. I really didn't mind the extra year since life was good on the farm and school was a blast. Besides, there was still a lot of uncertainty regarding a career and there was some hope that an extra year would trigger a few practical ideas. I was seriously entertaining the idea of becoming a commercial pilot but at this juncture such a wild notion got little support from Mother and Dad. Public transport by air was still in its infancy and no doubt they thought my interest in air travel was little more than a passing fancy. In any event the matter was more or less put on the back burner.

Meanwhile, Irene had completed her grade twelve in Calgary but having decided not to attend university, she was living in Standard and working for the Royal Bank. We didn't have her home every day but did see her on weekends and that offered some pleasant interludes.

As it turned out, my school year was rather light and slightly boring. A full course would have been hectic but a half load was almost ridiculous and not particularly challenging. Indeed, it had the potential of making me incredibly lazy. Fortunately the village opened a brand new skating rink and once again hockey became a dominant part of my activities. To make it even better, I was elected captain by my team colleagues. We also dressed up the whole gang with brand new white and green uniforms. At the suggestion of Johnny Grant, each new jersey was emblazoned with a large crest spelling out "Wheat Kings." Everyone liked the name and while we were still without a league, we looked great as we played a whole mess of ragtag teams. Despite the fact that we had been without ice the previous year, we had a solid team and won most of our games.

****

To the surprise of many, King George VI passed away in February. He had been a reluctant ruler but having seen him during his visit to Canada prior to the war, we were sorry to learn of his passing. While he had lived through the dark days of the war, his contribution to the final victory was probably minimal. He did however, chose to remain in England throughout the severe bombing of London and in so doing endeared himself to The United Kingdom and members of the Commonwealth.

****

Winter was winding down when Dad made a hurried trip to Minneapolis for a visit with his mother. She had lived in a delightful senior citizen home for many years, but now with failing health, she was in a nursing home. We were all pleased that Dad was able to spend a few weeks visiting with Grandmother. This became particularly meaningful since he had been home from the States for less than three weeks when Grandmother's tired and worn out body succumbed to her extended years.

She had lived eighty four years and while she had enjoyed good health, her life had been beset with hardship. As the daughter of a lowly stonecutter, you can be sure that Grandmother's childhood and youth featured only the barest of necessities. She was only thirty five when her husband gave way to tuberculosis, leaving her with the formidable task of raising five young boys. With her seamstress skills and the early, and I expect painful dismissal of her sons into the work force, she managed but it certainly could not have not have been easy. Enduring such adversity without complaint, she was clearly a remarkable woman.

****

The war in Korea was in full swing and while there weren't large numbers of Canadians in the conflict, this could change rather quickly and was of universal concern.

The United Nations forces (mostly United States) were attempting to stabilize the scene of battle along the historic boundary (38th Parallel) but at times they were forced to yield to the invading hordes of Chinese from the north. At other times the U. N. troops would push north, giving the impression that they planned to carry the battle into China and beyond. This seesaw action was particularly disquieting since the Soviet Union was constantly making threats that hinted of widening the fracas into adjacent areas.

While not a direct adversary, Joseph Stalin, the Soviet despot, clearly looked upon the Korean conflict as an extension to his own cold war policies. He was certainly in lock step with the Chinese forces who were supplying most of the impetuous and fuel for North Korea's irreverent invasion of the South. Indeed, most of the war materials in their arsenal were of Soviet origin and that source of supply seemed limitless.

Adding to the seriousness of the situation, General MacArthur, the commander of USA and United Nations forces, was making some brash pronouncements which were particularly inflammatory and not always in keeping with the agreed policies of the United Nations. With little regard for these objectives, he publicly announced that he wished to nuke the Chinese and bomb their air bases in Manchuria. This was all a bunch of insubordinate prattle, and while his ideas may have been legitimate, they caused some serious uneasiness with the allies and his superiors in Washington. President Truman quickly relieved him of command, replacing him with the less flamboyant General Matthew Ridgeway whose notion of fighting a war took a more conventional tone. Much of the tension eased under Ridgeway's command.

Moreover and perhaps most importantly, it was less than a month after Ridgeway's appointment that the United States detonated the first ever "Hydrogen Bomb." Following this awesome exhibition of nuclear strength, the North Koreans and Soviets became much more conciliatory. No one really thought that the United States would use this awesome weapon in Korea but there is little doubt that its availability made the enemy much more receptive to a settlement of the conflict at the negotiating table.

****

With the summer of 1952 came my last opportunity to have a temporary job in a unique setting. John Chapman requested my return to Kinbasket but I was looking for adventure beyond the benign business of changing tires and selling gasoline. In preparation for a change of venue, I pursued the relationships that had been made during the previous summer with various members of T. Connors Diamond Drillers. It was assumed that a job with this firm, if available, would be back in British Columbia, drilling a potential mine site. That was not to be. Instead, the forthcoming job offer put me with a crew working the Alberta foothills where the company was drilling seismic shot holes for California Standard Oil Company.

With the completion of my departmental exams, I immediately made my way to Olds, Alberta where the T. Connors foreman was to meet me for final transport to the job site. This was somewhere west of Olds and as I had been looking for a wild, remote, and adventurous summer, there was certainly no disappointment with the location. No one could have anticipated a more backwoods job site than the one to which I was delivered.

It was late afternoon when our four wheel drive vehicle reached a "go no further" point on the Burnt Timber River. From here the camp and my summer home, some four miles beyond, could only be reached by horseback or shank's mare. We didn't have horses so we walked.

By any standard, the camp was a primitive setup. The main focus was the cook tent, a large weather stained side wall canvas shelter. Within its shabby interior stood a rough table made of freshly sawn planks. This crude piece of furniture was flanked on both sides by green lumber benches whose still wet, uneven surfaces provided a particularly unpleasant seat. At the extreme end stood a thin metal cook stove with its requisite black stove pipe piercing the canvas roof through an asbestos ring. Resting under one low side of the tent was an array of vessels and an enormous stack of kindling wood. On the side opposite, but still without headroom, stood a pile of boxes showing labels of canned goods ranging from Burn's Ham to Dole's Hawaiian Pineapple.

Hanging from the bark covered ridge pole were long wires which supported pots, pans, and a high test gas fired Coleman lantern.

Except for the chilled but clear water of the Burnt Timber, washing facilities were nonexistent. The toilet, affectionately known as the snort pole, was in fact a horizontal pine log, suspended over a gaping dry gravel wash, leaving the user with the need for both courage and balance before taking a position over the abyss.

Scattered around this center piece of civilization were five khaki army surplus tents, one of which was assigned to me. It featured two army cots, at least one wet mattress and a room mate, Bob Fletcher, a third year university student from Vancouver. We hit it off immediately but he quickly warned me that my already long day was not yet over. He was right. After a generous supper in the cook tent, we took off for the night shift at the drill site. This was located approximately two miles away and every step was uphill. En route, we met the crew which, having just left the drill, were on their way back to camp.

Arriving at the rig, the V-8 Ford engine which powered the unit was still warm. A hole was in progress and I was assigned the job of getting the water source started. This vital element was supplied by means of a small gasoline engine, a portable pump and about two hundred yards of tough rubber hose. With the help of a kerosene lantern, I walked this snake like hose to a small mountain spring from which a small pump and engine moved a flow of water to the drill bit. The engine worked well but the distance and location of the pump put considerable pressure on the line causing frequent ruptures in the over stressed hose. A continuous flow of water was essential and throughout most of the shift I stumbled through the brush and shin tangle searching for and repairing the constantly occurring water leaks.

After my first ten hour shift and no sleep for what seemed an eternity, I was more than ready for some good sac time. It was still a two mile hike back to camp but fortunately, it was mostly downhill. The tent leaked and my cot was wet but I slept like a well fed baby.

Our role and the reason for the portable diamond drill was to produce shot holes at locations which were inaccessible to a conventional shot hole rig. All of our activity was at or near timber line and almost always on a steep slope. In most cases drilling a fifty foot shot hole took at least four full days, or put in other terms, a minimum of eight, ten hour shifts. The big job was moving from one location to the next and this momentous task consumed most of the time. Sliding and moving the rig was accomplished by means of a winch and as such was dependent on the availability of trees large enough to anchor the pull. For this reason timber line was slightly beyond the limits of our drilling activity.

The job paid well but it was truly brutal work. All of the materials and supplies had to be hand carried from the camp to the drill site. This often produced an exhausted crew even before the drilling started. To make matters worse, every move was taking the drill site farther and farther from camp. To cope with these problems the foreman hired a wrangler, Pinto Pete, who brought with him a string of saddle horses.

The horses helped our travel to and from work but more importantly, Pinto Pete and his well trained team were able to pack in gasoline, rod grease, and other items used at the rig site. While the burden of grunt work was reduced, my horsemanship hadn't improved much since Dad and I tilled the garden together. Moreover, being the youngest and the usual subject of a camp joke, I was assigned the sorriest cayuse of the bunch.

Pinto Pete was the quintessential cowboy or at least he thought so. Despite his somewhat earthy name, he was in fact a competent horseman and certainly looked the part. His dress was right out of a Hollywood western and his gaunt scraggly face seemed to suit the large sweat stained Stetson that he wore with considerable pride. Even during meals in the cook tent, Pinto's hat remained firmly in place. He made every effort to identify with his chosen field of endeavor and in his verbal emulations, even a brief sentence was laced with profanities. Clearly his notion of being a cowboy included tough and dirty talk and in this regard his inventiveness was quite remarkable. When for example he was telling you the time, he would decorate the number with an unrepeatable explicative. Also he quickly rechristened everyone with not so nice nick names. In deference to my youthful appetite, I became "Long Gut." Believe it or not, that was the most socially acceptable of his colorful monikers.

It was early July when Pinto and his horses arrived in camp. He was probably one of the most unsavory characters ever to cross my path but I liked him. So did everyone else and within a few days he had everyone convinced that a few days at the Calgary Stampede would be a good idea. Being the lone holdout with a desire to make a few dollars, it was agreed that for ten dollars a day, I would remain behind and watch over the camp. Ten dollars was less than half of what could be expected in a work situation but there wasn't much choice since the rest of the crew were off to the Stampede.

There was no discussion regarding my roll but it could be assumed that I would be obliged to defend the groceries and camp, should anyone wish to walk off with them. Not a likely scenario, but if nature should intervene with a terrific storm, it is possible that the river could threaten a few of the leaky bell tents.

Actually the idea of taking in the Stampede was a hasty decision and just before everyone's departure, the cook advised that fresh bread was in preparation and that all I needed to do was to bake it in the oven.

The crew had traversed less than a mile when I proceeded to bake the three loaves that had been left on top of the stove. Wood was the only fuel and while it was chopped into kindling, it was wet. With almost continuous rain this was not unusual but there was every reason to believe that a little kerosene would get things going. Taking the kerosene can, I doused the wood before striking a match to start the fire. Bang! It wasn't kerosene that I had used, it was high test gasoline. The can labeled "kerosene" was clearly in error as the explosion that ensued lifted the stove lids about ten feet and the concussion of the blast split the tent almost in half.

It had been quite an explosion and while the bread was eventually baked, the rip in the tent would be hard to explain.

In the end, the crew stayed away for five days during which time all of Pinto Pete's horses vanished. They had been hobbled in an adjacent meadow but obviously the hobbles didn't stop them from drifting away. A quiet restful period had been expected but their disappearance caused me to spend several days searching the nearby valleys and creek bottoms. Despite continuous threats from an ill-tempered cow moose with a young calf, I finally managed to locate the ponies about three miles down river. I made no effort to retrieve them, leaving that job for Pinto Pete, our resident expert.

Being alone in the bush for five days was a most unusual experience filled with a previously unknown period of calm and speechlessness. I didn't actually become lonesome but not hearing a human voice for that interval was a curious ordeal that I don't ever wish to repeat. Even Pinto Pete's swearing sounded good after all that silence.

By early August I had enjoyed nearly all of the backwoods adventure that one could be expected to endure. Also Pinto Pete had a disagreement with the foreman and withdrew himself and his horses from the camp. It hardly mattered since Pinto's modest oat supply had run out and without this tempting bribery, it was seldom that anyone could catch one of the hobbled but ornery steeds.

Walking to and from work was nasty, but without Pinto and his vagrant plugs, we once again found ourselves carrying gasoline and supplies by way of a pack board. Moreover, by this time the drill was at least four miles from camp. It was miserable work and the driller who managed the other crew decided that there were better ways to make a living. To fill his role, Bob Fletcher was promoted to head up the other shift as their driller. This reduced our modest gang to me and Ben, an old experienced hand who had worked T Connor's rigs for many years. He certainly knew his stuff but with me as the only helper our production slowed down to a walk.

By mid August, I too felt the need for a shave, some dry clothes and a warm bath. Besides, I had almost doubled the money earned the previous summer and felt that a little rest would be in order. The summer had been an eventful and treasured experience but not something that I was anxious to repeat.

****

My final year at Dana High was very much like the one just past. The first half of grade twelve had been filled with pleasant episodes and while a Rhodes Scholarship wasn't in the offing, I was nonetheless halfway to my senior matriculation. Now if I didn't have that pesky French III to contend with maybe this, my final year, could be semi interesting and hopefully pleasant. The whole class was of course getting tired of the process and most of us were anxious to finish so that we could get on with the important business of moving into the real world and making our own living.

It was late fall, well before Christmas when the tempo changed ever so slightly. School was starting to become a big bore when the girls in our room decided that we should have a Students Union. They had no notion of the organizations function or purpose but that fact was totally irrelevant in their deliberations. Most of us were ambivalent to the idea but in due course a vote was taken. Not only did we end up with a Students Union, I had been elected to the office of president. While it was flattering to have the confidence of my peers, I didn't want the job. Complaining about it didn't seem to matter and in the end the job was mine.

Getting nominated and winning the job happened without any help from me but now that the job was mine, I didn't have the faintest idea of what to do with this fledgling organization. To make matters worse, neither did anyone else, including Mr. Bragg who thought the whole matter rather amusing. As I understood things, unions were designed to deal with grievances. We didn't have any and while we all tried, no one could think of anything to complain about. Even

356

the girls who organized the whole mess were mum on the subject. We could only conclude that everyone was happy since we couldn't find a single scab to pick on.

Finally, it was agreed that we should endeavor to make some money. Theoretically, this should give credibility to our new organization and with cash we could fix something that wasn't broken. What a deal!

I had absolutely nothing to do with it but after a few recess "think tanks", the same group of girls, namely, Wilda, Lillian, and Geraldine, who invented the problem in the first place decided that we should sponsor a community dance. Such an event could be held in the spanking new hall next to Tommy Frazer's Reliable Motors garage. The girls were really excited about it, but more importantly, they were absolutely certain that such a momentous event would produce incredible financial rewards.

Filled with tremendous enthusiasm, it wasn't long before these adventurous and optimistic colleagues prepared and distributed billboards throughout the surrounding communities. The Buster Schultz Orchestra was hired and we were away.

Dancing, like music, was not my strong suit but as president, I felt obliged to attend this gala fund raiser. Moreover, to ensure that the invading rogues and Lotharios from nearby towns did not run off with our inventive female students, it was deemed fitting that all of the male members of the class make an appearance, albeit a reluctant one.

Admission was three dollars. I was happy to have gone since without my three bucks, our net gain would have been a paltry six dollars. Yes, after all the fuss, we made nine dollars, enough to purchase a new Websters Dictionary for the High School library. We didn't really need it, but what the heck.

****

The death of King George a year earlier was in sharp contrast with the death of Joseph Stalin on the fifth of March. Although there was a tremendous state funeral for the Soviet leader, everyone knew what a scoundrel he really was. Few if any expressed sorrow at his death and in fact the local press was joyful. There was also a brief hope that the cold war would slow down or end. This was not to be but three years later his successor Nikita Khrushchev denounced his predecessor as "a brutal, deranged torturer who had committed atrocious acts of mass murder in creating and sustaining his powerful reign of terror."

****

When finally the ice melted and hockey was over for the year, three hard facts emerged from the slush and mud that ensued. First of all, it was more than likely that I would never again use my hockey equipment. While I could probably find reason to use my skates, graduating and moving away from Standard would most assuredly spell the end of my hockey days. This fact was reinforced by the second obvious revelation which in truth had been clear to me for sometime. Although not previously admitted, the dressing room's smell of wet socks and wintergreen liniment was starting to nauseate me. Sore muscles, cracked fingers, almost frozen lungs along with an occasional whack on an essentially unprotected ankle from a frozen puck no longer represented a source of fun. Even worse, the seemingly constant practice sessions had lost their luster and were no longer interesting. Put in simple terms, I was sick and tired of hockey.

The third and final truth that came with the spring melt was the formal realization that my youthful fantasies of becoming a Toronto hockey star had in fact been dead for years. Had I developed the required talent on the ice, which I hadn't, my zest for the game had long since vanished.

Even the much less demanding pursuit of an American college-athletic scholarship was of little interest. Although Mr. Bragg, my coach and high school teacher urged me to give it a try with Colorado College, I couldn't bring myself to think of another four years of practice, practice and more practice. Moreover, while Mr. Bragg may have had some insight regarding hockey at Colorado Springs, he was totally unaware of my growing lack of interest and fervor for an athletic challenge. It was a secret that only I could know but no game, whether it be hockey, baseball or tennis could fire up my competitive spirit. I had lost the required killer instinct, if indeed it had ever existed. It was after all just a game, the results of which were not terribly important.

I truly envied my teammate's zeal for victory and their perpetual dedication for the sport. I sincerely wished for a similar attitude but despite every effort, I could no longer stimulate my subconscious to the required level of interest and commitment for anything approaching athletic excellence on the ice. In this my last year and indeed, last few months of school, it was much more important that I commit my efforts to the serious and vital business of clearing the graduation hurdle.

****

Hardly a day would go by when our teachers didn't remind us of the horrific "Departmental Exams" that were looming ahead. Except for the diminished hockey schedule, everything was focused on this foreboding event and my final days in high school. The process of honest learning was virtually set aside as the entire graduating class tried to predict the questions that would require answers if graduation was to become a reality. To help with this, we were provided

359

with exams from past years. They showed the probable format for the questions but offered little real help in selecting the answers. These old tests only served to make the forthcoming exams seem more ominous than they really were.

No doubt about it, the exams were both tough and important since passing or failing could easily determine the agenda for one's future. Fear of failure overshadowed most of my thoughts and the dreaded "Departmental Exams" garnered most of my attention. Also, there was some anxiety with the knowledge that I would soon be losing the umbrella of parental support. It was to be wished that none would be necessary but more importantly, it was my firm resolve that none would be sought. Indeed, in the spirit of adventure, most of these disquieting thoughts were more than offset by the excitement of the task ahead and my eagerness to get on with my life and into the foray of matching wits with the real world. Any new venue was sure to offer fresh challenges and promised to be much more than just a game.

While plans had been made for post graduation employment, I regarded the arrangements as temporary since over the longer term, it was my intention to become an airline pilot.

It is almost certain that Tommy Enevoldsen and his private planes were at least partially responsible for this keen interest in flying. This nearest neighbor to the north, had always enjoyed the use of at least one airplane. Despite the interference of the relatively new power line, Tommy's east quarter continued to feature two grass runways which crossed and traced their way through his grain fields. Although I had never been bold enough to ask for a ride, there was hardly a weekend when either Tommy or his son, Lyle, didn't fly circuits and bumps over these well marked grass strips. It looked like fun and besides Trans Canada Airlines, a growing concern, was seeking flight personnel.

For some considerable time I had harbored a secret desire to fly but knew that neither Mother or Dad would be impressed with such a revolutionary idea. In theory, leaving home should have given me the mandate to learn the nuances of levitation, but at this stage I was sensitive to their advice and council and not anxious to displease them. Having this in mind, interm employment seemed a prudent choice even though I knew that these initial plans were but a stepping stone to my long term aspirations..

Flying lessons cost money and would have to wait for a more propitious time. Also pursuit of a university degree was not in the cards since this was not a requirement in flying for Trans Canada or Canadian Pacific Airlines. (At the time, the need for eyeglasses was never given a thought, although within the next two years this changed everything.)

A few weeks before final exams were written, grades ten and eleven feted those of us who were leaving with a graduation party. It was truly a fine gesture but with exams still to come, it seemed a bit premature. In hindsight, it was of course totally proper since none of us would have returned for another year regardless of the outcome. This fact became absolutely clear when a few days later I started to make specific plans to leave home and take up my new job in the city. There was something terribly final about it, but leaving school and Standard filled me with excitement and anticipation. Hometown friends would of course be retained, and frequent return visits would be a certainty. Although these were comforting thoughts, after nineteen years of farm life, moving away to the city was sure to be different.

To be sure there were many things to regret and feel sad about, not the least of which were my Outdoor Life magazines. It may seem trivial but Mother insisted that I clean up my room and that included disposing of my nearly eight year collection of shooting and hunting journals. These had been read and reread and were carefully cataloged so that

I could find specific articles about guns and equipment. To Mother, they were nothing more than a pile of dog-eared, ragged periodicals but to me they were a veritable encyclopedia. I hated to burn them but they did make a big fire.

Thinking that I wouldn't look quite so country for my new life in the city, two brand new imitation alligator Samsonite bags were acquired. I was proud of these slick suitcases each of which came with a key. The keys opened both bags and of course every other Samsonite in the entire world but so what, I now had a key- my first ever.

With my departure, virtually all of my earthly goods could fit into these simple cases. I would of course be obliged to leave my shotgun and two rifles at home but apart from these bulky items, all else of importance could be carried off with me.

Embarking on a new job and venue was particularly stimulating for me but there is little doubt that my leaving home would suddenly immerse Mother and Dad into an unfamiliar chapter of their lives. For starters, the house was sure to seem empty and much less cluttered. Their day to day activities would be much less complicated as the rigors of a school schedule could be ignored for the first time in over a dozen years.

In addition, Irene's involvement at home was about to enter a new plateau which was sure to register a significant impact with Mother and Dad. For several years she had worked for The Royal Bank of Canada in Standard but had recently requested and received a transfer to Calgary. This had occurred several months earlier and she had now met a young fellow to whom she had just recently become engaged. Indeed, Irene and Dave had already set the date and had scheduled their wedding for September. My leaving combined with a new son-in law were certain to inject some fresh diversity into Mother and Dad's future activities.

****

It was the night before I was set to leave for Edmonton and my new job. The Samsonites were packed and all was ready for an early departure the next morning. Mother had gone to bed but Dad and I still had much to talk about. We were in the cool comfort of the living room where we shared many thoughts and ideas. We reminisced well into the night and may even have read a few Bible verses.

Some of our conversation has been forgotten but I well remember that Dad produced one of his favorite novels from which he read a few pages regarding a young man who was leaving home for college. Regrettably, I can't recall the book's title but will never forget the story which told of a father giving advice to his son. The young man in the story was from a family of modest means but was planning to attend a school beset with wealthy students having a penchant for parties and wild living. These were known as the Greeks (Fraternity members) while the rest were labeled Barbarians (Independents). The overall story line is unimportant but the message was clear. The father admonished his son not to fall into the clutches of wild living but to remain true to himself and his humble background. Without preaching, it was Dad's delicate way of giving me the same message. It was truly a tender moment on which I could reflect as I sat in the government office in Edmonton.

****

Suddenly, and without warning, my musings of the past were shattered as the single door to my temporary sanctuary burst open. To my dismay, there in the opening stood my recent antagonist, Mr. Olsen. But wait a minute, he looked different. His rotund frame was now draped in a suit jacket and his tie was tightened with the knot carefully centered on his shirt collar. While these elements had most assuredly changed his appearance, the most notable transformation was his scowl which had apparently been traded off for a broad smile. Even his eyes were smiling and as he moved toward me, he looked downright friendly. You would have thought that I was a long lost cousin as he reached out and fumbled for my confused hand.

"Son, you handled yourself well today," he said with a smile as he pumped my arm with a firm handshake. Then shifting his tone he went on to announce, "Tillykke med dit nye arbejde. Ver verlig at mode I Edmonton Lufthaven I morgen tidlig."

While the message wasn't totally clear, it was sufficiently understandable to know that the job was mine and that I would be expected to start my training the next day.

With apologies to Denmark, the translation went something like this, "Congratulations with your new job. Please report to the Edmonton airport early tomorrow."

I was in total shock but managed to mumble, "Manga tak."Gosh, maybe my Danish wasn't as bad as I thought.

Now it was unequivocal, I had left my rural home and the good life in Standard. The hustle and bustle of city streets would soon become as familiar as were the gopher mounds in Alfred Petersen's pasture. I would probably forget the favorite locations of the many Hungarian Partridge coveys that enjoyed living on Dad's farm. Even worse, it may not even matter.

I was enthusiastic with the prospects of a new and exciting venue, but these intoxicating thoughts were quickly dampened by a nostalgic and remorseful sense of knowing that my new persona would leave behind and probably disqualify many of the simple attributes of life in the country. There had been rare but memorable occasions when in solitude, I experienced and heard some of the first trickles of the snow melt. After the wrath of a cruel winter, this accompanied by the coy, yet unmistakable sweet smells arising from the rebirth of a willow grove, supplied a never to be forgotten and unsurpassed feeling of well-being.

To be sure, there had been times of concern and hardship but through it all, I had survived and developed a modicum of realistic confidence in myself and the world in which I was a part. Could I ever expect to retrace my way back to a spring day in a thicket of willows? Would I ever again commune with the quiet of the country and become entwined in nature's forgiving rhythms? Probably not, but the memories of a happy childhood, loving parents and caring family and friends would always be with me. Moreover, the community of my youth would continue to evoke warm and comfortable thoughts.

With care and vigilance, even the grind and energy of a city could not destroy my country spirit nor totally obstruct opportunities for quiet interludes with God. For sure, circumstances would be different but change itself could become the adventure.

With all of this, I also realized that the awesome and unfamiliar responsibility of making my own living was about to begin. Except for short visits, Mother's cooking would no longer be available. Open soft collars would give way to the stiffness of starched shirts and floppy neckties. One thing for sure, I could now expect to permanently lose my dubious immunity to the cleansing peculiarities of the water from Mother and Dad's farm well.

EPILOGUE

Dreams and a good deal of planning are the usual prerequisites for development of a career, but even the most carefully contrived strategies can be upset by unforeseen circumstances and unpredictable events. Not surprisingly, my own painstaking attempts to find employment with a commercial airline were thwarted by a totally unanticipated problem.

In keeping with my original blueprint, I learned to fly and experienced the freedom that only flight in a multidimensional medium can provide. Unfortunately, for some unknown reason, I lost a part of my previously excellent long range vision. Neither of Canada's national airlines were interested in myopic pilots with eyeglasses and it quickly became obvious that my journey through life would require some serious adjustment.

In the end, I chose to attend university where a degree in petroleum engineering was earned. With this fresh start, there were various work venues, including Texaco Exploration Ltd, The Royal Bank of Canada Oil and Gas Department, Oakwood Petroleum's Ltd, and Thomson Jensen Energy. While I am certain that the life of an airline pilot would have been enjoyable, my engineering degree served me well. Actually, on reflection, it is hard to imagine that being an airplane jockey could have been more enjoyable and rewarding than was the petroleum industry. I thoroughly enjoyed its people and the challenge of financing, drilling and producing oil and gas.

In 1959, I married Irene Larsen, a terrific girl with a Western Canadian farm background that was not unlike my own. We raised and educated two children, Philip and Sandy both of whom have opted for life in the city.

Whether it is the residual effects of playing hockey on a frigid January rink or creeping age, I now find Canadian winters to be inordinately cold and uncomfortable. To accommodate this malady, my wife and I moved and retired to the warmth of Arizona where for each month of the year we can enjoy our continuously growing garden and the inherent frustrations of bogie golf.

Order Form

DON'T DRINK THE WATER
The Uptown Musings of a Country Boy

Tempo Distributors
12190 East Arabian Park Drive
Scottsdale, Arizona 85259

E-mail: irjensen@mindspring.com

Name _____

Address _____

City _____ Province/State _____

Postal Code / Zip Code _____

Enclosed is my cheque for:

$24.95 (tax included) per book x _____ books = _____

$2.00 Shipping and Handling   x _____ books = _____

Total = _____

Please allow 4-6 weeks for delivery
Orders must be prepaid; no C.O.D.'s